The
Hunting *and* Exploring
Adventures
of
Theodore Roosevelt

BOOKS BY DONALD DAY

BACKWOODS TO BORDER *Edited with Mody C. Boatright*
(A Texas Folklore Society Publication)

FROM HELL TO BREAKFAST *Edited with Mody C. Boatright*
(A Texas Folklore Society Publication)

BIG COUNTRY: TEXAS
(American Folkways Series)

THE AUTOBIOGRAPHY OF WILL ROGERS, *Editor*

FRANKLIN D. ROOSEVELT'S OWN STORY, *Editor*

WILL ROGERS ON HOW WE ELECT OUR PRESIDENTS, *Editor*

WOODROW WILSON'S OWN STORY, *Editor*

UNCLE SAM'S UNCLE JOSH, *Editor*

THE AUTOBIOGRAPHY OF SAM HOUSTON
Edited with Harry Ullom

THE EVOLUTION OF LOVE

Hunting *and* Exploring
Adventures
of
Theodore Roosevelt

Told in His Own Words
and Edited by

DONALD DAY

Introduction
by
ELTING E. MORISON

THE DIAL PRESS · **1955** · NEW YORK

ACKNOWLEDGMENTS

The Publishers wish to express their gratitude for permission to reprint selections from the works of these authors and publishers listed below:

Cherrie, George K., *Dark Trails*. Copyright 1930. Used by permission of the publishers, G. P. Putnam's Sons.

Hagedorn, Hermann, *Roosevelt in the Badlands*. Copyright 1930. Used by permission of the publishers, Houghton Mifflin Company.

Morison, Elting E., "The Strenuous Life of TR" Copyright 1954 by Time, Inc., and used by permission of the author. This article first appeared in *Sports Illustrated*.

Roosevelt, Theodore, *African Game Trails*. Copyright 1910 by Charles Scribner's Sons, 1938 by Edith Carow Roosevelt. Used by permission of the publishers.

A Book Lover's Holiday in the Open. Copyright 1916 by Charles Scribner's Sons, 1944 by Edith Carow Roosevelt. Used by permission of the publishers.

Outdoor Pastimes of an American Hunter. Copyright 1905 by Theodore Roosevelt, 1933 by Edith Carow Roosevelt. Used by permission of the publishers, Charles Scribner's Sons.

Theodore Roosevelt, An Autobiography. Copyright 1913 by The Macmillan Company, 1941 by Edith Carow Roosevelt. Used by permission of Charles Scribner's Sons.

Through the Brazilian Wilderness. Copyright 1914 by Charles Scribner's Sons, 1942 by Edith Carow Roosevelt. Used by permission of the publishers.

Willis, John, *Roosevelt in the Rough*. Copyright 1931 by Ives Washburn, Inc. and used with their permission.

DESIGNED BY WILLIAM R. MEINHARDT

PRINTED IN THE UNITED STATES OF AMERICA

BY THE HADDON CRAFTSMEN, INC., SCRANTON, PA.

Contents

Introduction

IN THE year 1903 a son of the President of
the United States asked his father whether he should play
on the second squad at Groton. The President replied in a
long letter which began, simply enough, with some thoughts
on the joys and virtues of the manly sport of football. But
then he became distracted by something that Pliny had
written to the Emperor Trajan about athletics in the first
century after the birth of Christ. This led him to think
about the commissioned personnel of the British army, and
that, naturally enough, put him in mind of his old Army
regiment. From there he proceeded to a series of reflections
—on Groton School, a horse named Bleistein who crashed
through a jump, and the character of Abraham Lincoln.
Then he took up the various qualities a good government
officer ought to possess, the state of his own tennis game

(not so good), and his tendency to preach. He concluded finally that it was indeed a good thing to have a sound mind in a sound body.

The presidential letter suggests some of the difficulties confronting anybody who sets out to make a simple statement about who or what Theodore Roosevelt really was. One thing always leads to another. He did so many things; he had so many ideas; he said so much. He can't be trapped and stuffed and mounted in a single attitude.

This is as true of sports as anything else in his life. Among American Presidents, Roosevelt must have been the greatest sportsman. Leastwise, there is little doubt he was the most active sportsman while in office. The only encompassing description of the restless and energetic Roosevelt's omnivorous appetite for physical exercise was one coined by T.R. himself, "The Strenuous Life." Before and after Roosevelt most Presidents have felt that they have fulfilled the athletic requirements of high office if they caught a small trout, broke a hundred or drew to two pair. For Roosevelt, these didn't amount to a beginning.

As governor of New York, for instance, he had a difficulty with the state comptroller who would not make public funds available for the purchase of a wrestling mat. The watchdog of the treasury said he would permit a billiard table, but while it was apparently appropriate for a chief executive to chalk a cue, it was unbecoming in a governor to try an occasional fall with the middleweight champion of America. And a few years later, as President, Roosevelt had another difficulty with a doctor who would not let him box after a presidential eye had been permanently damaged by a right cross. Thus circumscribed by higher authority, he turned to the daily practice of jiu jitsu. Wrestling, boxing, jiu jitsu were, however, only secondary athletic interests of Theodore Roosevelt. At one time or another, he rode to hounds, engaged in single stick (a form of fencing) and harpooned fish. He could hit an ibis stork or a duck on the wing, play polo and hold the stern paddle in white water. He could hit a ball on the backhand, handle a rope from the saddle, kill a charging bull elephant at 40 yards, jump a horse five feet and, no doubt, build a fire without matches.

The list could be extended, but to no real purpose. It need only be said that in whatever place Theodore Roosevelt found himself, he entered with immense good pleasure into the sporting opportunities offered by local custom and terrain. Sometimes, indeed, he improved on or, according to one's taste, outraged local custom. Through a deep ravine in the city of Washington there runs lovely Rock Creek. Often in late fall or early spring it delighted the President to end a long tramp by swimming naked through the creek's freezing waters. Once, he loved to recall, he and the French ambassador had thus concluded a walk through the ravine, although the ambassador kept his gloves on because, as he explained, "we might meet ladies."

As adaptive as the President was to existing conditions, he always had his favorite forms of sport. The greatest was hunting. He shot and killed all kinds of game in this country, in England, in Europe, in South America and, of course, in Africa. The African bag was 296. In all there were 70 different kinds of game represented—from the lion to the python, from Coke's Hartebeests to the Lesser Bustard.

Some part of the joy he had in the hunt he has himself described well in his book on Africa. One day he and his native bearer and an English lady became separated from their party during a lion hunt. Simba, the bearer, and Roosevelt, who had dismounted from his horse, Tranquillity, faced the animal on the ground. "Now," he says, "an elderly man with a varied past which includes rheumatism does not vault lightly into the saddle, as his sons, for instance, can; and I had already made up my mind that in the event of the lion's charging it would be wise for me to trust to straight powder rather than try to scramble into the saddle and get under way in time. The arrival of my two companions settled matters. I was not sure of the speed of Lady Pease's horse; and Simba was on foot and it was, of course, out of the question for me to leave him. So I said, 'Good, Simba, now we'll see this thing through,' and gentle-mannered Simba smiled a shy appreciation of my tone, though he could not understand the words.

"I was still unable to see the lion when I knelt, but he was now standing up, looking first at one group of horses and then at the other, his tail lashing to and fro, his head held low and his lips dropped over his mouth in peculiar fashion, while his harsh and savage growling rolled thunderously over the plain. Seeing Simba and me on foot, he turned toward us, his tail lashing quicker and quicker. Resting my elbow on Simba's bent shoulder, I took steady aim and pressed the trigger; the bullet went in between the neck and shoulder, and the lion fell over on his side, one foreleg in the air. He recovered in a moment and stood up, evidently very sick and once more faced me, growling hoarsely. I think he was on the eve of charging. I fired again at once, and this bullet broke his back just behind the shoulders; and with the next I killed him outright, after we had gathered around him."

This is, in a way, a rather slight situation—one of nine lions killed by Theodore Roosevelt on this African trip. But there is in this episode picked at random from a score of similar descriptions something of the meaning of the hunt to Theodore Roosevelt. Here is the skillful organization of a crowded moment; the fully mobilized powers of a very acute observer; the great, unstated excitement of the tight situation. Such situations—when things could be seen really to hang in the balance—whether on battleground, convention floor, or hunting field called all the elements in Theodore Roosevelt most brilliantly to life.

It was not all lions and wilde-beests, however. Once in his youth he set out in pursuit of three horse thieves who had stolen one of his boats in their getaway from his land. This was in the early spring of 1886, but before he could set out, a great blizzard roared in over the Dakota Bad Lands. "All snowed up," Roosevelt stayed in his ranch house writing another chapter of his biography of Thomas Hart Benton and, in between times, building a new boat with the help of two of his men. The idea was that when the snow stopped, Roosevelt and his two ranch hands would pursue the thieves down river.

By the end of March they set out on the "very rough work." A day or two out the party ran out of food and had "an awful time in the river, as there were ice gorges, the cold being intense." But in the end they reached the enemy encampment on a bank of the river. They crept noiselessly up to within a few yards of the thieves, who sat unaware on the ground, and then challenged them. In short order they took away their rifles and captured them "in fine style." The chase turned out the easy part. On the return trip the boats got stuck in an ice jam, delaying the whole party for several days. After this, Roosevelt sent his two men along by boat while he took the three thieves to the sheriff in a wagon borrowed from a ranch. For two days he had them alone. At night they all camped in the open—Roosevelt with a cocked rifle in his right hand. In his left was a book from which he read throughout the night. He had considered taking the works of Matthew Arnold, but had finally decided on Tolstoy's *Anna Karenina*. He read through the thousand-page work with "very great interest" before he found the sheriff. Roosevelt finished his great ordeal "done out" with lack of sleep and the strain of watchfulness, but convinced that Tolstoy was a great writer.

Roosevelt was obviously proud to bring back a big bag of game. He was excited by plunges into the wilderness and dangerous trips down uncharted, doubtful rivers. But these things were not all of it; they were not even perhaps the greatest part of it. Reflecting one time on the huge toll of animals, reptiles and birds he had killed in Africa, he concluded that "the mere size of the bag indicates little as to a man's prowess as a hunter and almost nothing as to the interest or value of his achievement." For him much of the interest and all of the value of his long hunt in Africa were to be found in the scientific results. Over 164 mammals, large and small, were observed and carefully described in the course of the trip. Probably no previous exploration had produced so comprehensive and reliable a study of African natural history.

Then there were other things to be derived from the hunt. Not number killed, nor number studied, nor memories persisting after years of a lion's charge, a buffalo "sullen . . . under his helmet of horn," nor the rhinoceros "truculent and stupid, in the bright sunlight on the empty plains." These things, he said, could be told. But there were not words for the "hidden spirit of the wilderness—its mystery, its melancholy, its charm." There were not words for "the awful glory of sunrise and sunset in the wide waste spaces of the earth, unworn of man."

For all its unpredictability, there was a philosophy in Roosevelt's love of sport. In its briefest form, he stated it once to some Harvard undergraduates: First, he said, "it is of far more importance that a man should play something himself, even if he plays it badly, than that he should go with hundreds of companions to see someone else play well"; and second, "I trust I need not add that in defending athletics I would not for one moment be understood as excusing that perversion of athletics that would make it the end of life instead of merely a means in life. . . ."

This last was the great point for Roosevelt. He had little use for the pure sportsman—the man, not a professional athlete, who devoted himself exclusively to the life of sport. For this figure—more frequently found in the '90s than now —he reserved his greatest irritation. Equally, however, he had severe words for those who devoted themselves exclusively to industry or commerce. Indeed, he once said that prize fighting was not half so brutalizing or demoralizing as many forms of big business and of legal work carried on in connection with big business.

What irritated him was taking one small section of exis-

tence—law, business, politics, or athletics—and calling it
life. Each was useful only in so far as you worked in it until
you were competent and then worked to establish connec-
tions between it and all other parts of life.

Roosevelt used to love to point out he was not a gifted
athlete. He was not a natural shot nor a born horseman.
Neither boxing nor wrestling came readily to him. He got
started in the sports at 14 and only after his father had sent
him to Maine to get over asthma. He was not particularly
frail at the time, as legend has it, but he believed his father's
advice that if he were to accomplish much in life he had to
have a strong body. By hard work and numerous lessons he
became a fairly accomplished wrestler and boxer, but even
at Harvard he never won a championship. And it was the
same on the court, the playing field and hunting ground.

In all his sports, whether he was having the time of his life
hitting a ball or winging a grouse, Roosevelt always reached
out to relate them to natural history, to the state of nations
and to his own philosophy. And so when he hunted thieves
he brought along Tolstoy, and when he wrote his son about
the second squad at Groton, at just about the time he and
President Eliot were engaged in their altercation over the
state of Harvard football, his mind naturally ran on to the
Emperor Trajan, British officers, and government service.
At other times a concern for our diplomatic relations with
Venezuela would just as naturally make him think of the
Olympic games or his excellent friend Robert Fitzsimmons.
They were all parts of life and he loved them all.

                                        ELTING E. MORISON

PART ONE

The Child That Fathered the Man

Chapter 1

The Raw Elements

THEODORE ROOSEVELT was born on October 27, 1858, at 28 East Twentieth Street in New York City. On his father's side he was of Dutch, Welsh, English, Irish and German extraction, and from his mother came Scotch, Huguenot and English blood. Added to these warring and stimulating elements of heredity was the environmental one: his father was from the North and his mother from the South. The only discord that he experienced in his home was "a partial but alert understanding of the fact that the family were not one in their views" on the Civil War.

Theodore's father was interested in every "social reform movement, and did an immense amount of practical charitable work himself. He was a big, powerful man, with leonine face, and his heart filled with gentleness for those who needed help or protection, and with the possibility of much wrath against a bully or oppressor. He was very fond of riding, both on the road and across the country, and was also a great whip. He usually drove four-in-hand, or else a spike team, that is a pair with a third horse in the lead."

Theodore called him the best man he ever knew. He "always excelled in improving every spare half-hour or three-quarters of an hour, whether for work or enjoyment," and killed himself with overwork by the time he was forty-six. "He was always preaching caution to his boys, but did not practise his preaching overmuch. . . . He liked to take chances. Generally they came out right. Occasionally they did not. Once when we were driving into New York late at night the leaders stopped. He flicked them, and the next moment we could dimly make out that they had jumped. It then appeared that the street was closed and that a board had been placed across it, resting on two barrels, but without a lantern. Over this board the leaders had jumped, and there was considerable excitement before we got the board taken off the barrels and resumed our way."

Theodore said of his mother that she "was a sweet, gracious, beautiful Southern woman, a delightful companion and beloved by everybody. She was entirely 'unreconstructed' to the day of her death."

When still a small boy his interest in animal life was aroused to a high pitch by seeing a dead seal on Broadway. "That seal filled me with every possible feeling of romance and adventure," he wrote. "As long as it remained there I haunted the neighborhood of the market day after day." Immediately he determined to be a naturalist, and with some of his cousins and friends established a museum and began collecting specimens.

"What excitement," he wrote his father when he was ten. "My mouth opened wide with astonish [sic] when I heard how many flowers were sent in to you. I could revel in the buggie ones. I jumped with delight when I found you heard the mocking-bird. Get some feathers if you can. In the letter you write to me tell me how many curiosities and living things you have got for me." At the same time he told his sister in a letter that he had "four mice, two white-skinned, red eyed, velvety creatures very tame, for I let them run over me" and "they trie to get down the back of my neck and under my vest," and "two brown-skinned, black-eyed, soft as the others but wilder." He had named the white mice Lordy and Rosa, and as they were male and female, he stated that he kept "them in different cages."

This same year Theodore was taken to Europe for his first visit. Perhaps due to bad health he did not enjoy the trip very much although a climb up to the crater of Mt. Vesuvius gave him some excitement. Three years later, however, it was different. For one thing he made a month's trip up the Nile, with a shotgun his father had given him as his constant companion. He "procured between one and two hundred skins" of birds.* From Egypt the family went for a long stay in Germany where Theodore did considerable collecting. "My scientific pursuits cause the family a good deal of consternation," he wrote on June 13, 1873. "My arsenic was confiscated and my mice thrown (with the tongs) out of the window. In cases like this I would approach a refractory female, mouse in hand, corner her, and hang the

* The specimens that he collected on this trip are in the Smithsonian Museum.

mouse very near her face until she was thoroughly convinced of the wickedness of her actions."

One of the letters to his father, from Dresden on June
29, 1873, tells of his chronic sickness with a humor that
indicates his determination not to let it control his life. "I
am at present suffering under a very slight attack of
Asthma," he wrote. "However it is but a small attack and
except for the fact that I can not speak, without blowing
like an abridged edition of a hippopotamus, it does not in-
convenience me much."

Back in the United States, Theodore prepared himself
under tutors to enter Harvard where he intended to study to
become a naturalist. After enrolling however, he soon abandoned the idea when he found that this field was considered
"a science whose adherents were to spend their time in the
study of minute forms of marine life, or else in section-
cutting and the study of tissues of the higher organisms
under the microscope." Such a course of action had little
appeal for a boy who was already dreaming of lions and
grizzly bears.

The general instruction at Harvard, however, appealed to
him because it taught a man to respect and glorify what he
did himself, which he felt was as it should be. On the other
hand he deplored the absence of instruction and emphasis
on the necessity for the individual "to join with others in
trying to make things better for the many by curbing the
abnormal and excessive development of individualism in a
few."

Most important, by taking long walks in the country,
through boxing lessons and boxing bouts, by riding to the

hounds, and by trips into the wildernesses of upper New York and Maine, Theodore strengthened and toughened his sickly body and improved his general health. His father's death while he was at Harvard, although he was left a sizable sum of money, made it more important that he become self-reliant.

On his first trip to Maine, when he was nineteen, he met a man who had a profound influence on his entire life. One of his companions on the trip, his former tutor, Arthur Cutler, took aside their guide, brawny thirty-four-year-old Bill Sewall, and cautioned him about Theodore. "He is not very strong and he has got a great deal of ambition and grit," Cutler told Sewall, "and if you should take such a tramp as you are in the habit of taking, and take him with you, you never would know that anything ailed him. The first thing you knew he would be down, because he would go until he fell."

Theodore and Bill Sewall became fast friends at once. "They admired each other immensely, and while Roosevelt, footing the bills of the expeditions, was inevitably boss and felt free to express his mind as such," Hermann Hagedorn wrote, "on occasion Sewall was not hesitant in 'going for Theodore bow-legged,' when he thought the younger man needed an application of unadorned Maine English."

It was not long before Sewall realized that he had a different fellow to guide from any he had seen before. "I had never seen anybody that was like him," he said, and forty-two years later added, "and I have held that opinion ever since." Above all, Theodore learned from Sewall that genuine character and real worth are not necessarily found in fancy houses or clothes.

In February, 1880, Theodore became engaged to Alice Lee, a Brookline, Massachusetts girl whom he had met while at Harvard. "I have been in love with her for nearly two years now," he wrote a friend in explanation of his failure to continue collecting plants and birds with him, "and have made everything subordinate to winning her, so you can perhaps understand a change in my ideas as regards science." Theodore was always to make everything subordinate to doing the task at hand with all his abilities.

In September, 1880, as a sort of bachelor adventure before marrying, Theodore and his brother, Elliott, went for a week's hunt to Iowa. "Elliott revels in the change to civilization and epicurean pleasures," he wrote from Chicago after their hunt. "As soon as we got here he took some ale to get the dust out of his throat; then a milk punch because he was thirsty; a mint julep because it was hot; a brandy smash 'to give him an appetite.' He took a very simple dinner—soup, fish, salmi de grouse, sweetbread, mutton, venison, corn, macaroni, various vegetables and some pudding and pies, together with beer, later claret and in the evening shandigaff. I confined myself to roast beef and potatoes. When I took a second help he marvelled at my appetite—and at bed time wondered why in the thunder he felt 'stuffy' and I didn't. The good living also reached his brain, and he tried to lure me into a discussion about the intellectual development of the Hindoos, coupled with some rather discursive and scarcely logical digressions about the Infinity of the Infinate [sic], the Sunday School system and the planet

Mars, together with some irrelevant remarks about Texan 'Jack Rabbits' which are apparently as large as good sized cows. Elliott says that these remarks are incorrect and malevolent but I say they pay him off for his last letter about my eating manners.

"We had had very good fun so far, in spite of a succession of untoward accidents and delays. I broke both my guns, Elliott dented his, and the shooting was not as good as we expected. I got bitten by a snake and chucked head-foremost out of the wagon."

Chapter 2

"Enough Peril to Make It Exciting . . . "

THEODORE AND Alice Lee were married on October 27, 1880, at Brookline, Massachusetts, and, for the moment, went to his mother's house to live. "We breakfast at ten, dine at two, and take tea at seven," he wrote. "In the morning we go out driving in the buggy, with Lightfoot, who is in splendid trim. In the afternoon we play tennis or walk in Fleets woods. In the evening I read aloud —Pickwick Papers, Quentin Durward or Keats Poems. We are having an ideal honeymoon."

It takes little imagination to realize how long such an existence would satisfy this restless young man. In the spring they went to Europe for a few months. "We had a splendid passage," Theodore wrote back from Cork, "very nearly as gay as a funeral. If ever a person heartily enjoyed a sea trip, Alice did. She enjoyed it so much that she stayed in bed about all the time, the stewardess and myself being her devoted attendants. I fed her every blessed meal she ate and held her head when, about twenty minutes later, the meal came galloping up into the outer world again. I only rebelled once. That was when she requested me to wear a mustard plaster first to see if it hurt. About every half hour during the night I turned out to superintend matters while Alice went through a kind of stomachic earthquake."

After hearing a contemptuous remark in England about American prowess in mountain climbing, Theodore proceeded to conquer both Jungfrau and the Matterhorn. For doing so he was elected to the London Alpine Club. In a letter he set forth his ideas of what he had done. "Accidents are generally due either to rashness, or else to a combination of timidity and fatigue. A fairly hardy man, cautious but not cowardly, with good guides has little to fear. Still, there is enough peril to make it exciting, and the work is very laborious."

"Cautious but not cowardly," "enough peril," and "laborious work" were already his dominant characteristics.

Back in the United States there were more troublesome, if not more dangerous, "Matterhorns" to climb. What now? This man had to have activity. He first turned to the study of law but soon found that "the caveat emptor side of law, like the caveat emptor side of business," as well as the lack of a physical and action challenge, repelled him. There was not even the pull of having to make a living to urge him on.

Disregarding the advice of his family and friends that politics were "low" and that machines were not controlled by "gentlemen," Theodore stopped the study of law and ran for the legislature, in opposition to the machine candidate, and was elected. At Albany, although he was from the "silk-stocking" district of New York, his best friend was a cross-roads country storekeeper from a backwoods county. Both of them abhorred demagogy and corruption, and both worked for a progressive, clean government, operated with efficiency.

Much of Theodore's leisure time was taken up in finishing his The Naval War of 1812, a book that is still considered authoritative on the subject, particularly in England, and which was no doubt instrumental later in getting an appointment for him as Assistant Secretary of the Navy. At the same time he read all the books on the west that he could find and even this early began projecting a historical work on the winning of the territory between the eastern seaboard mountains and the Mississippi River.

Theodore's attention was directed towards the Bad Lands by a letter in an 1882 New York newspaper, and by a chance acquaintance with a naval officer named Gorringe, who was making a spirited fight for a better Navy. The two of them planned a hunt there, where Gorringe had some ranching interests, but at the last moment Gorringe could not go and Theodore went alone.

The Bad Lands at that time "was still the Wild West, the far West, the West of Owen Wister's stories and Frederic Remington's drawings, the West of the Indian and the buffalo hunter, the soldier, and the cowpuncher. It was a land of vast and silent spaces, of lonely rivers, and of plains where the wild game stared at the passing horseman. It was a land of scattered ranches, of herds of long-

*horned cattle, and of reckless riders who, unmoved, looked
in the eye of life or of death."*

This was the territory known as the northern cattle plains.
It stretched from the rich wheat farms of central Dakota
to the Rocky Mountains and took in all of the land drained
by the Big Missouri, before it takes its long trend to the
southeast, and all its tributaries. This included all of Montana, northern Wyoming and extreme western Dakota Territory.

It was a high, nearly treeless region, of little rainfall,
which was crossed by streams that were sometimes raging
torrents and at other times merely strings of shallow pools.
In places it stretched out into deserts of alkali and sage-
brush or into nearly level prairies of short grass, extending
many miles without a break. Elsewhere there were rolling
hills, some of considerable height, and in other parts the
ground was rent and broken into the most fantastic shapes,
mostly from erosion although here and there of volcanic
origin. This broken country had been called by the Indians,
French *voyageurs*, and American trappers alike, the Bad
Lands, partly from its dreary and forbidding aspect and
partly from the difficulty experienced in traveling through it.

The faces of the terraced cliffs, where erosion had taken
place, showed various bands of soil, often being of a dozen
different colors. Mostly they were bare of all but the scantiest vegetation. Some of the buttes spread out into level
plateaus, many miles in extent; others formed chains, or
rose as steep, isolated mesas. Those that were of volcanic
origin were composed of masses of scoria, and in coloring

were as bizarre as in form. Many of them had in them veins of coal which, catching on fire, turned the clay above them into brick. Then as the water wore away the side of a hill, the exposed parts were streaked with black and red, often mingled with grays, purples and browns.

The country had been but little over half a dozen years before won from the Indians. They had been the only remaining great hunting grounds, and toward the end of the 1870's all of the Northern plains tribes went on the warpath in a final desperate effort to preserve them. After bloody fighting and protracted campaigns, the Indians were defeated, and the country thrown open to the whites, while the building of the Northern Pacific Railroad gave immigration an immense impetus.

The inhabitants were few, the frontier independent spirit still prevailed, and one man was as good as another, "if not a little better." When a man worked for another, he expected his employer to do the same kind of work that he did and to be treated as an equal.

Under strict orders from his doctor not to take violent exercise, after an attack of cholera morbus, Theodore nevertheless headed for the Bad Lands with the avowed intention of hunting buffalo before that noble animal disappeared forever as game from the American scene. His destination was the squalid little frontier town of Little Missouri, on this tributary of the Big Missouri where the Northern Pacific crossed it, and near where Medora in Western Dakota is today.

"I first reached the Little Missouri on a Northern Pacific

train about three in the morning of a cool September day in 1883," he wrote. "Aside from the station, the only building was a ramshackle structure called the Pyramid Hotel. I dragged my duffle-bag thither, and hammered on the door until the frowsy proprietor appeared, muttering oaths. He ushered me upstairs, where I was given one of the fourteen beds in the room which by itself constituted the entire upper floor."

The slim young man whom the other occupants of the room must have stared at, particularly after he put on his glasses, bore little resemblance to the burly, intense figure that millions later knew so well. Even his slight, silky mustache was worlds apart from the heavy drooping one that later became, along with his flashing teeth, his trademark. The steady eyes that looked out from under thick hair which grew over a serene brow had not taken on the grimness and defiance which later were habitual. If any of the occupants of the room had challenged him then, however, he undoubtedly would have found that the spirit to resist wrongs was just as strong then as later.

PART TWO

Ranching and Hunting in the West

Chapter 1

A Buffalo Hunt

Now THAT Theodore was in the Bad Lands, he was raring to go. But the next day he sought in vain for someone to guide him to the hunting grounds. It seemed that no one wanted to "trundle a tenderfoot," and particularly one who wore glasses. This weakness, to the Bad Landers, constituted a deficiency in character. But then, as later, Theodore was not to be gainsaid. He eventually met Joe Ferris, whose brother, Sylvane, and William Merrifield, had a small ranch. With considerable misgivings Joe agreed to take Theodore on a hunt. They went out to spend the night at the ranch—the Chimney Butte.

"The ranchhouse was a log structure with a dirt roof, a corral for the horses near by, and a chicken-house jabbed against the rear of the house," Theodore wrote. "Inside there was only one room, with a table, three or four chairs, a cooking-stove, and three bunks. That evening we all played old

sledge round the table, and at one period the game was
interrupted by a frightful squawking outside which told us
that a bobcat had made a raid on the chicken house."

Theodore's hearty good-humor in the card game and his
eagerness in going out to help in trying to kill the bobcat
broke down some of the resistance. Nevertheless, by morning, Joe was not at all enthusiastic about the hunt. When
Theodore found that Joe intended to go in a buckboard, he
promptly stated that he wanted to go on horseback. This
even more dampened Joe's enthusiasm. He tried to worm
out of it by stating that there was no horse for the tenderfoot
to ride. In the end Theodore bought a horse and they rode
off to the ranch of Gregor Lang, a Scotchman some fifty
miles away, which they were going to use for headquarters.

Roosevelt stayed up most of the night talking with Lang
who was well-educated and well-informed. The next morning it was raining and Joe wanted to postpone the hunt.
Nothing doing. They went. For a week they hunted in the
rain, returning to Lang's place at night, with Joe so exhausted that he fell into bed immediately after supper.
Theodore continued his talks with Lang until way into the
night, and then was raring to go by daylight. They were
unsuccessful in finding buffalo. Then, as it cleared up, they
decided to make a final big push. Theodore told what happened:

We left early in the morning and after crossing the Little
Missouri threaded our way through the narrow defiles and
along the tortuous divides of a great tract of Bad Lands.
We saw two or three blacktail deer some distance off but

not in shooting range. After we were a couple of hours on our way we came across the fresh track of a bull buffalo. The tracks were easily followed as long as he had kept to the soft creek bottom, but when he left this and turned up a winding coulee, which branched out in every direction, his hoofs scarcely made any marks in the hard ground. Late in the afternoon we saw three black specks in the middle of a large plain, which proved to be buffalo bulls. Our horses had come a great distance without water and were in no condition for running. Therefore, although the ground was unfavorable, we determined to creep up on the buffalo. We left the ponies in a hollow half a mile from the game, and started off on our hands and knees, using every sage brush as cover. After a while we had to lie flat on our bodies and wriggle like snakes. To my chagrin I blundered into a bed of cactus and filled my hands with spines. After taking advantage of every hollow, hillock, or sage brush, we got within a hundred and twenty-five yards of the bulls. As all between was bare ground I drew up and fired. Confused by the bulk and shaggy hair of the beast, I aimed too far back at one that was standing nearly broadside toward me. The bullet told on his body with a loud crack, the dust flying up from his hide. Away went all three, with their tails up, disappearing over a light rise in the ground.

Much disgusted, we trotted back to where the horses were picketed, jumped on them, out of breath, and rode after the flying game. We thought that the wounded one might turn out and leave the others, and so followed them, though they had over a mile start. For seven or eight miles we loped our jaded horses along at a brisk pace, occasionally seeing the buffalo far ahead. Finally, when the sun had just set, all three came to a stand in a gentle hollow. There was no cover anywhere near them and, as a last desperate resort, we concluded to try to run them on our wornout ponies.

As we cantered toward them they faced us for a second and then turned round and made off, while with spurs and quirts we made the ponies put on a burst that enabled us to close in with the wounded one just about the time that the lessening twilight had almost vanished. The pony I was on could barely hold his own, after getting up within sixty or seventy yards of the wounded bull. My companion, better mounted, forged ahead, a little to one side. The bull saw him coming and swerved from his course, and by cutting across I was able to get nearly up to him. When within twenty feet I fired my rifle, but the darkness, and especially the violent labored motion of my pony, made me miss. I tried to get in closer, when suddenly up went the bull's tail, and, wheeling, he charged me with lowered horns. My pony, frightened into momentary activity, spun round and tossed up his head. I was holding the rifle in both hands, and the pony's head, striking it, knocked it violently against my forehead, cutting quite a gash, from which, heated as I was, the blood poured into my eyes. Meanwhile the buffalo, passing me, charged my companion, and followed him as he made off, and, as the ground was very bad, for some little distance his lowered head was unpleasantly near the tired pony's tail. I tried to run in on him again, but my pony stopped short, dead beat, and by no spurring could I force him out of a slow trot. My companion jumped off and took a couple of shots at the buffalo, which missed in the dim moonlight, and, to our unutterable chagrin, the wounded bull labored off and vanished in the darkness. I made after him on foot, in hopeless and helpless wrath, until he got out of sight.

Our horses were completely done out. We did not mount them again, but led them slowly along, trembling, foaming and sweating. The ground was moist in places, and after an hour's search we found in a reedy hollow a little mud pool with water so slimy that it was almost gelatinous. Thirsty though we were, for we had not drunk for twelve hours, neither man nor horse could swallow more than a mouthful or two of this water. We unsaddled the horses, and made our beds by the hollow, each eating a biscuit. There was not a twig with which to make a fire, nor anything to which we might fasten the horses. Spreading the saddle blankets under us, and our own over us, we lay down, with the saddles as pillows, to which we had been obliged to lariat our steeds.

Although the ponies stood about, almost too tired to eat, they were very watchful and restless, continually snorting or standing with their ears forward, peering out into the night. The day before we had had a false alarm from supposed hostile Indians, who turned out to be merely half-breed Crees. As we were in a lonely part of the wilderness, we knew we were in the domain of both white and red horse thieves, and that the latter might, in addition to our horses, try to take our scalps. It was some time before we dozed off.

About midnight we were rudely wakened by having our pillows whipped out from under our heads. As we started from the bed, we saw, in the bright moonlight, the horses galloping madly off with the saddles, tied to the lariats, whose other ends were around their necks, bounding and trailing after them. Our first thought was that they had been stampeded by horse thieves, and we rolled over and crouched down in the grass with our rifles. However, nothing could be seen except a shadowy four-footed form in the hollow, and in the end we found that the horses must have taken alarm at a wolf or wolves that had come up to the edge of the bank and looked over at us, not being able at first to make out what we were.

"*I ain't never committed any crime that makes me deserve this,*" *Joe said plaintively. Then he turned to Theodore, whose face was plainly visible in the moonlight, and asked, in a voice in which was mingled comic despair. "Have you?"*

"*Joe,*" *Theodore said solemnly, "I never have."*

"*Then I can't understand why we are running into such hard luck."*

Theodore grinned and chuckled; Joe grinned and chuckled. This broke down the last barriers between them.

"*Bad luck followed us like a yellow dog follows a drunkard,*" *Joe said later.*

We did not expect to find the horses again that night, but nevertheless took up the broad trail made by the saddles as they dragged through the dewy grass, and followed it well in the moonlight. Our task proved easier than we had feared. They had not run much over half a mile, and we found them standing close together and looking intently round when we came up. Leading them back we again went to sleep.

The weather was rapidly changing and by three o'clock a fine rain began to come steadily down. We cowered and shivered under our wet blankets till morning. At the first streak of dawn, having again eaten a couple of biscuits, we were off, glad to bid goodbye to the inhospitable pool in whose neighborhood we had spent such a comfortless night. A fine drizzling mist hid from sight all distant objects and, at times, there were heavy downpours of rain. For some hours we kept a nearly straight course, travelling by compass, over the formless, shapeless plain, drenched through and thoroughly uncomfortable. As we rose over a low divide, the fog lifted for a few minutes, and we saw several black objects slowly crossing some rolling country ahead of us, and a glance satisfied us they were buffalo. Picketing the horses, we ran up as near the game as we dared, and then began to stalk them, creeping forward on our hands and knees through the soft, muddy prairie soil, while a smart shower of rain blew in our faces, as we advanced up wind. The country was favorable, and we got within less than a hundred yards of the nearest, a large cow, though we had to creep along so slowly that we were chilled through, and our teeth chattered behind our blue lips. To crown my misfortunes, I now made one of those misses which a man to his dying day always looks back upon with wonder and regret. With the rain beating in my face and the drops standing out in the sights of the rifle, I either overshot or else at the last moment gave a nervous jerk and pulled the rifle clear off the mark. I missed clean, and the whole band plunged down into a hollow and were off before, with my stiffened and numbed fingers, I could get another shot. In wet, sullen misery we plodded back to the ponies.

All that day the rain continued, and we passed another wretched night. Next morning, however, it had cleared off. As the sun rose brightly we forgot our hunger and sleepiness, and rode cheerily off up a large dry creek, in whose bottom pools of rain-water still stood.

So far the trip had certainly not been a success. But a man who is fond of sport and yet is not naturally a good hunter, soon learns that if he wishes any success at all he must both keep in memory and put in practice Anthony Trollope's famous precept, "It's dogged as does it."

Shortly after midday we left the creek bottom, and skirted a ridge of broken buttes, out up by the gullies and winding ravines, in whose bottoms grew bunch-grass. While passing near the mouth and to leeward of one of these ravines both ponies threw up their heads and snuffed the air, turning their muzzles toward the head of the gully. Feeling sure that they had smelt some wild beast, either a bear or a buffalo, I slipped off my pony and ran quickly but cautiously up along the valley. Before I had gone a hundred yards, I noticed in the soft soil at the bottom the round prints of a bison's hoofs. I immediately afterward got a glimpse of the animal himself, as he fed slowly up the course of the ravine, some distance ahead of me. The wind was just right, and no ground could have been better for stalking. Hardly needing to bend down, I walked up behind a small sharp-crested hillock and, peeping over, there below me, not fifty yards off, was a great bison bull. He was walking along, grazing as he walked. His glossy fall coat was in fine trim and shone in the rays of the sun, while his pride of bearing showed him to be in the lusty vigor of his prime. As I rose above the crest of the hill, he held up his head and cocked his tail to the air. . . .

Joe Ferris, who had followed Theodore, pointed out a yellow spot on the buffalo, just back of the shoulder, and whispered, "If you hit him there, you'll get him right through the heart. . . ."

Before he could go off, I put the bullet in behind his shoulder. The wound was an almost immediately fatal one, yet with surprising agility for a large and heavy animal, he bounded up the opposite side of the ravine, heedless of two more balls, both of which went into his flank, and ranged forward, and disappeared over the ridge at a lumbering gallop, the blood pouring from his mouth and nostrils. We knew he could not go far, and trotted leisurely along on his bloody trail. In the next gully we found him stark dead, lying almost on his back, having pitched over the side when he tried to go down it. His head was a remarkably fine one, even for a fall buffalo.

With the enthusiasm that was to be his all of his life Theodore did an Indian war dance around the dead buffalo, expressing his delight in every conceivable way, in addition to giving Joe Ferris a hundred dollars.

"I never saw any one so enthused in my life," Joe Ferris said, "and, by golly, I was enthused myself for more reasons than one. I was plumb tired out, and, besides, he was so eager to shoot his first buffalo that it somehow got into my

blood; and I wanted to see him kill his first one as badly as
he wanted to kill it."

The flesh of a cow or calf is better eating than is that of
the bull, although the so-called hump meat—the strip of
steak on each side of the backbone—is excellent and tender
and juicy. The flesh of this bull tasted uncommonly good
to us, for we had been without fresh meat for a week. Until
a healthy, active man has been without it for some time, he
does not know how painfully hungry for flesh he becomes.
And the very toil I had been obliged to go through, in order
to procure the head, made me feel all the prouder of it when
at last it was in my possession.

Chapter 2

Theodore Becomes a Bad Lands Rancher

THEODORE'S LONG talks with Lang had been, it turned out, more than mere curiosity. He was seriously considering going into the ranching business—perhaps even for his life's work—in the Bad Lands. When he suggested a partnership with Lang, the Scotchman had to refuse reluctantly —for he had developed a great admiration and affection for this young Easterner—because of other commitments. He suggested, however, that Theodore would do well to tie up with Sylvane Ferris and William Merrifield. These two had a commitment with another group of men but were willing to see if their backers would sell out. In another week Theodore found out that they would and he wrote out a check to his two new partners for $14,000 with which to purchase cattle.

"Don't you want a receipt?" Ferris asked.

"Oh, that's all right," Theodore replied. "If I didn't trust you men, I wouldn't go into business with you."

This was hardly the way that his ancestors made the money that he was now using.

Theodore was now in the ranching business not in a big way but certainly on a substantial level. Back in New York the level-headed, business-minded members of the Roosevelt clan were not as sanguine about his adventure as he was. But Theodore did not have time to do much worrying. He was up for re-election to the legislature and, to his delight if to his worry, Alice was going to have a baby.

Theodore was re-elected easily and in his new term in the legislature continued to carry on his vigorous fight for better government. However this wasn't enough of a challenge to take up all of his energy and initiative.

But he was to receive a challenge that rocked him to the outmost reaches of his imagination. At ten o'clock in the morning, February 12, 1884, Alice gave birth to a baby girl. At five o'clock the next morning, Theodore's mother died, and six hours later Alice also died.

His new-born baby girl, also named Alice, was put in the care of his sister. He turned his attention to his work at Albany with savage intensity, but there was no one to whom he could turn in his grief and loneliness. The house that he had planned for Alice, to be built on a plot of ground he had bought at Oyster Bay, was already rising. But it was only a hollow mockery of what was to have been. In desperation his thoughts turned more and more to the Bad Lands.

In the spring he wrote Sylvane Ferris about the advisability of adding another thousand head of cattle to the small herd they had started with.

"Don't put in any more money until you're sure we've scattered the other dollars right," Ferris wrote back. "Better come out first and look around."

This was exactly what Theodore wanted to do. He went back to the Bad Lands in June.

In buying out Ferris and Merrifield, and the Maltese Cross brand, Theodore had bought only the cattle and the stock. The two men still owned the building and the land was owned by the Northern Pacific railroad and the government. The range claimed by the "Maltese Cross" had a fronting of four miles on both sides of the river and extended back on both sides about thirty miles.

Theodore determined to make cattle raising his main business and he authorized Ferris and Merrifield to buy a thousand more head.

Theodore plunged into the life of a ranchman with his usual energy. Very soon he convinced Ferris and Merrifield that he was not just a tenderfoot, playing around with a ranch, but that he intended to pull his own weight. Very soon after he got there, while out hunting for lost horses, he proved that he was able to take care of himself. He told about it in his Autobiography:

The only time I ever had serious trouble was at a primitive little hotel. It was on an occasion when I was out after lost horses. Below, the hotel had merely a barroom, a dining room, and a lean-to kitchen; above was a loft with fifteen or twenty beds in it. It was late in the evening when I reached the place. I heard one or two shots in the barroom as I came up, and I disliked going in. But there was nowhere else to go, and it was a cold night. Inside the room were several men, who, including the bartender, were wearing the kind of smile worn by men who are making believe to like what they don't like. A shabby individual in a broad hat with a cocked gun in each hand was walking up and down the floor talking with strident profanity. He had evidently been shooting at the clock, which had two or three holes in its face.

He was not a "bad man" of the really dangerous type, the true man-killer type, but he was an objectionable creature, a would-be bad man, a bully who for a moment was having things all his own way. As soon as he saw me he hailed me as "four eyes," in reference to my spectacles, and said, "Four-eyes is going to treat." I joined in the laugh and got behind the stove and sat down, thinking to escape notice. He followed me, however, and though I tried to pass it off as a jest this merely made him more offensive, and he stood leaning over me, a gun in each hand, using very foul language. He was foolish to stand so near, and, moreover, his heels were close together, so that his position was unstable. Accordingly, in response to his reiterated command that I should set up the drinks, I said, "Well, if I've got to, I've got to," and rose, looking past him.

As I rose, I struck quick and hard with my right just to one side of the point of his jaw, hitting with my left as I straightened out, and then again with my right. He fired the guns, but I do not know whether this was merely a convulsive action of his hands or if he was trying to shoot me. When he went down he struck the corner of the bar with his head. It was not a case in which one could afford to take chances, and if he had moved I was about to drop on his ribs with my knees. But he was senseless. I took away his guns, and the other people in the room, who were now loud in their denunciation of him, hustled him out and put him in a shed. I got dinner as soon as possible, sitting in a corner of the dining room away from windows, and then went upstairs to bed where it was dark so that there would be no chance of any shooting at me from the outside. However, nothing happened. When my assailant came to, he went down to the station and left on a freight.

Instead of frightening Theodore away from the Bad Lands this encounter added a touch of peril that made him want to stay even more badly. There were to be other stimulating forces.

One of them was Antoine de Vallombrosa, Marquis de Mores. This young French nobleman, married to the daughter of a wealthy New York banker, came to the Bad Lands in March, 1883, with the intention of going into the cattle business on a big scale. He was a member of an Orleans family, son of a duke, and a graduate of Saint Cyr. Twenty-six years old, a magnificent rider and a dead shot with rifle and pistol, he was a fine figure of a man, tall, with a military carriage, handsome, with black hair and mustache. "He had no judgment," said Bill Merrifield later, "but he was a fighter from hell." On arriving at Little Missouri he announced that he had his father-in-law's ten million dollars back of him and that he could borrow that much more. "I've got Armour and the rest of them matched dollar for dollar," he said. His plans called for buying up all of the beef, sheep and hogs that came over the Northern Pacific Railroad, slaughter them there in an abattoir which he built and then ship the meat products on to market in refrigerator cars. When he could not get the deal that he wanted in Little Missouri, he moved across the river and started a new town, christened Medora after his wife, and set up operations to make the new place, as he said, rival Omaha and Chicago. Some distance from Little Missouri, across the river from his abattoir, he built a twenty-six room chateau.

The grandiose schemes of the Marquis (which later shifted to sheep and cabbage raising), in addition to bringing many people to the region ran headlong into the interests of others. In the spring of 1884, before Theodore returned to the Bad Lands, the Marquis directed his foreman to drive fifteen hundred head of cattle to be pastured on range claimed by Ferris and Merrifield for the use of Theodore's cattle. Merrifield told the foreman in charge of the cattle to move them. He refused. Although it was late at night Merrifield rode into Medora to see the Marquis and found him at his office.

"We want them cattle moved by daylight," Merrifield told him.

"And if I don't?"

"We'll move them."

The Marquis tried to hedge by asking for three-weeks' grace. Merrifield, knowing the frontier advice, "Never draw your gun unless you mean to use it," refused.

The Marquis wrote out the order in a surly manner. Whether Merrifield told Theodore or not is not known.

However his actions were those Theodore would have demanded.

The chief thing which bothered Theodore was the lack of space and of privacy at the little Chimney Butte ranchhouse in which to do his reading and writing. As he looked around at great tracts of land still open for anyone who had the courage to use them, plans for a big ranching operation began to shape up. This was one way to forget Alice. He determined to bring out his old guide and friend, Bill Sewall, and to start another ranch. Thirty-five miles up the Little Missouri he found an ideal site for a ranchhouse with enough untaken range for a few thousand additional cattle. He wrote Bill Sewall asking him if he would come out, bring his nephew, Wilmot Dow with him, and take charge of this ranch.

"Now a little plain talk," he said in the letter, "though I think it unnecessary for I know you too well. If you are afraid of hard work and privation, don't come out west. If you expect to make a fortune in a year or two, don't come west. If you will give up under temporary discouragements, don't come out west. If, on the other hand, you are willing to work, especially the first year; if you realize that for a couple of years you cannot expect to make much more than you are now making; if you also know at the end of that time you will be in the receipt of about a thousand dollars for the third year, with an unlimited field ahead of you and a future as bright as you yourself choose to make it, then come."

Sewall and Dow agreed to come.

Theodore was pretty much of a joke to the working cow-men and cowboys the first part of that summer in 1884. He made a number of the local roundups doing what he could and trying to understand the picturesque language used around the cowcamps.

In one of the roundups some cows broke away from the herd. Theodore tried to head them back but failed. "Hasten forward quickly there," he shouted to one of his men.

That did it. This Harvardian phrase got belly laughs from all of them and was thereafter made a part of the language of the Bad Lands. He was to hear again and again, instead of the usual "head them cattle" spiced with juicy oaths, "Hasten forward quickly there!"

But he in turn had his laugh on them. Merrifield and Fisher, an employee of the Marquis, thought they would have some fun with him. They agreed to take Theodore for a hunt on the Sully Trail and see him get thrown by his horse. This trail ran along the sides of steep buttes to the southeast of Medora and was almost impassable. In addition, rain had made it slippery. They came to a steep, grassy slope that dipped away at an angle of forty-five degrees to a dry creek bed.

"There goes a deer!" Merrifield shouted, heading his horse down the trail. Theodore raced after him with Fisher coming along behind. Somehow the plan went awry. At the bottom of the trail Theodore was still on his horse and somewhere, halfway up, Merrifield was off his and rolling down toward the creek.

"Now see what you've done, Merrifield," Theodore said, in mock anger. "That deer is probably in Montana now."

As for Theodore he had a glorious time. "The country is growing on me, more and more," he wrote his sister. "It has a curious, fantastic beauty of its own, and as I own six or eight horses, I have a fresh one every day and ride on the lope all day long. How sound I do sleep at night now! I have never been in better health."

Before going east to bring out Sewall and Dow, he went off for a hunt by himself. "I wanted to see if I could not do perfectly well without a guide. . . ."

I took a trip in June, 1884, with antelope hunting for its chief object. The rest of the men were busy on the roundup. We had been living on salt pork, beans, potatoes, and bread. Finding I had a few days to spare, I thought I should take a short trip on the prairie and get a little sport and a little fresh meat out of the bands of pronghorn bucks which I was sure to encounter. Intending to be gone but a couple of days, it was not necessary to take many articles. Behind my saddle I carried a blanket for bedding, an oilskin coat to ward off the wet, a large metal cup with the handle riveted, not soldered, on, so that water could be boiled in it, a little tea and salt, some biscuits, and a small waterproof bag containing my half-dozen personal necessaries—not forgetting a book.

I started in the very earliest morning before the first streak of dawn. By the time I left the river-bottom and struck off up the valley of a winding creek, which led through the Bad Lands, the eastern sky was growing rosy, and soon the buttes and cliffs were lit up by the level rays of the cloudless summer sun. The air was fresh and sweet, and odorous

with the sweet scents of the springtime that was but barely
passed. The dew lay heavy, in glittering drops, on the leaves
and the blades of grass, whose vivid green, at this season,
for a short time brightened the desolate and sterile-looking
wastes of the lonely Western plains. The rose-bushes were
all in bloom, and their pink blossoms clustered in every
point and bend of the stream. The sweet, sad songs of the
hermit-thrushes rose from the thickets, while the meadow
larks perched boldly in sight as they uttered their louder
and more cheerful music.

Leaving the creek, I struck off among a region of scoria
buttes, the ground rising into rounded hills, through whose
grassy covering the red volcanic rock showed in places,
while boulder-like fragments of it were scattered all through
the valleys between. There were a few clumps of bushes
here and there, and near one of them were two magpies,
who lit on an old buffalo skull, bleached white by sun and
snow. . . .

After passing the last line of low, rounded scoria buttes,
the horse stepped out on the border of the great, seemingly
endless stretches of rolling or nearly level prairie.

I rode over the land in a general southerly course, bending
to the right or left according to the nature of the ground
and the likelihood of finding game. Most of the time the
horse kept on a steady single-foot, but this was varied by a
sharp lope every now and then, to ease the muscles of both
steed and rider. The sun was well up, and its beams beat
fiercely down on our heads from out of the cloudless sky.
My glass was slung alongside the saddle, and from every
one of the scattered hillocks the country was scanned care-

fully far and near. The greatest caution was used in riding up over any divide, to be sure that no game on the opposite side was scared by the sudden appearance of my horse or myself.

Nowhere, not even at sea, does a man feel more lonely than when riding over the far-reaching, seemingly never-ending plains. Their very vastness and loneliness and their melancholy monotony have a strong fascination. Nowhere else does one seem so far off from all mankind.

Although I could see so far, yet all objects on the outer-most verge of the horizon, even though within the ken of my vision, looked unreal and strange; for there was no shade to take away from the bright glare, and at a little distance things seemed to shimmer and dance in the hot rays of the sun. The ground was scorched to a dull brown, and against its monotonous expanse any objects stood out with a prominence that made it difficult to judge of the distance at which they were. A mile off one could see, through the strange shimmering haze, the shadowy white outlines of something which loomed vaguely up till it looked as large as the canvas top of a prairie wagon. But as I came nearer it shrunk and dwindled and took clearer form, until at last it changed into the ghastly staring skull of some mighty buffalo, long dead and gone to join the rest of his vanished race.

When I left the grassy prairies and entered a region of alkali desert and sage-brush, the look of the country became even more grim and forbidding. In places the alkali formed a white frost on the ground that glanced in the sunlight like the surface of a frozen lake. The dusty little sage-brush, stunted and dried up, sprawled over the parched ground, from which it could hardly extract the small amount of nourishment necessary for even its wizened life. The spiny cactus alone seemed to be really in its true home.

During the morning I came in sight of several small bands of antelope. Most of them saw me as soon as or before I saw them, and after watching me with intense curiosity as long as I was in sight and at a distance, made off at once as soon as I went into a hollow or appeared to be approaching too near. Twice, in scanning the country narrowly with the glasses, from behind a sheltering divide, I saw bands of antelope that had not discovered me. In each case I left the horse to graze, while I started off after the game nearly a mile distant. For the first half-mile I walked upright or went along half stooping. Then, as the distance grew less, I crawled on all fours and kept behind any little broken bank, or took advantage of a small, dry watercourse, and toward the end, flat on my face, I wriggled like a serpent, using every stunted sage-brush or patch of cactus as a cover, bareheaded under the blazing sun. In each case, after nearly an hour's irksome, thirsty work, the stalk failed. One band simply ran off without a second's warning, alarmed at some awkward movement on my part and without giving a chance for a shot. In the other instance, while still at very long and uncertain range, I heard the sharp barking alarm-note of one of the pronghorn, the whole band instantly raising their heads and gazing intently at their would-be destroyer. They were a very long way off but, seeing it was hopeless to try to get nearer, I rested my rifle over a little mound of earth and fired. The dust came up in a puff to one side of the nearest antelope. The whole band took a few jumps and turned again; the second shot struck at their feet, and they went off like so many race-horses, being missed again as they ran. I sat up by a sage-brush, thinking they would, of course, not come back, when to my surprise I saw them wheel round with the precision of a cavalry squadron, all in line and fronting me, the white and brown markings on their heads and throats showing like the facings on soldiers' uniforms. Then back they came charging up till again within long range, when they wheeled their line as if on a pivot and once more made off, this time for good, not heeding an ineffectual fusillade from the Winchester.

By midday I reached a dry creek and followed up its course for a mile or so, till a small spot of green in the side of a bank showed the presence of water, a little pool of which lay underneath. Both my horse, Manitou, and I satisfied our thirst, and Manitou was turned loose to graze, with his saddle off, so as to cool his back, and I, after eating a biscuit, lay on my face on the ground—there was no shade of any sort near—and dozed until a couple of hours' rest and feed had put the horse in good trim for the afternoon ride.

For some time after leaving the creek I saw nothing until, on coming over the crest of the next great divide, I came in sight of a band of six or eight pronghorn about a quarter of a mile off to my right hand. There was a slight breeze from the southeast, which blew diagonally across my path toward the antelope. The latter, after staring at me a minute, as I rode slowly on, suddenly started at full speed to run directly up wind, and therefore in a direction that would cut the line of my course less than half a mile ahead of where

I was. Knowing that when antelope begin running in a
straight line they are very hard to turn, and seeing that they
would have to run a longer distance than my horse would to
intercept them, I clapped spurs into Manitou, and the game
old fellow, a very fleet runner, stretched himself down to the
ground and seemed to go almost as fast as the quarry. As I
had expected, when the antelope saw me running, they
merely straightened themselves out and went on, possibly
even faster than before, without changing the line of their
flight, keeping right up wind. Both horse and antelope fairly
flew over the ground, their courses being at an angle that
would certainly bring them together. Two of the antelope
led, by some fifty yards or so, the others, who were all
bunched together. Nearer and nearer we came, Manitou, in
spite of carrying myself and the pack behind the saddle,
gamely holding his own. When the two leading animals
crossed the line of my flight ahead of me, I pulled short up,
leaped from Manitou's back, and blazed into the band as
they went by not forty yards off, aiming well ahead of a fine
buck who was on the side nearest me. As the smoke blew
off I saw the buck roll over like a rabbit, with both shoulders
broken.

I cut off the hams and strung them beside the saddle. Then
after securing the buck's head—the horns were unusually
long and fine—I pushed rapidly on without stopping to
hunt, to reach some large creek which would contain both
wood and water, for even in summer a fire added greatly to
the comfort and coziness of a night camp. When the sun
had nearly set I went over a divide and came in sight of a
creek. It wound its way through a valley of rich bottom-

land, cottonwood trees growing in thick groves along its banks, while its bed contained many deep pools of water, some of it fresh and good. I rode into a great bend, with a grove of trees on its right and containing excellent feed. I loosed Manitou with the lariat round his neck to feed where he wished until I went to bed, when he was to be taken to a place where the grass was thick and succulent, and tethered out for the night. There was plenty of wood with which a fire was started for cheerfulness, and some of the coals were soon raked off apart to cook over. The metal cup was soon filled with water and simmering over the coals to make tea, while an antelope steak was roasting on a forked stick. It is wonderful how cozy a camp, in clear weather, became if there was a good fire and enough to eat, and how sound the sleep was afterward in the cool air, with the brilliant stars glimmering through the branches overhead.

Early in the morning I was awakened by the shrill yelping of the prairie-dogs, whose town was near me. The sun had not risen, and the air had the peculiar chill it always takes on toward morning, while little wreaths of light mist rose from the pools. Getting up and loosing Manitou to let him feed round where he wished and slake his thirst, I took the rifle, strolled up the creek-valley a short distance, and turned off out on the prairie. Overhead a skylark was singing, soaring up above me so high that I could not make out his form in the gray morning light. I listened for some time, and the music never ceased for a moment, coming down clear, sweet, and tender from the air above. Soon the strains of another answered from a little distance off, and the two kept soaring and singing as long as I stayed to listen.

The sun was just appearing when I walked back to the creek bottom. A doe came slowly out of a patch of brushwood, going down to drink—her great, sensitive ears thrown forward as she peered anxiously and timidly round. She was very watchful, lifting her head and gazing about between every few mouthfuls. When she had drunk her fill she snatched a hasty mouthful or two of the wet grass, and then cantered back to the edge of the brush, when a little spotted fawn came out and joined her. The two stood together for a few moments, and then walked off into the cover. The little pond at which they had drunk had other tenants in the shape of a mallard duck, with a brood of little ducklings, balls of fuzzy yellow down, that bobbed off into the reeds like little corks as I walked by.

Breaking camp was a simple operation for one man. A few minutes after breakfast Manitou and I were off, the embers of the fire having been extinguished with the care that comes to be almost second nature with the cattleman, one of whose chief dreads is the prairie fire that sometimes robs his stock of such an immense amount of feed. Very little game was seen during the morning. The sweat drenched the horse even when we were walking. Before noon we halted for rest by a bitter alkaline pool with border so steep and rotten that I had to bring water up to the horse in my hat. When leaving this halting-place, I spied three figures in the distance, loping toward me. They turned out to be cowboys, looking up a band of strayed ponies, and, as they had exhausted their supply of food, I gave them the antelope hams, trusting to shoot another for my own use.

I headed the horse toward the more rolling country where

the prairies begin to break off into the edges of the Bad Lands. Toward evening, when only about a mile from a wooded creek on whose banks I intended to sleep, I came across a solitary buck, just as I was topping the ridge of the last divide. As I was keeping a sharp lookout at the time, I reined in the horse the instant the head of the antelope came in sight, and jumping off crept up till I could see his whole body, when I dropped on my knee and took steady aim. He was a long way off (three hundred yards by actual pacing), and not having made out exactly what we were he stood still, looking intently in our direction and broadside to us. I held well over his shoulder, and at the report he dropped like a shot, the ball having broken his neck. Taking the hams and saddle, I rode on down to the creek and again went into camp among timber.

On this trip I was never successful in outwitting antelope on the several occasions when I pitted my craft and skill against their wariness and keen senses, always either failing to get within range or else missing them. Nevertheless I got two by taking advantage of the stupidity and curiosity which they occasionally show.

The middle part of the days having proved so very hot, and as my store of biscuits was nearly gone, and as I knew, moreover, that the antelope meat would not keep over twenty-four hours, I decided to push back home next day; and, accordingly, I broke camp at the first streak of dawn, and took Manitou back to the ranch at a smart lope.

A few days later Theodore went East to bring out his two new partners.

Chapter 3

Life on the Ranch

THEODORE RETURNED to the Bad Lands on
July 31, 1884 with Sewall and Dow. Sewall was not impressed with the place as ranching country.

"Bill," Theodore said emphatically, "you don't know anything about it. Everybody says that it is."

Sewall did not argue. As soon as possible Theodore set to
work building his ranchhouse out of cottonwood trees. "I
could chop fairly well for an amateur," he wrote, "but I
could not do one-third the work that Sewall and Dow could.
One day when we were cutting down the cottonwood trees,
to begin our building operations, I heard some one ask Dow
what the total cut had been, and Dow, not realizing that I
was within hearing, answered, 'Well, Bill cut down fifty-
three, I cut down forty-nine, and the boss, he beavered down
seventeen.' Those who have seen the stump of a tree which
46

has been gnawed down by a beaver will understand the force of the comparison."

This ranching life appealed to Theodore. He even liked the costumes. "I wear a sombrero, silk neckerchief, fringed buckskin shirt, sealskin chaparajos or riding-trousers, and alligator-hide boots," he wrote his sister, "and with my pearl-hilted revolver and beautifully finished Winchester rifle, I feel able to face anything."

By the end of the next summer both Sewall and Dow had brought their wives out. From then on the food, the quarters and general living at the Elkhorn ranch were much better, Theodore described his layout:

My home ranch lay on both sides of the Little Missouri, the nearest ranchman above me being about twelve, and the nearest below me about ten, miles distant. The general course of the stream here was northerly, but, while flowing through my ranch, it took a great westerly reach of some three miles, walled in, as always, between chains of steep, high bluffs, half a mile or more apart. The stream twisted down through the valley in long sweeps, leaving oval wooded bottoms, first on one side and then on the other.

In an open glade among the thick-growing cottonwoods stood the long, low house of hewn logs. Just in front of the ranch veranda was a line of old cottonwoods that shaded it during the fierce heats of summer, rendering it always cool and pleasant. But a few feet behind these trees came the cut-off bank of the river, through whose broad, sandy bed the shallow stream wound as if lost, except when a freshet filled it from brim to brim with foaming yellow water. The bluffs that walled in the river valley curved back in semicircles, rising from its alluvial bottom generally as abrupt cliffs, but often as steep, grassy slopes that led up to great level plateaus. The line was broken every mile or two by the entrance of a dry creek whose head branches might be twenty miles back. Above us, where the river came round the bend, the valley was very narrow, and the high buttes bounding it rose, sheer and barren, into scalped hill peaks and naked knife-blade ridges.

From the low, long veranda, one looked across sand-bars and shallows to a strip of meadowland, behind which rose a long line of sheer cliffs and grassy plateaus. This veranda was a pleasant place in the summer evenings when a cool breeze stirred along the river and blew in the faces of tired men, who lolled back in their rocking chairs (what true American does not enjoy a rocking chair?), book in hand— though they did not often read the books, but rocked gently to and fro, gazing sleepily out at the weird-looking buttes opposite, until their sharp lines grew indistinct and purple in the afterglow of the sunset.

The other buildings stood in the same open glade with the ranch house, the dense growth of cottonwoods and matted, thorny underbrush making a wall all about, through which we had chopped our wagon roads and trodden out our own bridle paths. The cattle had trampled down this brush a little, but deer still lay in it, only a couple of hundred yards from the house. From the door sometimes in the evening one could see them peer out into the open, or make their way down, timidly and cautiously, to drink at the river. The stable, sheds, and other outbuildings, with the hayricks and the pens for such cattle as we brought up during winter were near the house. The patch of fenced garden land was on the edge of the woods. Near the middle of the glade stood the high circular horse corral, with a snubbing-post in the center, and a wing built out from one side of the gate entrance, so that the saddle band could be driven in without trouble. As it was very hard to work cattle where there was much brush, the larger cow corral was some four miles off on an open bottom.

Our routine of life at the ranch was always much the same, save during the excessively bitter weather of mid-winter when there was little to do except to hunt, if the days were fine enough.

We breakfasted early—before dawn when the nights had grown long, and rarely later than sunrise, even in the summer. The instant this meal was over the horse wrangler rode off to hunt up and drive in the saddle band. He drove these into the corral, the other men (who had been lolling idly about the house or stable, fixing their saddles or doing any odd job) coming out with their ropes as soon as they heard the patter of the unshod hoofs and the shouts of the cowboy driver. Going into the corral, and standing near the center, each of us picked out one of his own string from among the animals that were trotting and running in a compact mass round the circle. When all had caught their horses, the rest were again turned loose, together with those that had been kept up overnight.

Once saddled, the men rode off on their different tasks, for almost everything was done in the saddle, except that in the winter we cut fire-wood and quarried coal—both on the ranch—and in summer attended to the garden and put up what wild hay we needed.

If any horses had strayed, one or two of the men would go look for them, for hunting lost horses was one of the commonest and most irksome of our duties. Every outfit always had certain of its horses at large and, if they remained out long enough, they became as wild and wary as deer and had to be regularly surrounded and run down.

If the men did not go horse-hunting, they might ride off over the range, for there was generally some work to be done among the cattle.

During the early spring months, before the round-up began, the chief work was in hauling out mired cows and steers. As long as everything was frozen solid there was no danger from miring, but when the thaw came, along toward the beginning of March, a period of danger set in. The streams were left with an edging of deep bog, and the quicksand was at its worst. As the frost went out of the soil, the ground round every little alkali spring changed into a trembling quagmire, and deep holes of slimy, tenacious mud formed in the bottom of all gullies. The cattle which had lived on snow for three or four months, were very eager for water, and were weak and in poor condition. They rushed heedlessly into any pool and stood there drinking gallons of the icy water and sinking steadily into the mud. When they tried to get out they were already too deep down, and too weak to make a prolonged struggle. After one or two fits of desperate floundering, they resigned themselves to their fate with dumb apathy and were lost, unless some one of us riding about discovered and hauled them out. They might be lost in a wonderfully small mud hole, often found dead in a gulch not over two or three feet across, or in the quicksand of a creek so narrow that it could almost be jumped. An alkali hole, where the water oozed out through the thick clay, was the worst of all, owing to the ropy tenacity with which the horrible substance stuck and clung to any unfortunate beast that got into it. More cattle died from getting mired than from any other cause.

In addition to this, mud holes often proved very annoying to the rider himself, as getting his horse mired or caught in a quicksand was one of the commonest of the accidents that beset a horseman in the far West. This usually happened in fording a river, although I once saw a horse and rider suddenly engulfed while leisurely walking over what appeared to be dry land. They had come to an alkali mud hole, an old buffalo-wallow, which had filled up and was covered with a sun-baked crust that let them through as if they had stepped on a trap door. There being several of us along, we dragged both unfortunates out in short order.

While the river was up it was a very common thing for a horseman to have great difficulty in crossing, for the swift, brown water ran over a bed of deep quicksand that was ever shifting. An inexperienced horse became mad with fright in such a crossing, and, after speedily exhausting its strength in wild struggles, would throw itself on its side and drown unless the rider got off. An old horse used to such work would, on the contrary, take matters quietly and often push along through really dangerous quicksand. Old Manitou never lost his head for an instant but, now resting a few seconds, now feeling his way cautiously forward, and now making two or three desperate plunges, would go on wherever a horse possibly could.

Nor were mud holes the only danger the horseman had to fear. In much of the Bad Lands the buttes were so steep and broken that it needed genuine mountaineering skill to get through them, and no horse but a Western one, bred to the business, could have accomplished the feat. In many parts of our country it was impossible for a horseman who did not know the land to cross it, and it was difficult enough even for an experienced hand. For a stretch of nearly ten miles along the Little Missouri above my range, and where it passed through it, there were but three or four places where it was possible for a horseman to get out to the eastern prairie through the exceedingly broken country lying back from the river. In places this very rough ground came down to the river; elsewhere it lay back near the heads of the creeks. In such very bad ground the whole country seemed to be one tangled chaos of canyon-like valleys, winding gullies and washouts with abrupt, unbroken sides, isolated peaks of sandstone, marl, or gumbo clay, which rain turned into slippery glue, and hill chains, the ridges of which always ended in sheer cliffs. After a man had made his way with infinite toil for half a mile, a point might be reached around which it was an absolute impossibility to go, and he had nothing to do but painfully retrace his steps and try again in a new direction, as likely as not with the same result.

Once I was overtaken by darkness, while trying to get through a great tract of very rough land, and, after once or twice nearly breaking my neck, in despair had to give up all attempts to get out, and until daybreak simply stayed where

I was, in a kind of ledge or pocket on the side of the cliff, luckily sheltered from the wind. It was midsummer and the nights were short, but this particular one seemed quite long enough, and, though I was on the move by dawn, it was three hours later before I led the horse, as hungry, numb, and stiff as myself, out on the prairie again.

Occasionally it was necessary to cross some of the worst parts of the Bad Lands with a wagon, and such a trip was exhausting and laborious beyond belief. Often the wagon had to be taken to pieces every few hundred yards in order to get it over a ravine, lower it into a valley, or drag it up a cliff. One outfit that tried to take a short cut through some of the Bad Lands of the Powder River made just four miles in three days, and then had to come back to their starting-point after all.

The long forenoon's work, with its attendant mishaps to man and beast, being over, the men came riding in. The midday dinner was variable as to time, for it came when the men had returned from their work. It was the most sub-stantial meal of the day and we felt that we had little fault to find with a table on which were spread platters of smoked elk meat, loaves of good bread, jugs and bowls of milk, saddles of venison or broiled antelope-steaks, perhaps roast and fried prairie chicken with eggs, butter, wild plums, and tea or coffee.

The afternoon's tasks were usually much the same as the morning's, although often spent in doing odd jobs as, for instance, breaking in a new horse.

Horses were cheap, each outfit had a great many, and the wages for breaking an animal were but five or ten dollars. Three rides, of an hour or two each, on as many consecutive days, were the outside number a bronco-buster deemed necessary before turning an animal over as "broken." The average bronco-buster, however, handled horses so very roughly that we preferred, aside from motives of economy, to break our own. The best and quietest horses on the ranch were far from being those broken by the best riders. On the contrary, they were those that had been handled most gently, although firmly, and that had the greatest number of days devoted to their education.

If doing nothing else the cowboys would practise roping. A man could not practise too much with this if he wished to attain even moderate proficiency. A forty-foot lariat was the one commonly used, for the ordinary range at which a man could throw it was only about twenty-five feet.

When the day's work was over we had supper, and bedtime came soon afterward, for the men who lived on ranches slept well and soundly.

A ranchman's work was, of course, free from much of the sameness attendant upon that of a mere cowboy. One day he might ride out with his men among the cattle, or stray horses; the next he might hunt, so as to keep the ranch in meat. Then he could make the tour of his outlying camps, or, again, he might join in one of the roundups.

There were few sounds to break the stillness of summer. From the upper branches of the cottonwoods—whose shimmering, tremulous leaves if there was the least bit of wind rustled and quivered and sighed all day long—came now and then the soft, melancholy cooing of the mourning dove, whose voice always seemed far away and expressed more than any other sound in nature the sadness of gentle, hopeless, never-ending grief. The cattle, that had strung down in long files from the hills, lay quietly on sand bars, except that some of the bulls kept traveling up and down, bellowing and giving vent to long, surly grumblings as they pawed the sand and tossed it up with their horns.

No life could be pleasanter than during the months of fall. The weather was cool and inviting. In the evenings and on the rare rainy days we were glad to sit by the great fireplace, with its roaring cottonwood logs. But on most days not a cloud dimmed the serene splendor of the sky. The fresh pure air was clear with the wonderful clearness of the high plains. We were in the saddle from morning until night. The fall was the time for riding. In the keen, frosty air neither man nor beast would tire, though out from the dawn until the shadows had again waxed long, warning all to push straight for home without drawing rein. Then deer-saddles and elk-haunches hung from the trees near the house, and one could always have good sport right on the sand of the river bed, for we always kept shotgun or rifle at hand to be ready for any prairie chickens or passing water fowl that might light on the river.

When the days had dwindled to their shortest, and the nights seemed never-ending, then all the great northern plains were changed into an abode of iron desolation. Sometimes furious gales blew out of the north, driving before them the clouds of blinding snow-dust, wrapping the mantle of death round every unsheltered being that faced their unshackled anger. They roared in a thunderous bass as they swept across the prairie or whirled through the naked canyons. They shivered the great brittle cottonwoods, and beneath their rough touch the icy limbs of the pines that clustered in the gorges sang like the chords of an Aeolian harp. Again, in the coldest midwinter weather, not a breath of wind might stir. Then the still, merciless, terrible cold that brooded over the earth like the shadow of silent death seemed even more dreadful in its gloomy rigor than in the lawless madness of the storms. All the land was like granite. The great rivers stood still in their beds, as if turned to frosted steel. In the long nights there was no sound to break the lifeless silence. Under the ceaseless, shifting play of the Northern Lights, or lighted only by the wintry brilliance of the stars, the snow-clad plains stretched out into dead and endless wastes of glimmering white.

Then the great fireplace of the ranch house was choked with blazing logs, and at night we had to sleep under so many blankets that the weight was fairly oppressive. Outside, the shaggy ponies huddled together in the corral, while long icicles hung from their lips, and the hoarfrost whitened the hollow backs of the cattle.

A ride in midwinter was fascinating. The great white country wrapped in the powdery snow-drift seemed like another land. The familiar landmarks were so changed that a man must be careful lest he lose his way. When the sun was out the glare from the endless white stretches dazzled the eyes. If the gray snowclouds hung low and only let a pale, wan light struggle through, the lonely wastes became fairly appalling in their desolation.

There were few moments more pleasant than the home coming, when, in the gathering darkness, after crossing the last chain of ice-covered buttes, or after coming round the last turn in the wind-swept valley, we saw, through the leafless trees, or across the frozen river, the red gleam of the firelight as it shone through the ranch windows and flickered over the trunks of the cottonwoods outside, warming a man's blood by the mere hint of the warmth awaiting him within.

The long winter evenings were spent sitting round the hearthstone, while the logs roared and crackled, and the men played checkers or chess, in the firelight.

Rough board shelves held a number of books without which some of the evenings would have been long indeed. As for Irving, Hawthorne, Cooper, Lowell, and the other standbys, I suppose no man, East or West, would willingly be long without. For lighter reading there were dreamy Ik Marvel, Burroughs' breezy pages, and the quaint, pathetic character-sketches of the Southern writers—Cable, Craddock, Macon, Joel Chandler Harris, and sweet Sherwood Bonner. And when one was in the Bad Lands he felt as if they somehow looked just exactly as Poe's tales and poems sounded.

Chapter 4

Wildlife at the Ranch

IN THE still fall nights, if we lay awake, we could listen to the clanging cries of the water fowl, as their flocks sped southward, and, in cold weather, the coyotes occasionally came near enough for us to hear their uncanny wailing. The larger wolves, too, now and then joined in, with a kind of deep, dismal howling.

The wolf was not nearly as common with us as the little coyote. When the cattlemen came they soon perceived in the wolves their natural foes, and followed them unrelentingly. They shot at and chased them on all occasions, killed great numbers by poisoning, and as a result they hardly ever stirred abroad by day and they were rarely seen. At night it was different. The wolves then wandered far and wide, often coming up round the outbuildings of the ranches. The prey was invariably seized by the haunch or flank, and the entrails afterwards torn out, while a cougar, on the contrary, grasped the neck or throat.

On a neighboring ranch there was an ill-favored hybrid, whose mother was a Newfoundland and whose father was a large wolf. It was stoutly built, with erect ears, pointed muzzle, rather short head, short bushy tail, and a brindled color. Funnily enough, it looked more like a hyena than like either of its parents, and both barked and howled.

The parent wolf carried on a long courtship with the Newfoundland. He came round the ranch regularly and boldly every night, and she would at once go out to him. In the daytime he would lie hid in the bushes at some little distance. Once or twice his hiding place was discovered, and then the men would amuse themselves by setting the Newfoundland on him. She would make at him, but when they were a good way from the men he would turn round and wait for her and they would go roaming off together, not to be seen again for several hours.

The cougar was hardly ever seen round my ranch but, toward the mountains, it was very destructive both to horses and horned cattle. One would generally lie in wait for the heifers or young steers as they came down to water, and, singling out an animal, reach it in a couple of bounds and fasten its fangs in the throat or neck.

The skunks were a nuisance around the ranch in more ways than one.

A number of us, among whom was a huge, happy-go-lucky Scotchman who went by the name of Sandy, were sleeping in a hut when a skunk burrowed under the logs and got in. Hearing it moving about among the tin pans Sandy struck a light, was much taken by the familiarity of the pretty black-and-white animal, and, as it seemed to his eyes a curiosity, took a shot at it with his revolver. He missed and, for a wonder, the skunk retired promptly without taking any notice of the attack. The rest of the alarmed sleepers, when informed of the cause of the shot, cursed the Scotch-man up hill and down dale for having so nearly brought dire confusion on them all. Sandy took the abuse very philosophi-cally, merely remarking, "I'm glad a did nay kill him mysel'. He seemed such a dacent wee beastie."

Neither the skunk nor Sandy had learned any wisdom, however. Half an hour later the "dacent wee beastie" came back and this time Sandy fired at him with fatal effect. Of course the result was a frantic rush of all hands from the hut, Sandy exclaiming with late but sincere repentence, "A did nay ken 't wad cause such a tragadee."

Rattlesnakes were only too plentiful along the river bot-toms, in the broken, hilly ground, and on the prairies and the great desert wastes alike. Every cowboy killed dozens each season. To a man wearing top boots there was little or no danger while he was merely walking about, for the fangs could not go through the leather, and the snake did not strike as high as the knee. It was, of course, both a dangerous and a disagreeable neighbor, and one of its annoying traits was the fondness it displayed for crawling into a hut or taking refuge among the blankets left out on the ground. Except in such cases, men were rarely in danger from it, unless they happened to be stooping over, or unless the snake was encountered while stalking an animal.

Once I was creeping up to an antelope under cover of some very low sage brush—so low that I had to lie flat on my face and push myself along with my hands and feet.

While cautiously moving on in this way I was electrified by hearing almost by my ears the well-known ominous "whi-r-r" of a rattlesnake, and on hastily glancing up there was the reptile, not ten feet away from me, all coiled up and waiting. I backed off and crawled to one side, the rattler turning its head round to keep watch over my movements. When my stalk was over (the antelope took alarm and ran off before I was within rifle shot) I came back, hunted up the snake and killed it.

The mighty bird of rapine, the war-eagle, which on the great plains and among the Rockies supplanted the bald-headed eagle of better watered regions, was a dangerous foe of the young antelope. It was even said that under exceptional circumstances eagles would assail a full-grown prong-horn.

On one occasion while riding over the range I witnessed an attack on a jack rabbit. The eagle was soaring overhead, and espied the jack while the latter was crouched motionless. Instantly the great bird rushed down through the humming air, with closed wings, checked itself when some four yards above the jack, hovered for a moment, and again fell like a bolt. Away went long-ears, running as only a frightened jack can, and after him the eagle, not with the arrowy rush of its descent from high air, but with eager, hurried flapping. In a short time it had nearly overtaken the fugitive when the jack dodged sharply to one side, and the eagle overshot it precisely as a greyhound would have done, stopping itself by a powerful, setting motion of the great pinions. Twice this maneuver was repeated, then the eagle made a quick rush, caught and overthrew the quarry before it could turn, and in another moment was sitting triumphant on the quivering body, the crooked talons driven deep into the soft, furry sides.

Once while hunting mountain sheep in the Bad Lands I killed an eagle on the wing with the rifle. I was walking beneath a cliff of gray clay, when the eagle sailed into view over the crest. As soon as he saw me he threw his wings aback, and for a moment before wheeling poised motionless, offering a nearly stationary target, so that my bullet grazed his shoulder, and down he came through the air, tumbling over and over. As he struck the ground he threw himself on his back, and fought against his death with the undaunted courage proper to his brave and cruel nature.

This grand bird, the war-eagle of the Sioux, was not very common in the Bad Lands, but was sometimes still seen with us and, as everywhere else, its mere presence added a certain grandeur to its lonely haunts.

One cool afternoon in the early fall of 1884 while sitting on the veranda of the ranchhouse, we heard a long way off the ha-ha-honk, ha-honk of wild geese. They came in sight, in a V-shaped line, flying low and heavily toward the south along the course of the stream, flying within a hundred yards of the house, and alighted about a mile past us. I took the rifle, as the ground was flat and without cover, and hurried after them on foot. As I came to the place where I thought they were, as wild geese are very watchful and wary, I crept along with as much caution as if the game had been a deer. Peering through a thick clump of bullberry bushes, I saw them clustered on a high sand bar in the middle of the river. The only way to get at them was to crawl along the river bed, which was partly dry, using the patches of rushes and the sand hillocks and driftwood to shield myself. I dropped over the bank and crept along on my hands and knees through the sand and gravel, keeping in line with a great log washed up on the shore which was some seventy-five yards from the geese. On reaching it and looking over I was annoyed to find that in the fading light I could not distinguish the birds clearly enough to shoot, as the dark river bank was behind them. I crawled quickly back a few yards and went off a good bit to the left into a hollow. Peeping over the ridge I could now see the geese, gathered into a clump with their necks held straight out, sharply outlined against the horizon. I fired into the thickest of the bunch, and as the rest flew off, with discordant clamor, ran forward and picked up my victim, a fat young Canada goose.

On another occasion while out riding along the river bottoms, just at dawn, I heard a splashing and low cackling in the stream where the water deepened in a wide bend which swept around a low bluff. Leaving my horse where he was, I walked off toward the edge of the stream and lying on the brink of the bank looked over into the water of the bend. Only a faint streak of light was visible in the east. Little wreaths of mist that rose from the river were between me and the geese. But I could plainly hear their low murmuring and splashing, and once one of them, as I judged from the sound, stood up on end and flapped its wings vigorously. Pretty soon a light puff of wind blew the thin mist aside, and I caught a glimpse of them. They were wild geese, five of them, resting on the water, drifting down stream. The fog closed over them again, but it was growing light very rapidly, and in a short time I knew they would be in the still water of the bend just below me, so I rose on my elbows and held my rifle ready at poise. In a few minutes, before the sun was above the horizon, but when there was plenty of light by which to shoot, another eddy in the wind blew away the vapor and showed the five geese in a cluster, some thirty yards off. I fired one shot, and one of the geese, kicking and flapping frantically, fell over, its neck half cut from the body, while the others, with laborious effort, got under way. Before they could get their heavy bodies fairly off the water and out of range, I took three more shots but missed. Waiting until the dead goose drifted into shore, I picked it up and tied it on the saddle of my horse to carry home to the ranch. Being young and fat it was excellent eating.

Another time I was out after antelope, starting before there was any light in the heavens, and pushing straight out toward the rolling prairie. After two or three hours, when the sun was well up, I neared where a creek ran in a broad, shallow valley. On looking over the crest with the glasses, my eye was at once caught by a row of white objects stretched straight along it, and another look showed me that they were snow geese. They were feeding, and were moving abreast of one another slowly down the length of the meadow toward the end nearest me, where a patch of small trees and brushwood lay. I slipped back over the crest and ran down to the bed of the creek, round a turn of the hill, where the geese were out of sight. I walked up to the trees without any special care, as they screened me from view, and looked cautiously out from behind them. The geese were moving along with their necks stretched out before them, nibbling and jerking at the grass as they tore it up by mouthfuls. Geese will not come near any cover in which foes may be lurking if they can help it, and so I feared that they would turn before coming near enough to the brush to give me a good shot. I therefore dropped into the bed of the creek, which wound tortuously along the side of the meadow, and crept on all fours along one of its banks until I came to where it made a loop out toward the middle of the bottom. Here there was a tuft of tall grass which served as a good cover, and I stood upright, dropping my hat, and looking through between the blades. The geese, still in a row, with several yards' interval between each of them, were only sixty or seventy yards off, still feeding toward me. I tried to get two in line, but could not. There was one gander much larger than any other bird in the lot that went by just opposite my hiding place. He stopped still, broadside to me, and I aimed just at the root of the neck. Away flew the others, and in a few minutes I was riding along with the white gander dangling behind my saddle.

It was possible in the sloughs and pools nearby, particularly during migrations, to get good bags of duck, "both among the young flappers (as tender and delicious birds for the table as any I know) and among the flights of wild ducks that made the region a stopping place." Theodore told about one good hunt when meat was low:

While out with the wagon we halted for the midday meal on the bank of the river. Noticing a bunch of teal fly past, I took my double-barrel and followed them on foot. On getting round the bend of the river I poked my head through the bushes and saw them on a sand bar in the middle of the stream. I aimed for the thickest part of the flock and fired. At the report they sprang into the air, and I leaped to my feet to give them the second barrel, when two spoonbills rose, and I took them instead, knocking both over. When I fished out the two spoonbills, I waded over to the sand bar and picked up eleven teal, making thirteen ducks with two barrels.

Another time, in 1884, out of fresh meat, I sallied forth intent not on sport but on slaughter. It was late fall, and as I rode along in the dawn a small pack of prairie fowl passed over my head and lit on a dead tree that stood out some distance from a grove of cottonwoods. They paid little attention to me, but they were so shy at that season that I did not dare to try to approach them on foot, but let the horse jog on at the regular cow pony gait—a kind of single-foot pace between a walk and a trot—and as I passed by, fired into the tree and killed four birds. Now I would not have dreamed of taking either of these shots had I been out purely for sport. Neither needed any more skill than would have been shown in killing hens in a barnyard. But when one is hunting for one's dinner he takes an interest in his success which he would otherwise lack, and on both occasions I felt a most unsportsmanlike glee when I found how many I had potted.

One of the strangest, and to me one of the most attractive

sounds of the prairie was the hollow booming made by the cocks in the spring. Before the snow had left the ground they would begin, and at the break of morning their deep resonant calls sounded from far and near, for in still weather they could be heard at immense distance. The call cannot be described in words. It has a hollow, vibrant sound like that of some wind instrument, and would hardly be recognized as a bird note at all. It was as strange and weird a form of natural music as any I have known.

Frequently, when out among the cattle I rode my horse almost over a hen with a brood of chicks. The little chicks first attempted to run off in single file but if discovered, scattered and squatted down under clods of earth or tufts of grass. Holding one in my hand near my pocket, it scuttled into it like a flash. The mother, when she saw her brood discovered, tumbled about through the grass as if wounded, in an effort to decoy the foe after her.

On more than one occasion I would have gone foodless had it not been for some of these grouse. One November, about the middle of the month, I determined to visit a little bunch of cattle which was some thirty-five miles down the river, under the care of one of my men. There was so much business to settle that it was an hour and half after noon before I put spurs to the smart little cow pony and loped briskly down the valley. It was a sharp day, the mercury well down toward zero. Darkness set in so early at this season that I had not gone many miles before I began to fear that I would not reach the shack by nightfall. After making a wide circle of twelve miles, the trail came back to the Little Missouri and led along the bottoms between the rows of high bluffs, continually crossing and recrossing the river. These crossings were difficult and disagreeable for the horse, as they always were when the ice was not quite heavy enough to bear his weight. The ice, after bearing the cautiously stepping pony for a few yards, would suddenly break and let him down to the bottom, and he would then have to plunge and paw his way through to the opposite shore. If the horse had slipped and fallen, it would have been a serious matter, for a wetting in such cold weather, with a long horseback journey to make, was no joke.

I was still several miles from the hut when the sun set. I hurried the willing little fellow all I could without distressing him, for, though I knew the road pretty well, yet I doubted if I could find it easily in darkness. When we came to the last crossing the pony was stopped and watered, and we splashed through over a rapid where the ice had formed only a thin crust. On the opposite side was a large patch of cottonwoods, thickly grown up with underbrush. The cowboy's shack was in this but as it was now pitch dark I was unable to find it until I rode clean through to the cow corral, which was out in the open on the other side. Here I dismounted, groped around till I found the path, and then followed it to the shack.

To my annoyance, the cowboy was away, having run out of provisions, as I afterwards learned and, of course, had left nothing to eat behind him. The tough little pony was turned loose to shift for himself. I went into the low, windowless hut, which was less than twelve feet square. In one end was a great fireplace, and it took but a short time to start a roaring fire which speedily made the hut warm and comfortable. Then I went down to the river with an axe and a pail, got some water, and the tea kettle was soon simmering away. I should have liked something to eat, but as I did not have it, the tea did not prove such a bad substitute for a cold and tired man.

Next morning I sallied out at the break of day with the rifle, for I was pretty hungry. As soon as I stepped from the hut I heard the prairie fowl crowing and calling to one another from the tall trees. There were many score—many hundreds would perhaps be more accurate—scattered through the wood. As the dawn brightened, perched up among the bare limbs of the trees, sharply outlined against the sky, they were very conspicuous. I kept out of their sight, and sometimes got two or three shots at the same bird before it flew off. I did not have much trouble in killing five, almost all of them shot very nearly where the neck joins the body. Salt, like tea, I carried with me, and it was not long before two of the birds, plucked and cleaned, were split open and roasting before the fire.

Chapter 5

Whitetail and Blacktail Deer

VENISON FURNISHED the staple meat for both the Chimney Butte and the Elkhorn Ranches. There were two types of deer to hunt: "the low-scudding, brush-loving whitetail" which was far more plentiful near the ranch and the blacktail which preferred the ravines and the rocky uplands for its habitat.

Often Theodore hunted by himself. At other times, when it was necessary to lay in a supply of meat for several weeks, several of his men went with him, taking the ranch wagon along for a protracted hunt. These were holiday trips for all of them. One of them was particularly exciting:

All was bustle and laughter as we started. I was to ride a horse named Whitefoot, who had been a confirmed and very bad bucker three years before, but had grown quieter with years. Nevertheless I found he had some fire left. A hasty vault into the saddle on my part was followed on his by some very resolute pitching. I lost my rifle and hat, and my revolver and knife were bucked out of my belt, but I kept my seat all right, and finally got his head up and mastered him without letting him throw himself over backwards, a trick he sometimes practised.

We followed the old Keogh trail, which had been made by the heavy army wagons that journeyed to Fort Keogh in the old days when the soldiers were, except for a few daring trappers, the only white men to be seen on the last great hunting-ground of the Indians.

We had at first very bad weather. Leaving the ranch in the morning, two of us, who were mounted, pushed on ahead to hunt, the wagon following slowly, with a couple of spare saddle-ponies leading behind it. Early in the afternoon, while riding over the crest of a great divide, which separated the drainage-basins of two important creeks, we saw that a tremendous storm was brewing with that marvellous rapidity which is so marked a characteristic of weather changes on the plains. A towering mass of clouds gathered in the northwest, turning that whole quarter of the sky to an inky blackness. From there the storm rolled down toward us at a furious speed, obscuring by degrees the light of the sun, and extending its wings toward each side, as if to overlap any that tried to avoid its path. Against the dark background of the mass could be seen pillars and clouds of gray mist, whirled hither and thither by the wind, and sheets of level rain driven before it. The edges of the wings tossed to and fro, and the wind shrieked and moaned as it swept over the prairie. The prairie fowl rose in flocks before the storm, scudding with spread wings toward the thickest cover, and the herds of antelope ran across the plain like racehorses to gather in the hollows and behind the low ridges.

We spurred hard to get out of the open, riding with loose reins for the creek. The center of the storm swept by behind us, fairly across our track, and we only got a wipe from the tail of it. Yet we could not have faced this in the open. The first gust almost took us from the saddle, and drove the rain and hail in stinging level sheets against us. We galloped to the edge of a deep washout, scrambled into it at the risk of our necks, and huddled up with our horses underneath the windward bank. Here we remained pretty well sheltered until the storm was over. The air became very cold. Where the center of the whirlwind struck, it did great damage, sheets of hailstones as large as pigeons' eggs striking the earth with the velocity of bullets. Next day the hailstones could have been gathered up by the bushel from the heaps that lay in the bottom of the gullies and ravines. One of my cowboys came across some antelope so numb and stiffened that they could barely limp out of the way.

It rained all night, and there was a thick mist, with continual sharp showers, all the next day and night. The wheeling was very heavy, and, after striking the Keogh trail, we were able to go along it but a few miles before the approach of evening warned us that we should have to go into camp while still a dozen miles from any pool or spring. Accordingly, we made what would have been a dry camp had it not been for the incessant downpour of rain, which we gathered in the canvas wagon-sheet and in our oilskin overcoats in

sufficient quantity to make coffee, having with infinite difficulty started a smouldering fire just to leeward of the wagon.
The horses, feeding on the soaked grass, did not need water.
An antelope came up within two hundred yards of us as
we were building the fire, but though one of us took a shot
at him, it missed. Our chaps and oilskins had kept us perfectly dry, and as soon as our frugal supper was over, we
coiled up among the bundles and boxes inside the wagon
and slept soundly until daybreak.

When the sun rose next day, the third we were out, the
sky was clear, and two of us prepared to make a hunt. Some
three miles off to the south of where we were camped, the
plateau sloped off into a great expanse of broken ground,
with chains upon chains of steep hills, separated by deep
valleys, winding and branching in every direction, their
bottoms filled with trees and brushwood. Toward this place
we rode, intending to go into it some little distance, and
then to hunt along through it near the edge. As soon as we
got down near the brushy ravine we rode along without
talking, guiding the horses as far as possible on earthy places,
where they would neither stumble nor strike their feet
against stones, and not letting our rifle-barrels or spurs clink
against anything. Keeping outside of the brush, a little up
the side of the hill, one of us would ride along each side of
the ravine, examining intently with our eyes every clump of
trees or brushwood. For some time we saw nothing, but,
finally, as we were riding both together round the jutting
spur of a steep hill, my companion suddenly brought his
horse to a halt, and, pointing across the shelving bend to a
patch of trees well up on the opposite side of a broad ravine,

asked me if I did not see a deer in it. I was off the horse in a second, throwing the reins over his head. We were in the shadow of the cliff-shoulder, and with the wind in our favor, so were unlikely to be observed by the game. I looked long and eagerly toward the spot indicated, which was about a hundred and twenty-five yards from us, but at first could see nothing. By this time, however, the experienced plainsman who was with me was satisfied that he was right in his supposition, and he told me to try again and look for a patch of red. I saw the patch at once, just glimmering through the bushes, but should certainly never have dreamed it was a deer if left to myself. Watching it attentively I soon saw it move enough to satisfy me where the head lay. Kneeling on one knee and (as it was a little beyond point-blank range) holding at the top of the portion visible, I pulled trigger, and the bright-colored patch disappeared from among the bushes. The aim was a good one, for, on riding up to the brink of the ravine, we saw a fine whitetailed buck lying below us, shot through just behind the shoulder. He was still in the red coat, with his antlers in the velvet.

In coming home we made a long moonlight ride, passing over between sunset and sunrise what had taken us three days' journey on the outward march. For nine hours we rode steadily, generally at a quick lope, across the moonlit prairie. The hoofbeats of our horses rang out in steady rhythm through the silence of the night, otherwise unbroken save now and then by the wailing cry of a coyote. The rolling plains stretched out on all sides of us, shimmering in the clear moonlight. Occasionally a band of spectral-looking antelope swept silently away before our path. Once we went by a drove of Texan cattle, who stared wildly. As we passed they charged down by us, the ground rumbling beneath their tread, while their long horns knocked against each other with a sound like the clattering of a multitude of castanets. We could see clearly enough to keep our general course over the trackless plain, steering by the stars where the prairie was perfectly level and without landmarks. Our ride was timed well, for as we galloped down into the valley of the Little Missouri the sky above the line of the level bluffs in our front was crimson with the glow of the unrisen sun.

Hunting the blacktail was to Theodore "a far nobler sport than hunting the whitetail." Next to the bighorn, or mountain sheep, there was "no kind of plains hunting more fitted to bring out the best and hardiest of the many qualities which go to make a good hunter." He particularly enjoyed for himself and another good rider to gallop down opposite sides of a long ravine against the wind at breakneck speed. "The patter of the unshod hoofs over the turf made but little noise and the turns were so numerous and abrupt, and the horses went so swiftly, that the hunters came on the deer almost before the deer was aware of their presence. It often stood motionless for a few seconds, and offered a chance for a steady shot."

One mid-afternoon in mid-August, when the ranch was entirely out of meat, I started with one of my cowhands to kill a deer. After riding a mile or two down the bottoms we left the river and struck off up a winding valley, which led back among the hills. In a short while we were in a black-tail country, and began to keep a sharp lookout for game, riding parallel to, but some little distance from, one another. We skirted closely all likely-looking spots, such as the heavy brush-patches in the bottoms of the winding valleys, and the groves of ash and elm in the basins and pockets flanking the high plateaus. After a while we came to a coulee with a small muddy pool at its mouth, where there was much fresh deer sign. My companion rode up the middle, while I scrambled up one of the banks and, dismounting, led my horse along its edge, that I might have a clear shot at what-ever we roused. We went nearly to the head, and then the cowboy reined up and shouted that "there were no deer in the coulee." Instantly there was a smashing in the young trees midway between us, and I caught a glimpse of a blacktail buck speeding round a shoulder of the cut bank. I took a hurried shot and missed. Another buck with big antlers not yet clear of velvet jumped up, ran up the opposite bank, and I got a fair shot at him galloping broadside, and rolled him over with a broken back.

One of the best shots I ever made was while on a wagon trip to the fork of a plains river in western Montana. As we were out of meat two of us went back of the river after blacktail. The country was absolutely bare of trees except along the bed of the river. The rolling hills sloped steeply off into low valleys and deep ravines that were sparsely covered with coarse grass and sage brush, which in some places gathered into dense thickets.

Where the hilly country joined the alluvial river bottom, it broke short off into steep bluffs, up which none but a

Western pony could have climbed. In getting up from the bottom we went into a washout, and then led our ponies along a clay ledge, from which we turned off and went straight up a very steep sandy bluff. Just as my companion turned off the ledge, and as I was underneath him, his horse, in plunging to try to get up the sand bluff, over-balanced itself, and, after standing erect on its hind legs for a second, came over backward. The second's pause while it stood bolt upright gave me time to make a frantic leap out of the way with my pony, which scrambled after me, and we clung with hands and hoofs to the side of the bank, while the other horse took two as complete somer-saults as I ever saw, and landed with a crash at the bottom of the washout, feet uppermost. I thought it was done for, but not a bit. After a moment or two it struggled to its legs, shook itself, and looked round in rather a shamefaced way, apparently not in the least the worse for the fall. We now got my pony up to the top by vigorous pulling, and then went down for the other, which at first strongly objected to making another trial, but after much coaxing and a good deal of abuse, took a start and went up without trouble.

For some time after reaching the top of the bluffs we rode along without seeing anything. When it was possible, we kept one on each side of a creek, avoiding the tops of the ridges, because while on them a horseman could be seen at a very long distance, and going with particular cau-tion whenever we found a spur or came up over a crest. The country stretched away like an endless, billowy sea of dull-brown soil and barren sage-brush, the valleys making long parallel furrows, and everything having a look of dreary sameness. At length, as we came out on a rounded ridge, three blacktail bucks started up from a lot of sage-brush some two hundred yards away and below us, and made off down-hill. It was a very long shot, especially to try running, but, as game seemed scarce and cartridges were plenty, I leaped off the horse, and, kneeling, fired. The bullet went low, striking in a line at the feet of the hindmost. I held very high next time, making a wild shot above and ahead of them, which had the effect of turning them, and they went off round a shoulder of a bluff, being by this time down in the valley. Having plenty of time, I elevated the sights (a thing I hardly ever do) to four hundred yards and waited for their reappearance. Meanwhile, they had evidently gotten over their fright, for pretty soon one walked out from the other side of the bluff, and came to a standstill, broadside toward me. He was too far off for me to see his horns. As I was raising the rifle another stepped out and began to walk toward the first. I thought I might as well have as much of a target as possible to shoot at, and waited for the second buck to come out farther, which he did immediately and stood still just alongside of the first. I aimed above his shoulders and pulled the trigger. Over went the two bucks! And when I rushed down to where they lay I found I had pulled a little to one side, and the bullet had broken the backs of both. While my companion was dressing them I went back and paced off the distance. It was just four hundred and thirty-one long paces—over four hundred yards. Both were large bucks and very fat, with the velvet hanging in shreds from their antlers, for it was late in August. The day was waning and we had a long ride back to the wagon, each with a buck behind his saddle. When we came back to the river-valley it was pitch dark, and it was rather ticklish work for our heavily laden horses to pick their way down the steep bluffs and over the rapid streams. Nor were we sorry when we saw ahead under a bluff the gleam of the campfire, as it was reflected back from the canvas-topped prairie-schooner that for the time being represented home to us.

One of the finest blacktail bucks I ever shot was killed while lying out in a rather unusual place. I was hunting mountain-sheep, in a stretch of very high and broken country, and about midday crept cautiously up to the edge of a great gorge, whose sheer walls went straight down several hundred feet. Peeping over the brink of the chasm, I saw a buck, lying out on a ledge so narrow as to barely hold him, right on the face of the cliff wall opposite, some distance below, and about seventy yards diagonally across from me. He lay with his legs half stretched out, and his head turned so as to give me an exact center-shot at his forehead, the bullet going in between his eyes, so that his legs hardly so much as twitched when he received it. It was toilsome and dangerous work climbing out to where he lay. I have never known any other, even of this bold and adventurous species of deer, to take its noonday siesta in a place so barren of all cover and so difficult of access even to the most surefooted climber. This buck was as fat as a prize sheep, and heavier than any other I had ever killed, while his antlers, with two exceptions, were the best I ever got.

Chapter 6

Black and Grizzly Bears

THEODORE WAS contemptuous of the black bear as a game animal. Unless he needed the meat, he much preferred to watch their comical actions than to hunt them. He described one such bit of fun.

When I first saw him the bear was shuffling along and rooting in the ground, so that he looked like a great pig. Then he began to turn over the stones and logs to hunt for insects, small reptiles, and the like. A moderate-sized stone he would turn over with a single clap of his paw, and then plunge his nose down into the hollow to gobble up the small creatures which were still dazed by the light. The big logs and rocks he would tug and worry at with both paws. Once, over-exerting his clumsy strength, he lost his grip and rolled clean on his back. Under some of the logs when he found mice and chipmunks he would jump about with grotesque agility,

80

and make quick dabs here and there, as the little scurrying
rodent turned and twisted, until at last he put his paw
on it and scooped it up into his mouth. Sometimes, probably when he smelt the mice underneath, he would cautiously turn the log over with one paw, holding the other
lifted and ready to strike. Now and then he would halt and
sniff the air in every direction, and after one of these halts
he suddenly shuffled off into the woods.

Far different to Theodore was the ferocious grizzly bear,
king of the game beasts of temperate North America. This
giant man and beast killer, weighing many times more than
the black bear and often reaching twelve or thirteen hundred
pounds, was called "Old Ephraim" or "Moccasin Joe" by
the old-time trappers of the Rockies. By the time Theodore
came to the Bad Lands, the grizzly had become chiefly a
beast of the high hills and heavy timber. It had learned to
rely on cover to guard itself from man. However, before
the white man came with his gun it had wandered over the
plains at will, fearing nothing. A full-grown grizzly cared
little for cover, except as a weather-break, or because it happened to contain food he liked. Aside from man, the full-
grown grizzly had hardly any foe to fear.

Theodore's first big hunt was made in the summer of 1884
on a trip to the cattle country of southeastern Montana
and northern Wyoming in the Bighorn Mountains. A fortnight was spent here with Bill Merrifield chiefly in a hunt
for bears. With them was a weather-beaten old plainsman
who took care of their pack train. This old character had a
habit of going off on a hunt and not coming back to his

wife for several years. Before she would let him go on this hunt Theodore had to promise to furnish her food for three years unless her husband was returned to her after the hunt.

On the way to the hunting grounds Theodore wrote Henry Cabot Lodge that "whether this letter is, or is not, ever delivered depends partly on Providence, and partly on the good-will of an equally inscrutable personage, either a cowboy or a horse thief, whom we have just met, and who has volunteered to post it—my men are watching him with anything but friendly eyes, as they think he is going to try to steal our ponies. To guard against this possibility he is to sleep between my foreman and myself—delectable bedfellow he'll prove, doubtless."

Although it was still early in September, the weather was cool and pleasant, the nights being frosty. Every few days there was a flurry of snow which made tracking more easy. Our fare was excellent, consisting of elk venison, mountain grouse, and small trout—caught in one of the beautiful little lakes that lay almost up by the timber line. To us, who had for weeks been accustomed to make small fires from dried brush, or from sage brush roots, which we dug out of the ground, it was a treat to sit at night before the roaring and crackling pine logs. The old teamster quaintly put it, "We have at last come to a land where the wood grew on trees."

Sometimes we hunted in company, sometimes each of us went out alone, the teamster remaining to guard camp and cook. One day we had separated. I reached camp early in the afternoon and waited a couple of hours before Merrifield put in an appearance. At last I heard a shout—the familiar long-drawn *Eikoh-h-h* of the cattleman. He came in sight, galloping at full speed down an open glade, waving his hat. He had packed behind his saddle the fine glossy pelt of a black bear. Better still, he announced that he had been off about ten miles to a perfect tangle of ravines and valleys where bear sign was very thick—principally grizzly.

He had run across the black bear by accident while riding up a valley in which there was a patch of dead timber grown up with berry bushes. He noticed a black object which he first took to be a charred stump. On coming near, however, the object suddenly took to its heels. He followed over frightful ground until his pony stumbled and fell. Picking himself up, he rushed after the bear on foot. After running fifty yards the growling of the bear, which he had followed, stopped and he could not find the animal anywhere. Happening to glance up in a tree he saw it on a limb and shot it.

Merrifield's tale made me decide to shift camp at once to the spot where the bear tracks were plenty. By noon we pitched camp by a clear brook, in a valley with steep, wooded sides, and with good feed for the horses in the open bottom. We rigged the canvas wagon sheet into a small tent, sheltered by the trees from the wind, and piled great pine logs nearby where we wished to place the fire.

That afternoon I shot a fine bull elk. I came home alone toward nightfall, walking through a reach of burnt forest, where there was nothing but charred tree trunks and black mould. When nearly through it I came across the huge, half-human footprints of a great grizzly, which must have passed by within a few minutes. It gave me rather an eerie feeling in the silent, lonely woods, to see for the first time the unmistakable proofs that I was in the home of the mighty lord of the wilderness. I followed the tracks in the fading twilight until it became too dark to see them any longer, and then shouldered my rifle and walked back to camp.

Next day we went off on a long tramp through the woods and along the sides of the canyons. There were plenty of berry bushes growing in clusters, and all around these there were fresh tracks of bear. On visiting the place where Merrifield had killed the black bear, we found that the grizzlies had been there before us, and had utterly devoured the carcass with cannibal relish. We turned our steps toward where lay a bull elk I had killed. It was quite late in the afternoon when we reached the place. A grizzly had been at the carcass during the preceding night, for his great footprints were in the ground all around it, and the carcass itself was gnawed and torn, and partially covered with earth and leaves—for the grizzly buries all of his prey that he does not at the moment need.

The forest was composed mainly of ridge-pole pines, which grew close together, and did not branch out until the stems were thirty or forty feet from the ground. We walked beneath these trees over a carpet of pine needles upon which our moccasined feet made no sound. The silence of the vast and lonely woods was broken now and then by the strange noises always to be heard in the great forests and which seem to mark the sad and everlasting unrest of the wilderness. We climbed up along the trunk of a dead tree which had toppled over until its upper branches stuck in the limb crotch of another, and thus supported it at an angle halfway in its fall. When above the ground far enough to prevent the bear's smelling us, we sat still to wait for his approach, until, in the gathering gloom, we could no longer see the sights of our rifles, and could but dimly make out the carcass of the elk. As it was useless to wait longer, we clambered down and stole out to the edge of the woods. Once out from under the trees there was still plenty of light, although the sun had set, and we crouched down under a bush to see if some animal might not leave the cover. To our right the ravine sloped downward toward the valley of the Bighorn River, and far on its other side we could catch a glimpse of the great main chain of the Rockies, their snow peaks glinting crimson in the light of the set sun. The owls hooted dismally from the tops of the tall trees, and two or three times a harsh wailing cry, probably the voice of a lynx or wolverine, arose from the depths of the woods. As we were rising to leave, we heard the sound of the breaking of a dead stick from the spot where the carcass lay. It was a sharp, sudden noise, perfectly distinct from the natural creaking and snapping of the branches. Old Ephraim had come back to the carcass but it was entirely too dark to go in after him.

Early next morning we were at the elk carcass and, as we expected, found that the bear had eaten his fill during the night. His tracks showed him to be an immense fellow, and were so fresh that we made up our minds to follow him up and try to find his lair.

Merrifield was a skilful tracker, and we took up the trail at once. For some distance it led over the soft, yielding carpet of moss and pine needles. We made no sound ourselves, and every little sudden noise sent a thrill through me as I peered about with each sense on the alert. After going a few hundred yards the tracks turned off on a well-beaten path made by elk. The beast's footprints were perfectly plain in the dust, until the trail turned off into a tangled thicket within which it was almost certain we would find our quarry. When in the middle of the thicket we crossed a breastwork of fallen logs and Merrifield, who was leading, passed by the upright stem of a great pine. Suddenly, he sank on one knee, turning half round, his face fairly aflame with excitement. As I strode past him, with my rifle at the ready, there, not ten steps off, was the great bear, slowly rising from his bed among the young spruces. He had heard us, but apparently hardly knew exactly where or what we were, for he reared up on his haunches sideways to us. Then he saw us, and dropped down again on all fours, the shaggy hair on his neck and shoulders seeming to bristle as he turned toward us. As he sank down on his forefeet I raised the rifle. His head was bent slightly down, and when I saw the top of the white bead fairly between his small, glittering, evil eyes, I pulled trigger. Half rising up, the huge beast fell over on his side in the death throes, the ball having gone into his brain, striking as fairly between the eyes as if the distance had been measured by a carpenter's rule.

The whole thing was over in twenty seconds from the time I caught sight of the game. The grizzly did not have time to show fight or come a step toward us and I felt not a little proud as I stood over the great brindled bulk which

lay stretched out at length in the cool shade of the evergreens. He was a monstrous fellow. As near as we could
estimate he must have weighed about twelve hundred
pounds. He must have been very old, his teeth and claws
being all worn down and blunted. He was still in the summer coat, his hair being short, and in color a curious brindled
brown, somewhat like that of certain bulldogs.

We tried eating the grizzly's flesh, but it was not good,
being coarse and not well flavored. The flesh of the little
black bear, that Merrifield had killed, was excellent. It
tasted like that of a young pig.

One day, while camped near the Bitter Root Mountains
in Montana I found that a bear had been feeding on the
carcass of a moose which lay some five miles from the little
open glade in which my tent was pitched. I made up my
mind to try to get a shot at it that afternoon. I stayed in
camp till three o'clock, lying lazily back on the bed of
sweet-smelling evergreen boughs, watching the pack ponies
as they stood under the pines on the edge of the open,
stamping now and then, and switching their tails. The air
was still, the sky a glorious blue. The smoke from the
smouldering logs of the camp fire curled thinly upward.
Little chipmunks scuttled out from their holes to the packs,
which lay in a heap on the ground, and then scuttled madly
back again. A couple of drab-colored whiskey-jacks, with
bold mien and fearless bright eyes, hopped and fluttered
round, picking up the scraps, so tame that one of them lit
on my outstretched arms as I half dozed, basking in the
sunshine.

When the shadows began to lengthen, I shouldered my

rifle and plunged into the woods. A scramble through a rocky pass took me into a high, wet valley, where the thick growth of spruce was broken by occasional strips of meadow. In this valley the moose carcass lay, well at the upper end.

In moccasined feet I trod softly through the soundless woods. Under the dark branches it was already dusk, and the air had the cool chill of evening. As I neared the clump where the body lay, I walked with redoubled caution, watching and listening with strained alertness. Then I heard a twig snap and my blood leaped, for I knew the bear was at his supper. In another moment I saw his shaggy, brown form. He was trying to bury the carcass, twisting it to one side and the other with wonderful ease. Once he got angry and suddenly gave it a tremendous cuff with his paw, having in his bearing something half humorous, half devilish. I crept up within forty yards. For several minutes he would not keep his head still. Then something attracted his attention in the forest, and he stood motionless looking toward it, broadside to me, with his fore paws planted on the carcass. This gave me my chance. I drew a very fine bead between his eye and ear, and pulled the trigger. He dropped like a steer when struck with a poleaxe.

Chapter 7

Hunting Elk

IN MANY ways Theodore enjoyed hunting elk more than any other game animal. He particularly loved the "whistling" sound which the bulls make in rutting season, "It is a most singular and beautiful sound," he wrote, "and is very much the most musical cry uttered by any four-footed beast. When heard for the first time it is almost impossible to believe that it is the call of an animal. It sounds far more as if made by some strange wind instrument. It consists of quite a series of notes uttered continuously, in a most soft, musical, vibrant tone, so clearly that they can be heard half a mile off."

I saw and killed my first elk in the summer of 1884 in the Bighorn Mountains. Merrifield and I, with a weather-beaten old plainsman who possessed a most extraordinary stock of miscellaneous misinformation, went into the mountains with a pack train. We made a two days' journey before pitching camp in what we intended to be our hunting grounds.

It was on the second day, while leading the pack-ponies down the precipitous side of a steep valley, that I obtained my first sight of elk. The trail wound through a forest of tall, slender pines, standing very close together, and with dead trees lying in every direction. At last we got out into a succession of small, open glades, with boggy spots in them. As we reached the lowest glade, we saw a small band of cow elk disappearing into the woods on its other edge. I was riding a restive horse, and when I tried to jump off to shoot, it reared and turned round before I could get my left foot out of the stirrup. When I at last got free, I caught a glimpse of one elk vanishing behind a dead trunk. My hasty shot missed.

We pitched camp by a beautiful clear mountain brook. Being entirely out of meat, after lunch, all of us separated to hunt. The plainsman went upstream, Merrifield went down, while I followed the tracks of the band of cows and calves that we had started earlier. Their trail led along the wooded hill-crests parallel to the stream. There was a small growth of young spruce thick enough to give cover. In my moccasined feet, I trod without any noise.

The footprints of the band I was following showed that after getting through the first grove, the huddled herd had straightened itself out into a single file, and trotted off in a nearly straight line. A mile or two having been passed, the animals had slackened their pace into a walk, and soon afterwards scattered to each side, browsing and grazing.

While carefully looking to my footsteps I paid too little heed to the rifle which I held in my right hand, and let the barrel tap smartly on a tree trunk. Instantly there was a stamp and movement among the bushes ahead of me. The elk had heard but had neither seen nor smelt me. A second afterward I saw the indistinct, shadowy outlines of the band as they trotted downhill. I raced forward downhill, behind some large mossy boulders, and cut them fairly off, the band passing directly ahead of me and not twenty yards away, at a slashing trot, which a few of them changed for a wild gallop as I opened fire. I was so hemmed in by the thick tree trunks, that I caught little more than a fleeting glimpse of each animal, and though I fired four shots I only brought down one elk, a full-grown cow, with a broken neck.

After thrusting the hunting-knife into the throat of the cow I followed the trail of the band, but only succeeded in getting a calf I had previously wounded. The elk had run across Merrifield's path and he shot two. Leaving him to skin and cut up the dead animals, I walked back to camp, where I found the teamster who had brought in the hams and tongues of two deer he had shot. I sent him with a pack-pony for the hides and meat of the elk. We now had more than enough meat in camp and did not shoot at another cow or calf elk while on the mountains, though we saw quite a number.

Later on we made a camp at the head of a great natural meadow where two streams joined together and in times long gone by had been dammed by the beaver. This had at first choked up the passage and made a small lake. The dams were built higher, making chains of little ponds. By degrees these filled up, and the whole valley became a broad, marshy meadow through which the brook wound between rows of willows and alders.

We got a fine mess of spotted trout by taking a long and most toilsome walk up to a little lake lying very near timber line. Our rods and lines were most primitive, consisting of two clumsy dead cedars, about six feet of string tied to one and a piece of catgut to the other, with preposterous hooks. The trout were so ravenous, however, that we caught them at the rate of about one a minute.

One day Merrifield and I went out together and had a rather exciting chase after some bull elk. We saw nothing until we came to a large patch of burnt ground, where we at once found the soft, black soil marked up by elk hoofs. We had penetrated into it not more than a hundred yards before we came to tracks made but a few minutes before, and almost instantly afterward saw three bull elk. We had been running briskly uphill through the soft, heavy loam, and as a consequence, I was all out of breath and my hand so unsteady that I missed my first shot. The three elk trotted off in a direction quartering to us. I doubt if I ever went through more violent exertion than in the next ten minutes. We raced after them at full speed, opening fire. I wounded all three, but none of the wounds were immediately disabling. They trotted on and we panted afterward, slipping on the wet earth, pitching headlong over charred stumps, leaping on dead logs that broke beneath our weight, more than once measuring our full length on the ground, halting and firing whenever we got a chance.

At last one bull fell. We passed him by, after the others,

which were still running uphill. The sweat streamed into my eyes and made furrows in the sooty mud that covered my face. I sobbed for breath as I toiled at a shambling trot after them, as nearly done out as could well be. At this moment they turned downhill. It was a great relief. A man who is too done up to go a step up hill can still run fast enough down. With a last spurt I closed in near enough to fire again. One elk fell, the other went off at a walk. I kept on alone after him, not able to go at more than a slow trot myself, and too much winded to dare risk a shot at any distance. He got out of the burnt patch, going into some thick timber in a deep ravine. I closed pretty well and rushed after him into a thicket of young evergreen. I caught a glimpse of a yellow body moving out to one side, ran toward the edge and fired through the twigs at the moving beast. Down it went but when I ran up, to my disgust, I had killed a blacktail deer.

I at once took up the trail of the elk again, but after a little while the blood grew less and ceased. I lost the track and could not find it again hunt as hard as I might.

Early the next morning, just as the east began to grow gray, I waked. As I did so the sounds that smote on my ear caused me to sit up and throw off the warm blankets. Bull elk were challenging among the mountains on both sides of the valley, a little way from us, their notes echoing like the calling of silver bugles. Groping about in the dark, I drew on my trousers, an extra pair of thick socks, and my moccasins, donned a warm jacket, found my fur cap and gloves, and stole out of the tent with my rifle.

The air rang with the challenges of many wapiti. First

one bull challenged, then another answered, then another and another. The herds were approaching one another from opposite sides of the valley, and the master-bulls were roaring defiance as they mustered their harems.

I walked stealthily up the valley until I felt that I was nearly between the two herds and then stood motionless under a tall pine. The ground was quite open at this point, the pines, though large, being scattered. The little brook ran with a strangled murmur between its rows of willows and alders, for the ice along its edges nearly skimmed its breadth. The stars paled rapidly, the gray dawn brightened, and in the sky overhead faint rose-colored streaks were turning blood red. What little wind there was breathed in my face and kept me from discovery. Soon a bull on my right was evidently approaching one on my left, both uttering their challenges. The one on the right approached so near that I could hear him crack the branches and beat the bushes with his horns. I slipped quietly from tree to tree, so as to meet him when he came out into the more open woodland. Day broke, and crimson gleams played across the snow-clad mountains beyond.

At last, just as the sun flamed red above the hilltops, I heard the roar of the wapiti's challenge not fifty yards away. I cocked and half raised my rifle and stood motionless. In a moment more, the belt of spruces in front of me swayed and opened, and the lordly bull stepped out. He bore his massive antlers aloft as he snuffed the air and stamped on the ground as he walked. As I drew a bead, the motion caught his eye. Instantly his bearing of haughty and warlike self-confidence changed to one of alarm. My bullet smote through his shoulder blades and he plunged wildly forward and fell full length on the blood-stained snow.

The finest bull, with the best head that I got, was killed in the midst of very beautiful and grand surroundings. We had been hunting through a great pine wood which ran up to the edge of a broad canyon-like valley, bounded by sheer walls of rock. There were fresh tracks of elk about, and we had been advancing up-wind with even more than our usual caution when, on stepping out into a patch of open ground, near the edge of the cliff, we came upon a great bull, beating and thrashing his antlers against a young tree, about eighty yards off. He stopped and faced us for a second, his mighty antlers thrown in the air, as he held his head aloft. Behind him towered the tall and somber pines, while at his feet the jutting crags overhung the deep chasm below, that stretched off between high walls of barren and snow-streaked rocks, the evergreens clinging to their sides, while along the bottom the rapid torrent gathered in places into black and sullen mountain lakes. As the bull turned to run I struck him just behind the shoulder. He reeled to the death-blow but staggered gamely on a few rods into the forest before sinking to the ground with my second bullet through his lungs.

No sportsman can ever feel much keener pleasure and self-satisfaction than when, after a successful stalk and good shot, he walks up to a grand elk lying dead in the cool shade of the great evergreens, and looks at the massive and yet finely moulded form, and at the mighty antlers which are to serve in the future as the trophy and proof of his successful skill.

After returning from this hunt, in which he had gotten both grizzly bear and elk, Theodore remained in the Bad Lands most of the fall helping with the house and keeping an eye on both of his ranching operations.

While he had been gone on the hunt it became obvious that the Marquis and his men had not given up the idea of taking over the territory where his second ranch was. One of the Medora toughs, who was lined up with the Marquis and thereby had escaped a vigilante committee, claimed the cabin that Sewall and Dow lived in while building the ranchhouse, and asked five hundred dollars in payment for it. Theodore ignored the demand. The report got out that this man was going to kill him. Theodore, when he heard of it, saddled his horse and rode to the man's house where he knocked sharply. "I understand," he said, when the man came to the door, "that you have threatened to kill me on sight. If you have anything to say to me, say it; if not, then get busy." The man told Theodore that there had evidently been "a mistake" in what he had heard.

Theodore returned east in October, 1884, feeling that he was leaving his ranching interests in capable hands. However, he was back a month later with the intention of forming a Live Stock Association to be patterned after the one existing in Montana. In sub-zero weather he rode from ranch to ranch talking his idea. A meeting was called for December 19th when an active organization, under his leadership, came into being. Of course other efforts before this had paved the way but it was his ability that brought them into fruition. The next day he left for New York, to spend Christmas with his family, but in the meantime he had made another interesting hunt.

Chapter 8

Hunting Bighorns

BEFORE RETURNING *East Theodore heard that there was a small band of bighorns, or mountain sheep, in some steep and broken country, about twenty-five miles from his ranch headquarters. Quite naturally he went after them. After two or three fruitless efforts, balked primarily by bitter cold weather, he decided that he would have to spend several days in the neighborhood where the quarry was supposed to be. Consequently he sent the buckboard, with bedding and food, in charge of a cowboy to a deserted hunter's cabin in the general neighborhood to be hunted. Riding ahead of it on horseback he and Merrifield hunted through the country on their way to the camp.*

On our first day's hunt we clambered up the slippery, ice-covered buttes, clinging to the rocks, and slowly working our way across the faces of the cliffs, or cautiously peered over every crest long and carefully, from the peaks scanning

the ground all about with the field glasses. But we saw no
sheep, and but little sign of them.

The cold, as the day wore on, seemed gradually to chill
us through and through. Our hands and feet became numb
and our ears tingled under our fur caps. As the afternoon
was beginning to wane we mounted our shivering horses
for good and pushed toward the bend of the river where
we were to meet the buckboard. Our course lay across a
succession of bleak, wind-swept plateaus, broken by deep
and narrow pine-clad gorges. Getting on and off these table-
lands was real labor, their sides were so sheer. The horses
plunged and scrambled after us as we led them up, while
in descending they would sit back on their haunches and
half walk, half slide down the steep inclines. Some of them
were so steep that we had to turn the horses around and
back them over the edge. Then they would go down with
a rush. It warmed our blood to stay out of the way of their
hoofs.

We finally found the hut in which the cowboy had already built a fire. Throughout the night the temperature
sank lower and lower, and it was impossible to keep the
crazy old hut anywhere above freezing point. The wind
whistled through the chinks and crannies of the logs, and,
after a short supper, we were glad to cower down with our
great fur coats still on, under the pile of buffalo-robes and
bear-skins. My sleeping bag came in very handily and kept
me as warm as possible.

We were up and had taken breakfast next morning by
the time the first streak of dawn had dimmed the brilliancy
of the stars, and immediately afterward strode off on foot,

as we had been hampered by the horses on the day before. We walked briskly across the plain until, by the time it was light enough to see to shoot, we came to the foot of a great hill known as Middle Butte, a huge, isolated mass of rock, several miles in length, with high sides, very steep toward the nearly level summit. We hunted carefully through the outlying foot-hills and projecting spurs around its base, without result, finding but a few tracks, and those old ones. We then toiled up to the top, which, though narrow in parts, in others widened out into plateaus half a mile square. Having made a complete circuit of the top, peering over the edge and closely examining the flanks of the butte with field glasses, without having seen anything, we slid down the other side and took off through a streak of very rugged but low country. This day, though the weather had grown even colder, we did not feel it, for we walked all the while with a quick pace, and the climbing was very hard work. The shoulders and ledges of the cliffs had become round and slippery with the ice, and it was no easy task to move up and along them, clutching the gun in one hand, and grasping each little projection with the other.

Hunting for a day or two without finding game where the work is severe and toilsome is a good test of the sportsman's staying qualities. On this day I got rather tired and fired at small game while on ground where I might expect large. We came upon some sharptails in a hollow. One was quite near me, perched on a bush, its neck stretched up offering a beautiful mark. I could not resist, so knelt and fired. At the report a head suddenly appeared over a ridge, looked fixedly at us, and then disappeared. We feared it might be a bighorn, but on hurrying up to the place were relieved to find that the tracks were only those of a blacktail. After this lesson we proceeded in silence, making a long circle through the roughest kind of country.

When on the way back to camp, where the buttes rose highest and steepest, we came upon fresh tracks. As it was late in the afternoon we did not try to follow them that day. On the way in I killed a sharptail for supper, making rather a neat shot, the bird being eighty yards off.

The night was even colder than the preceding one, and all signs told us that we would soon have a change for the worse in the weather. Doubly anxious to get a sheep before the storm struck, we determined that next morning we would take the horses and make a quick push for the chain of high buttes where we had seen the fresh tracks, and hunt them through with thorough care.

We started in the cold gray of the next morning and pricked rapidly off over the frozen plain, columns of white steam rising from the nostrils of the galloping horses. When we had reached the foot of the hills where we intended to hunt, and tethered the horses, the sun had already risen. The air was thick and hazy, and away off in the northwest a towering mass of grayish-white clouds looked like a weather-breeder.

The country over which we now hunted was wilder and more mountainous than any we had yet struck. High, sharp peaks and ridges broke off abruptly into narrow gorges and deep ravines. They were bare of all but the scantiest vegetation, save on some of the sheltered sides where grew groves of dark pines, now laden down with feathery snow.

At first we went straight up the side of the tallest peak, and then along the knife-like ridge which joined it with the next. The ice made the footing very slippery as we stepped along the ledges or crawled round the jutting shoulders. The cold, thin air made us pant for breath. We had gone but a little way before we saw fresh signs of the animals we were after.

We left the high ground and, descending into a narrow chasm, walked along its bottom, which was but a couple of feet wide, while the sides rose up from it at an acute angle. After following this for a few hundred yards, we turned a sharp corner, and caught sight of fresh earth lying on the snow in front of our feet. On the sides, some feet above our heads, were marks in the snow which a moment's glance showed us had been made by a couple of mountain sheep that had come down one side of the gorge and had leaped across to the other, their sharp toes going through the thin snow and displacing the earth that had fallen to the bottom. The tracks had evidently been made just before we rounded the corner, and as we had been advancing noiselessly on the snow, with the wind in our favor, we knew that the animals could have no suspicion of our presence.

They had gone up the cliff on our right, but as that on our left was much lower and continued for some distance parallel to the other, we concluded that by running along its top we would be most certain to get a good shot. Clambering instantly up the steep side, digging my hands and feet into the loose snow, and grasping at every little rock or frozen projection, I reached the top, and then ran forward along the ridge a few paces, crouching behind the masses of queerly shaped sandstone, and saw, about ninety yards off across the ravine, a couple of mountain rams. The one with the largest horns was broadside toward me, his sturdy, massive form outlined clearly against the sky as he stood on the crest of the ridge. I dropped on my knee, raising the rifle as I did so. For a second he did not quite make me out, turning his head half round to look. I held the sight fairly on the point just behind his shoulder and pulled the trigger. At the report he staggered and pitched forward, but recovered himself and crossed over the ridge out of sight. We jumped and slid down into the ravine again, and clambered up the opposite side as fast as our lungs and the slippery ice would let us. The trail of the wounded ram was easy to find and we did not have to go far. We found him lying on his side a couple of hundred yards beyond the ridge, his eyes already glazed in death. The bullet had gone in behind the shoulder and ranged clean through his body crosswise, going a little forward. No animal less tough than a mountain ram could have gone any distance at all with such a wound. He had most obligingly run round to a part of the hill where we could bring up one of the horses without much difficulty. Accordingly, I brought up old Manitou, and the bighorn was soon strapped across his back. It was a fine ram, with perfectly shaped but not very large horns.

It was still early in the day and we made up our minds to push back for the home ranch, as we did not wish to be caught out in a long storm. In a little over an hour we were back at the log camp, where the ram was shifted from Manitou's back to the buckboard. In a few minutes we started for home. Merrifield and I rode on ahead, not sparing the horses, but before we got home the storm burst, and a furious blizzard blew in our teeth as we galloped along the last mile of the river bottom before coming to the ranchhouse. As we warmed our stiffened limbs before the log fire I congratulated myself upon the successful outcome of what I knew would be the last hunting trip I should take during that season.

Mountain mutton in the fall is the most delicious eating furnished by any game animal. Nothing else compares with it for juiciness, tenderness and flavor. At other times of the year it is tough and stringy.

A couple of years later, this time in the summer of 1886, Theodore made another interesting bighorn hunt. This time he was alone—except that he was not, since he was riding on his horse Manitou. His blanket and oilskin slicker were strapped behind his saddle; he had salt, hardtack, tea and sugar, with his tin cup in which to boil water, his rifle and a belt with a score of cartridges. He was ready for anything.

At first my route lay across grassy plateaus, and along smooth wooded coulees. In one of them I shot two prairie chickens. After a few miles the ground became very rugged and difficult. At last I got into the heart of the Bad Lands proper, where the hard, wrinkled earth was torn into shapes as sullen and grotesque as those of dreamland. The hills rose high, their barren flanks carved and channelled, their tops mere needles and knife crests. Bands of black, red, and purple varied the gray and yellow-brown of their sides. The tufts of scanty vegetation were dull green.

In the midst of this devil's wilderness, I came on a lovely valley. A spring trickled out of a cedar canyon, and below this spring the narrow, deep ravine was green with luscious grass and was smooth for some hundreds of yards. Here I unsaddled, and turned Manitou loose to drink and feed at his leisure. At the edge of the dark cedar wood I cleared a spot for my bed, and drew a few dead sticks for the fire. Then I lay down and watched drowsily until the afternoon shadows filled the wild and beautiful gorge in which I was camped. I was ready to see what game was near. Springing to my feet, I climbed the nearest ridge, and then made my way, by hard clambering, from peak to peak and from crest to crest, sometimes crossing and sometimes skirting the deep washouts and canyons. When possible I avoided appearing on the skyline, and I moved with utmost caution, walking in a wide sweep so as to hunt across and upwind. There was much sheep sign, some of it fresh, though I saw none of the animals themselves.

I walked back to camp in the gloaming, taking care to reach it before it grew really dark, for in the Bad Lands it is entirely impossible to travel, or find any given locality after nightfall. Old Manitou had eaten his fill and looked up at me with pricked ears, and wise, friendly face as I climbed down the side of the cedar canyon. He came slowly toward me to see if I had something for him. I rubbed his soft nose and gave him a cracker, then picketed him to a solitary cedar where the feed was good. I kindled a small fire, roasted both prairie chickens, ate one, and put the other by for breakfast, then rolled myself in my blanket, with the saddle for a pillow and the oilskin underneath. Manitou was munching the grass near by. I lay just outside the line of stiff black cedars; the night air was soft in my face; I gazed at the shining and brilliant multitude of stars until my eyelids closed.

The chill breath which comes before dawn awakened me. It was still and dark. Through the gloom I could indistinctly make out the loom of the old horse. I was speedily ready, and groped and stumbled slowly up the hill, and then along its crest to a peak. Here I sat down and waited a quarter of an hour or so, until gray appeared in the east, and the dim light-streaks enabled me to walk farther. Before sunrise I was two miles from camp. I crawled cautiously to a high ridge and, crouching behind it, scanned all the landscape eagerly. In a few minutes a movement about a third of a mile to the right, midway down the hill, caught my eye. Another glance showed me three white specks moving along the hillside. They were the white rumps of three fine mountain sheep, on their way to drink at a little alkaline pool in the bottom of a deep, narrow valley. In a moment they went out of sight round a bend of the valley.

I rose and trotted briskly toward them along the ridge. There were two or three deep gullies to cross, and a high shoulder up which to clamber, so I was out of breath when I reached the bend beyond which they had disappeared. Taking advantage of a scrawny sage brush as cover, I peeped over the edge, and at once saw the sheep, three big young rams. They had finished drinking and were standing beside the little miry pool, about three hundred yards distant. Slipping back I dropped down into the bottom of the valley, where a narrow washout zigzagged from side to side, between straight walls of clay. The pool was in the upper end of this washout, under a cut bank.

An indistinct game trail ran up this washout. The bottom was of clay, so that I walked noiselessly, and the crookedness of the washout's course afforded ample security against discovery by the sharp eyes of the quarry. In a couple of minutes I stalked stealthily round the last bend, my rifle cocked and at the ready, expecting to see the rams by the pool. However, they had gone, and the muddy water was settling in their deep hoof-marks. Running on, I looked over the edge of the cut bank and saw them slowly quartering up the hillside, cropping the sparse tufts of coarse grass. I whistled, and as they stood at gaze I put a bullet into the biggest, a little too far aft of the shoulder, but ranging forward. He raced after the others, but soon fell behind, and turned off on his own line, at a walk, with drooping head. As he bled freely I followed his tracks, found him, very sick, in a washout a quarter of a mile beyond, and finished him with another shot. After dressing him and cutting off the saddle and hams, as well as the head, I walked back to camp, breakfasted, and rode Manitou to where the sheep lay. Packing it securely behind the saddle, and shifting the blanket roll to in front of the saddle horn, I led the horse until we were clear of the Bad Lands, then mounted him, and was back at the ranch soon after midday.

Chapter 9

Working a Roundup

WHILE RANCHING in the Bad Lands Theodore participated in many roundups. He sometimes represented himself and sometimes other ranches. Often, in lieu of other work, he supplied the roundup with meat by hunting. At other times he worked as an ordinary rider, either in the actual rounding up of the cattle, or as "rider," or guard for the herds already gathered. "I am as much a cowboy as any of them," he stated in an interview in 1885. "I can shoot, ride, and drive in the roundup with the best of them. Oh, they are a jolly set of fellows, those cowboys, tiptop good fellows, too, when you know them, but they don't want any plug hat or pointed shoes foolishness around them." He was called "not a pretty rider but a good one," and though he was thrown a number of times, he always picked himself up and went back for more. This was part of the challenge of the life he had chosen and had to be met.

If the cattle stampeded, Theodore did as all good cowboys were supposed to do. "I kept on my side and the cowboy on the other," he wrote in describing one stampede, "and never in my life did I ride so hard. In the darkness I could but dimly see the shadowy outlines of the herd, as with whip and spurs I ran the pony along its edge, turning back the beasts at one point barely in time to wheel and keep them in at another. The ground was cut up by numerous little gullies, and each of us got several falls, horses and riders turning complete somersaults. We were dripping with sweat, and our ponies quivering and trembling like quaking aspens, when, after more than an hour of the most violent exertion, we finally got the herd quieted down."

In the Bad Lands there were a succession of roundups which began in May and ended toward the last of October. The spring roundup, which lasted about six weeks, was the most important one of the year:

In April we began to get up the horses. After running all winter free, even the most sober pony was apt to buck. We liked to ride every animal once or twice before we did real work with him. The captain or foreman of the roundup, an expert cowman, was chosen beforehand. He was, of course, acquainted with the country and had to be able to keep control of the wild riders he had under him.

At the appointed day all met at the place from which the roundup was to start. We had a four-horse wagon in which we carried bedding and food and on the back of which a mess-chest was rigged to hold the knives, forks, cans, etc. The teamster was also cook. A man who was really a first rate hand at both driving and cooking—and ours was—could command his own price. We had at least a dozen cowboys—besides representatives of other ranches—who did the actual cattle work. Each of these had a string of eight or ten ponies. Two herders, or horse wranglers—one for the day and one for the night—took charge of these.

At the meeting-place the heavy four-horse wagons jolted in from different quarters, the horse-wranglers rushing madly to and fro in an endeavor to keep the different saddle bands from mingling, while the cowboys jogged along in a body. Each wagon wheeled out of the way into some camping-ground not too near the others, the bedding was tossed out on the ground, and then everyone was left to do what he wished, while the different wagon bosses, or foremen, sought out the captain of the roundup to learn what his plans were.

On the days when there was no regular work, there would often be horse races, as each outfit was pretty sure to have some running pony which it believed could outpace any other. These contests were always short-distance dashes, for but a few hundred yards. Horse racing was a mania with most plainsmen, white or red. A man with a good racing pony would travel all about with it, often winning large sums, visiting alike cow ranches, frontier towns, and Indian encampments. Sometimes the race was "pony against pony," the victor taking both steeds. In racing the men rode bareback, as there were hardly any light saddles in the cow country. There would be intense excitement and very heavy betting over a race between two well-known horses, together with a good chance of blood being shed in the attendant quarrels. A race was usually run between two thick rows of spectators, on foot and on horseback, and as the racers passed, these rows closed in behind them, every man yelling and shouting with all the strength of his lungs, and all waving their hats and cloaks to encourage the contestants, or firing off their revolvers and saddle guns. The little horses were fairly maddened, as was natural enough, and ran as if they were crazy. If the distance had been longer, some would have been sure to have dropped in their tracks.

In the morning the cook prepared breakfast long before the first glimmer of dawn. As soon as it was ready, probably about three o'clock, he uttered a long-drawn shout, and all the sleepers knew it was time to be up on the instant, for there could be no such thing as delay on the roundup, under penalty of being set afoot. Accordingly, they bundled out, rubbing their eyes and yawning, drawing on their boots and trousers—if they had taken the latter off—rolled up and corded their bedding, and usually without any attempt at washing crowded over to the little smouldering fire, which was placed in a hole dug in the ground, so there might be no risk of its spreading. The men were rarely very hungry at breakfast, and it was a meal that had to be eaten in short-est order, so it was perhaps the least important. Each man, as he came up, grasped a tin cup and plate from the mess box, poured out his coffee, with sugar, but, of course, no milk, helped himself to one or two of the biscuits that had been baked in a Dutch oven, and perhaps also to a slice of fat pork swimming in the grease of the frying-pan, ladled himself out some beans, if there were any, and squatted down on the ground to eat his breakfast. Although the meal was not an elaborate one, he had to hurry if he ate it before the foreman sang out, "Come, boys, catch your horses." Then he had to drop everything and run out to the wagon with his lariat. The night wrangler was bringing in the saddle band, which he had been up all night guarding. A rope corral was rigged up by stretching a rope from each wheel of one side of the wagon, making a V-shaped space, into which the saddle-horses were driven. Men stood around to keep them inside, while others caught the horses. As soon as each rider had a horse the others were turned loose under the control of the day wrangler.

The organization from now on was simple but effective. The mess wagons, loose horses and cattle gathered the day before moved in a straight line through the country to be covered. The riders worked on both sides of the line the wagons took and went as far back into the country as any cattle might be. The captain of the roundup rode on ahead of the wagons to see that everything would be in readiness both for the wagons and for the cattle rounded up during the day.

The wagons always kept some little distance from one another, and the saddle bands did the same, so that the horses might not get mixed. It was rather picturesque to see the four-horse teams filing down at a trot through a pass among the buttes—the saddle bands being driven along at a smart pace to one side or behind, the teamsters cracking their whips, and the horse-wranglers calling and shouting as they rode rapidly from side to side behind the horses, urging on the stragglers by dexterous touches with the knotted ends of their long lariats that were left trailing from the saddle. The country driven over was very rough, and it was often necessary to double up teams and put on eight horses to each wagon in going up an unusually steep pitch, or hauling through a deep mud hole, or over a river crossing where there was quicksand.

To do good work in cutting out from a herd, not only should the rider be a good horseman, but he should also have a skilful, thoroughly trained horse. A good cutting pony was not common, and was generally too valuable to be used anywhere but in the herd. Such a one entered thoroughly into the spirit of the thing, and found out immediately the animal his master was after. He would then follow it closely of his own accord through every wheel and double at top speed. When looking through the herd it was necessary to move slowly and when any animal was found, it was taken to the outskirts at a walk, so as not to alarm the others. Once there, however, the cowboy had to ride like lightning, for as soon as the beast he was after found itself separated from its companions it endeavored to break back among them, and a young range-raised steer or heifer ran like a deer. In cutting out a cow and a calf two men had to work together. As the animals of a brand were cut out they were received and held apart by some rider detailed for the purpose, who was said to be "holding the cut."

As soon as the cows, calves and other animals had been cut out of the herd, the others were driven clear of the camp-

ing grounds and headed in the opposite direction from the
roundup.

It was now branding time. If there was a corral, each
band was driven into it; if not, a ring of riders held the cattle
together. A fire was built, the irons heated, and men dismounted and, as it was called, "wrestled," or threw the
calves. A roper caught the calf by both hind feet, and then,
having taken a twist with his lariat around the horn of the
saddle, dragged the bawling little creature, extended at full
length, up to the fire where it was branded.

If there were seventy or eighty calves in a corral, the
scene was one of the greatest confusion. The ropers, spurring
and checking the fierce little horses, dragged the calves up
so quickly that a dozen men could hardly hold them. The
men with the irons, blackened with soot, ran to and fro,
the calf-wrestlers, grimy with blood, dust and sweat, worked
like beavers, while with the voice of a stentor the tallyman
shouted out the number and sex of each calf. The dust rose
in clouds, and the shouts, cheers, curses, and laughter of
the men united with the lowing of the cows and the frantic
bleating of the roped calves to make a perfect babel. Now
and then an old cow turned vicious and put every one out
of the corral. Or a maverick bull—an unbranded bull—a
yearling or a two-year-old, was caught, thrown, and branded.
When he was let up there was sure to be a fine scatter.
Down went his head, and he bolted at the nearest man,
who made out of the way at top speed, amidst roars of
laughter from all of his companions.

The cattle gathered at the camp had to be kept together and guarded. There were the day and night herds. Guarding the day herd was the most monotonous work, the men being on from four in the morning till eight in the evening, the only rest at dinner time, when they changed horses. From eight in the evening till four in the morning the day herd became a night herd. Each wagon in succession guarded it for a night, dividing the time into watches of two hours apiece, a couple of riders taking each watch. This was "generally chilly and tedious, and at times accompanied by intense excitement and danger, when the cattle stampeded, whether by storm or otherwise."

The first and the last watches were those preferred. The others were disagreeable, the men having to turn out cold and sleepy, in the pitchy darkness, the two hours of chilly wakefulness completely breaking the night's rest.

The first guards bedded the cattle down. This took some time. When finally they had lain down and were chewing their cud or slumbering, the two night guards began riding round them in opposite ways, often, on very dark nights, calling or singing to them, as the sound of the human voice on such occasions seemed to have a tendency to quiet them. In inky-black weather, especially when rainy, it was both difficult and unpleasant work. The main trust had to be placed in the horse, which, if old at the business, would of its own accord keep pacing steadily around the herd and head off any animals that, unseen by the rider's eyes in the darkness, were trying to break out. Usually the watch passed off without incident, but on rare occasions the cattle became restless and prone to stampede. Anything might then start them—the plunge of a horse, the sudden approach of a coyote. Every animal in the herd would be on its feet in an instant, as if by an electric shock, and off with a rush, horns and tail up. Then, no matter how rough the ground nor how pitchy black the night, the cowboys must ride for all there was in them and spare neither their own nor their horses' necks. Perhaps their charges broke away and were lost altogether; perhaps, by desperate galloping, they might head them, get them running in a circle, and finally stop them.

But though there was much work and hardship, rough fare, monotony, and exposure connected with the roundup, yet there were few men who did not look forward to it and back to it with pleasure. It was superbly health-giving, and was full of excitement and adventure, calling for the exhibition of pluck, self-reliance, hardihood, and dashing horsemanship, and of all forms of physical labor the easiest and pleasantest was to sit in the saddle.

Chapter 10

"Sheriff" Roosevelt

EARLY IN the fall of 1885 the Marquis de Mores wrote Theodore: "If you are my enemy, I want to know it. Between gentlemen it is easy to settle matters of that sort directly." On September 6, Theodore wrote back, "Most emphatically I am not your enemy. If I were you would know it, for I would be an open one, and would not have asked you to my house nor gone to yours. As your final words, however, seem to imply a threat it is due to myself to say that the statement is not made through any fear of possible consequences to me. I too, as you know, am always on hand, and ever ready to hold myself accountable in any way for anything I have said or done."

The best evidence seems to indicate that although Theodore often visited at the chateau of the Marquis, and the Marquis and his wife often came to Elkhorn ranchhouse, there was no genuine friendship between the two. Actually, both of them were too strong-willed for a real friendship. The evidence also warrants the conclusion that the misunderstanding which caused this letter was fomented by troublemakers who would have liked to have seen the two lock horns.

Theodore's ability to take care of himself, no matter how rough-and-tumble the situation is best indicated when, in the following Spring, three thieves and so-called "bad men" stole his boat.

For a long time Theodore and some of his men had been anxious to run down the Little Missouri in a boat during the time of the spring floods, for duck and goose shooting, and it was decided that now was the time. But they left a little sooner than they intended.

One morning Sewall came up to the ranchhouse with the information that the boat had been stolen. There was little doubt about who had done it. The only other boat on the river was a small flat-bottomed scow owned by three hard characters who lived in a hut twenty miles above them, and who had narrowly missed lynching a few weeks earlier. They were suspected to have engaged both in cattle and horse stealing. Their leader was a well-built fellow named Finnegan, who had long red hair reaching to his shoulders, and always wore a broad hat and a fringed buckskin shirt.

Without waiting an hour, Theodore and his men began building a flat-bottomed scow in which to follow them. Sewall and Dow knew exactly how to do this. In three days they were ready to leave and Theodore, if he could have picked the country over, would not have wanted two better companions. They packed flour, coffee, and bacon enough to last a fortnight or so, plenty of warm bedding, and mess kits, into the boat, and early one cold March morning slid it into the icy current, took their seats, and shoved off down the river.

For several days before we started the weather had been bitterly cold, as a furious blizzard was blowing, but on the day we left there was a lull, and we hoped a thaw had set in. We all were most warmly and thickly dressed, with woolen socks and underclothes, heavy jackets and trousers, and great fur coats, so we felt we could bid defiance to the weather. Each carried his rifle, and we had in addition a double-barreled duck gun, for water-fowl and beaver. To manage the boat, we had paddles, heavy oars, and long iron-shod poles, Sewall steering while Dow sat in the bow. Altogether, we felt we were off on a holiday trip, and set to work to have as good a time as possible.

All through the early part of the day we drifted swiftly down between the heaped-up piles of ice, the cakes and slabs now dirty and unattractive-looking. Toward evening, however, there came long reaches where the banks on either side were bare, though even here there would every now and then be necks where the jam had been crowded into too narrow a spot and had risen over the side as it had done upstream, grinding the bark from the big cottonwoods and snapping the smaller ones short off. In such places the ice-walls were sometimes eight or ten feet high, continually undermined by the restless current; and every now and then overhanging pieces would break off and slide into the stream with a loud sullen splash, like the plunge of some great water beast. Nor did we dare to go too close to the high cliffs, as boulders and earth masses, freed by the thaw from the grip of the frost, kept rolling and leaping down their faces and forced us to keep a sharp lookout lest our boat should be swamped.

At nightfall we landed, and made our camp on a point of wood-covered land jutting out into the stream. We had seen very little trace of life until late in the day, for the ducks had not yet arrived; but in the afternoon a sharp-tailed prairie-fowl flew across stream ahead of the boat, lighting on a low branch by the water's edge. Shooting him, we landed and picked off two others that were perched high up in leafless cottonwoods, plucking the buds. These three birds served us as supper and shortly afterward, as the cold grew more and more biting, we rolled in under our furs and blankets and were soon asleep.

In the morning it was evident that instead of thawing it had grown decidedly colder. The anchor-ice was running thick in the river, and we spent the first hour or two after sunrise in hunting over the frozen swamp bottom for white-tail deer, of which there were many tracks; but we saw nothing. Then we broke camp and again started down-stream—a simple operation, as we had no tent, and all we had to do was to cord up our bedding and gather the mess-kit. For some time we went along in chilly silence, nor was it until midday that the sun warmed our blood in the least. The crooked bed of the current twisted hither and thither, but which ever way it went the icy north wind, blowing stronger all the time, drew steadily up it. One of us remarking that we bade fair to have it in our faces all day, the steersman announced that we couldn't, unless it was the crookedest wind in Dakota and, half an hour afterward, we overheard him muttering to himself that it was the crookedest wind in Dakota. We passed a group of tepees on one bottom, marking the deserted winter camp of some Grosventre Indians. It was almost the last point on the river with which we were acquainted. At midday we landed on a sandbar for lunch—a simple enough meal, the tea being boiled over a fire of driftwood that also fried the bacon, while the bread only needed to be baked every other day. Then we again shoved off. As the afternoon waned the cold grew still more bitter, and the wind increased, blowing in fitful gusts against us, until it chilled us to the marrow when we sat still. But we rarely did sit still; for even the rapid current was unable to urge the light-draft scow down in the teeth of the strong blasts, and we only got her along by dint of hard work with pole and paddle. Long before the sun went down the ice had begun to freeze on the handles of the poles, and we were not sorry to haul on shore for the night. For supper we again had prairie-fowl, having shot four from a great patch of bullberry bushes late in the afternoon. A man doing hard open-air work in cold weather is always hungry for meat.

During the night the thermometer went down to zero, and in the morning the anchor-ice was running so thickly that we did not care to start at once, for it is most difficult to handle a boat in the deep frozen slush. Accordingly we took a couple of hours for a deer-hunt, as there were evidently many whitetail on the bottom. We selected one long, isolated patch of tangled trees and brushwood, two of us beating through it while the other watched one end. Almost before we had begun four deer broke out at one side, loped easily off, evidently not much scared, and took refuge in a deep glen or gorge densely wooded with cedars, that made a blind pocket in the steep side of one of the great plateaus bounding the bottom. After a short consultation, one of our number crept round to the head of the gorge, making a wide detour, and the other two advanced up it on each side, thus completely surrounding the doomed deer. They attempted to break out past the man at the head of the glen, who shot down a couple, a buck and a yearling doe. The other two made their escape by running off over ground so rough that it looked fitter to be crossed by their upland-loving cousins, the blacktail.

This success gladdened our souls, insuring us plenty of fresh meat. We carried pretty much all of both deer back to camp and, after a hearty breakfast, loaded our scow and started merrily off once more. The cold still continued intense, and as the day wore away we became numbed by it, until at last an incident occurred that set our blood running freely again.

We were, of course, always on the alert, keeping a sharp lookout ahead and around us, and making as little noise as possible. Finally our watchfulness was rewarded, for in the middle of the afternoon of this, the third day we had been gone, as we came around a bend, we saw in front of us the lost boat, together with a scow, moored against the bank, while from among the bushes some little way back the smoke of a camp-fire curled up through the frosty air. We had come on the camp of the thieves. As I glanced at the faces of my two followers I was struck by the grim, eager look in their eyes. Our overcoats were off in a second, and after exchanging a few muttered words, the boat was hastily and silently shoved toward the bank. As soon as it touched the shore ice I leaped out and ran up behind a clump of bushes, so as to cover the landing of the others, who had to make the boat fast. For a moment we felt a thrill of keen excitement and our veins tingled as we crept cautiously toward the fire, for it seemed likely that there would be a brush.

The men we were after knew they had taken with them the only craft there was on the river, and so felt perfectly secure. Accordingly, we took them absolutely by surprise. Only one was in camp and his weapon was on the ground. He gave in at once. We made him safe, then sat down and waited for the others. In an hour or so they came in. We heard them a long way off and made ready, watching them for some minutes, as they walked toward us, their rifles on their shoulders and the sunlight glinting on the steel barrels. When they were within twenty yards we straightened up from behind a bank, covering them with our cocked rifles, while I shouted to them to hold up their hands. One of them obeyed at once, but Finnegan hesitated, his eyes wolfish. I walked a few paces closer, covering the center of his chest so as to avoid overshooting, and repeated the command. With an oath he let his rifle drop and held his hands up beside his head.

It was nearly dusk, so we camped where we were. While Sewall and Dow chopped down dead cottonwoods and dragged them up into a huge pile, to keep the fire going all night, I kept guard over the three prisoners who were huddled into a sullen group some twenty yards off, just the right distance for the buckshot from the double-barrel.

Having captured our men, we were in a quandary how to keep them. The cold was so intense that to tie them tightly hand and foot meant freezing both hands and feet off during the night, and not to tie tightly was no good at all. So nothing was left to us but to keep perpetual guard over them.

Our next step was to cord their weapons up in some bedding, which we sat on while we took supper. Immediately afterward we made the men take off their boots—it was a cactus country—and go to bed, all three lying on one buffalo robe and covering with another, in the full light of the blazing fire. We determined to watch in succession a half night apiece, thus each getting a full rest every third night. I took first watch, my two companions, revolver under head, rolling up in their blankets on the side of the fire opposite that on which the three captives lay, while I, in fur cap, gauntlets, and overcoat, took a position in which I could watch my men with absolute certainty of being able to stop any movement, no matter how sudden. For this night-watching we always used the double-barrel with buckshot.

Next morning we started downstream, having a well-laden flotilla, for the men we had caught had a good deal of plunder in their boat, including some saddles, as they evidently intended to get horses as soon as they reached a part of the country where there were any, and where it was possible to travel. Finnegan, who was the ringleader, and the man I was especially after, I kept by my side in our boat, the other two being put in their own scow, heavily laden and rather leaky, and with only one paddle. We kept them just in front of us, a few yards distant, the river being so broad that we knew, and they knew also, any attempt to escape to be perfectly hopeless.

They paddled and poled their way on until they came to a small ice jam, through which they worked their way, only to run into another one. A look from a high hill showed that a great ice jam that had passed the ranchhouse earlier had stopped here. It was impossible to go up the swift current of the Little Missouri, to walk meant abandoning all of their equipment, so there was nothing to do but to pitch camp and wait for a thaw.

"The next eight days," wrote Theodore, "were as irksome and monotonous as any I ever spent." Certainly there was little amusement in combining the work of an Arctic explorer with that of a sheriff. It was so cold that during the night the water in the camp pail froze into a solid mass. About noon the next day the ice in the pail would start melting but would freeze solid again in a few hours.

The great jam worked its way down the river and as it did so we followed behind in our scow. Our chief care, at the moment, was not to get too near to the jam and be sucked under by the current.

We had to be additionally cautious on account of being in the Indian country, having worked down past Killdeer Mountains, where some of my cowboys had run across a band of Sioux—said to be Tetons—the year before. Very probably the Indians would not have harmed us anyhow, but as we were hampered by the prisoners, we preferred not meeting them; nor did we, though we saw plenty of fresh signs, and found, to our sorrow, that they had just made a grand hunt all down the river, and had killed or driven off almost every head of game in the country through which we were passing.

As our stock of provisions grew scantier and scantier, we tried in vain to eke it out by the chase; for we saw no game. Two of us would go out hunting at a time, while the third kept guard over the prisoners. The latter would be made to sit down together on a blanket at one side of the fire, while the guard for the time being stood or sat some fifteen or twenty yards off. The prisoners being unarmed, and kept close together, there was no possibility of their escaping, and the guard kept at such a distance that they could not overpower him by springing on him, he having a Winchester or the double-barreled shotgun always in his hands cocked and at the ready. So long as we kept wide awake and watchful, there was not the least danger, as our three men knew us and understood perfectly that the slightest attempt at a break would result in their being shot down; but, although there was thus no risk, it was harassing, tedious work, and the strain, day in and day out, without any rest or letup, became very tiresome.

The country itself added to the monotony. When they rounded a bend, it was only to see on each hand the same lines of broken buttes dwindling off into the distance ahead as had dwindled off into the distance behind. The discolored river, whose eddies boiled into yellow foam, flowed always between the same banks of frozen mud or of muddy ice. Roosevelt wrote, "Our diet began to be as same as the scenery. Being able to kill nothing, we exhausted all our stock of provisions, and got reduced to flour, without yeast or baking powder, and unleavened bread, made with exceedingly muddy water, is not, as a steady thing, attractive."

The prisoners, finding that they were well treated, all in all behaved themselves excellently. They even became talkative. At one time the subject veered around to a man called "Calamity" who, when caught and ordered to hold up his hands, attempted instead to draw his revolver, with the result of having two bullets put through him. Finnegan remarked, "He was a damn fool for not knowing when a man had the drop on him." He turned to Theodore. "If I'd had any show at all," he said, "you'd have had to fight, Mr. Roosevelt, but there wasn't any use making a break when I'd only have got myself shot, with no chance of harming any one else."

The prisoners had quite a stock of books with them including dime novels, "the inevitable History of the James Brothers, and what was odd, "society" novels ranging from Ouida to Augusta J. Evans. Theodore had brought Anna Karenina along which he thought blended very well with the surroundings.

Finally the food supply diminished to a point where there was serious thought of abandoning the boats. The Indians had driven all the deer out of the country and the occasional prairie fowl that was shot did not go far.

A flock of geese passed us one morning, and afterward an old gander settled down on the river near our camp; but he was over two hundred yards off, and a rifle-shot missed him. Where he settled down the river was covered with thick glare ice that would just bear his weight and it was curious to see him stretch his legs out in front and slide forty or fifty feet when he struck, balancing himself with his outspread wings.

But when the day was darkest the dawn appeared. At last, having worked down some thirty miles at the tail of the ice-jam, we struck an outlying cow camp of the C Diamond ranch, and knew that our troubles were almost over. There was but one cowboy on it, but we were certain of his cordial help, for in a stock country all make common cause against either horse-thieves or cattle-thieves. He had no wagon, but told us we could get one up at a ranch near Killdeer Mountains, some fifteen miles off, and lent me a pony to go up there and see about it—which I accordingly did, after a sharp preliminary tussle when I came to mount the wiry bronco (one of my men remarking in a loud aside to our cowboy host, "the boss ain't no bronco-buster"). When I reached the solitary ranch spoken of, I was able to hire a large prairie-schooner and two tough little bronco mares, driven by the settler himself, a rugged old plainsman, who evidently could hardly understand why I took so much bother with the thieves instead of hanging them offhand. Returning to the river the next day, we walked our men up to the Killdeer Mountains. Sewall and Dow left me the following morning, went back to the boats, and had no further difficulty, for the weather set in very warm, the ice went through with a rush, and they reached Mandan in about ten days, killing four beaver and five geese on the way, but lacking time to stop to do any regular hunting.

Meanwhile I took the three thieves into Dickinson, the nearest town. The going was bad, and the little mares could only drag the wagon at a walk; so, though we drove during the daylight, it took us two days and a night to make the journey. It was a most desolate drive. The prairie had been burned the fall before, and was a mere bleak waste of blackened earth, and a cold, rainy mist lasted throughout the two days. The only variety was where the road crossed the shallow headwaters of Knife and Green Rivers. Here the ice was high along the banks, and the wagon had to be taken to pieces to get it over. My three captives were unarmed, but as I was alone with them, except for the driver, of whom I knew nothing, I had to be doubly on my guard, and never let them come close to me. The little mares went so slowly, and the heavy road rendered any hope of escape by flogging up the horses so entirely out of the question, that I soon found the safest plan was to put the prisoners in the wagon and myself walk behind with the inevitable Winchester. Accordingly I trudged steadily the whole time behind the wagon through the ankle-deep mud. It was a gloomy walk. Hour after hour went by always the same, while I plodded along through the dreary landscape—hunger, cold, and fatigue struggling with a sense of dogged, weary resolution. At night, when we put up at the squalid hut of a frontier granger, the only habitation on our road, it was even worse. I did not dare to go to sleep, but making my three men get into the upper bunk, from which they could get out only

with difficulty, I sat up with my back against the cabin door
and kept watch over them all night long. So, after thirty-six
hours' sleeplessness, I was most heartily glad when we at
last jolted into the long, straggling main street of Dickinson,
and I was able to give my unwilling companions into the
hands of the sheriff.

Under the laws of Dakota I received my fees as a deputy
sheriff for making the three arrests, and also mileage for the
three hundred odd miles gone over—a total of some fifty
dollars.

Theodore's first thought, after turning the prisoners over
to the sheriff, was to his feet. They were blistered and bloody.
Almost as if by an act of God the first man that he met,
after leaving the sheriff's office, was the only doctor in a
fifty-mile radius. "He was all teeth and eyes," this doctor
later said, "but he was unusually wide awake. He did not
seem to think that he had done anything particularly com-
mendable, but he was, in his own phrase, 'pleased as Punch'
at the idea of having participated in a real adventure. He was
just like a boy. We talked of many things that day while I
was repairing his blistered feet. He impressed me and
puzzled me, and when I went home to lunch, an hour later,
I told my wife that I had met the most peculiar, and at the
same time the most wonderful, man I had ever come to
know. I could see that he was a man of brilliant ability and
I could not understand why he was out there on the frontier."

The editor of the Newburyport, Massachusetts Herald
had a friend living in Dickinson who sent in news items on

odd happenings in the west. "When I saw him," this man wrote about Theodore, after describing the capture, "Mr. Roosevelt had been on the 'trail' for three weeks, and wore a cowboy's hat, corduroy jacket, flannel shirt, and heavy shoes, but was in excellent health and spirits. Said he, 'I don't know how I look, but I feel first rate.'

"The next morning he appeared in the justice's court, saw the outlaws indicted, and a little later took the train bound west, for his 'cow camp.'"

When pressed, back in Medora, as to why he had not killed these outlaws, as was customary on the frontier, instead of taking all the trouble and risk that he had, Theodore's answer was, "I didn't come out here to kill anybody. All I wanted to do was to defend myself and my property. There wasn't any one around to defend them for me, so I had to do it myself."

Chapter 11

Hunting White Goats in the Coeur d'Alene

In late Summer of 1886 Theodore wrote to a hunter, John Willis in Montana, "I want to shoot a white antelope goat. I have heard it is the hardest animal in the Rockies to find and the most difficult to kill. I have also heard that you are a great hunter. If I come to Montana, will you act as my guide, and do you think I can kill a white goat?"

After puzzling over Theodore's handwriting for several hours Willis scribbled across the letter, "If you can't shoot any better than you can write, no," and sent it back. Theodore immediately wired him back, "Consider yourself engaged," and left with Merrifield by train to meet him at a little frontier town.

It was not that easy. An extremely sour-visaged man, huge and broad-shouldered, met them at the train but one look at Theodore's corduroy knickers convinced him that he would have a real tenderfoot on his hands. If that was not enough, the glasses were to him the final and positive proof. But this tenderfoot was not to be gotten rid of so easily.

"He had red cheeks, like those of a brewer's son I knew," Willis later wrote, "and that didn't help any. The only thing about him that appealed to me at all was his eyes. They were keen and bright and dancing with animation. From them I knew he was honest and had a mind that worked fast and smoothly and was set on a hair-trigger."

It took all of that mind to turn the trick.

"When do we start?" Theodore cried impulsively.

"We are not going to start at all. You can go when you please."

Theodore offered Willis twenty-five dollars for every shot he got at a goat. This, Willis refused. He then offered to buy the grub.

"All the grub I'll take won't cost more than a couple of dollars," Willis said.

"By George, that's bully," said Theodore.

"You can't stand the sort of trip I am going to take," Willis countered.

"I'll train myself to walk as far as you can."

Grudgingly, Willis told them that he was going to leave for a hunt in a few days and that they could go along as his guests—as he saw no way of getting rid of this persistent man. This they agreed to. He strongly advised them to buy heavy, hobnailed shoes to replace the lightweight ones that Theodore had and the cowboy boots that Merrifield clung to. Both refused. Theodore did not want to delay for a moment getting on the trail. They started from "one of those most dismal and forlorn of all places, a dead mining town, on the line of the Northern Pacific Railroad."

In a day or two we were in the heart of the vast wooded wilderness. A broad, lonely river ran through its midst, cleaving asunder the mountain chains. Range after range, peak after peak, the mountains towered on every side, the lower timbered to the top, the higher with bare crests of gray crags, or else hooded with fields of shining snow. The deep valleys lay half in darkness, hemmed in by steep, tim- bered slopes and straight rock walls. The torrents, broken into glittering foam masses, sprang down through the chasms that they had rent in the sides of the high hills, lingered in black pools under the shadows of scarred cliffs, and reaching the rank, treechoked valleys, gathered into rapid streams of clear brown water, that drenched the drooping limbs of the tangled alders.

In places the mountain paths were very steep and the ponies could with difficulty scramble along them. Once or twice they got falls that no animals less tough could have survived. It was marvelous to see the philosophy with which the wise little beasts behaved, picking their way gingerly through these rough spots, hopping over fallen tree trunks, or stepping between them in places where an Eastern horse would have snapped a leg short off, and walking composedly along narrow ledges with steep precipices below.

Walla Walla, the little mule, was always in scrapes. Once we spent a morning in washing our clothes, then spread the half-clean array upon the bushes and departed on a hunt. On returning, we spied the miserable Walla Walla shamefacedly shambling off from the neighborhood of the washing, having partly chewed up every garment and completely undone all our morning's labor.

We first camped in a narrow valley, surrounded by mountains so tall that except at noonday it lay in the shadow. There were very few open glades, and these were not more than a dozen rods or so across. Even on the mountains it was only when we got up very high that we could get a glimpse into the open. A broad brook whirled and eddied past our camp, and a little below us was caught in a deep, narrow gorge, where the strangling rocks churned its swift current into spray and foam, and changed its murmurous humming and splashing into an angry roar.

Whitetail deer were plentiful, and we kept our camp abundantly supplied with venison, varying it with all the grouse that we wanted and with fresh trout.

For three or four days I hunted steadily and without success, and it was as hard work as any that I had ever undertaken. Merrifield and I were utterly unable to cope with the Missourian when it came to mountaineering.

We would start immediately after breakfast each morning, carrying a light lunch in our pockets, and go straight up the mountainsides for hours at a time, varying it by skirting the broad, terrace-like ledges or by clambering along the cliff crests. The slope was so steep that it was like going upstairs —now through loose earth, then through a shingle of pebbles or sand, then over rough rocks, and again over a layer of pine needles as smooth and slippery as glass, while brittle dry stick that snapped at a touch, and loose stones that rattled down if so much as brushed, strewed the ground everywhere. Often, too, we would encounter dense under-

brush, perhaps a thicket of little burnt balsams, as prickly
and brittle as so much coral, or else a heavy growth of laurel,
all the branches pointing downward, to be gotten through
only by main force.

The trails at which we looked with the most absorbed
interest were those that showed the large, round hoofmarks
of the white goats. They had worn deep paths to certain
clay licks in the slides, which they must have visited often
in the early spring, for the trails were little traveled when
we were in the mountains, during September. The clay
seemed to contain something that both birds and beasts
were fond of, for I frequently saw flocks of crossbills light
in the licks and stay there for many minutes at a time,
scratching the smooth surface with their little claws and
bills.

*By now Theodore's shoes were in shreds and Merrifield's
boots had made his feet so sore that he could not leave
camp. "Being accustomed to it," Willis wrote, "I walked
so fast that Roosevelt was forced into a jog trot most of the
time to keep up with me. But he never complained, nor did
he ever ask me to slacken my speed. Moisture would develop on his glasses, from perspiration, and he would pause
at intervals to wipe them off, but he kept right on coming.
His muscles were strong and after they became hardened,
which took about a week, he could keep up with me on
almost any trail, no matter how hard the going."*

The goat trails led away in every direction from the licks,
but usually went uphill. Although deeply worn, they showed
very little fresh goat sign. In fact we came across the recent

trails of only two of the animals we were after. One of these we came quite close to. I had been, as usual, walking and clambering over the mountains all day long, and in mid-afternoon reached a great slide, with a tree half-way across it. Under this I sat down to rest, my back to the trunk, and had been there but a few minutes when Willis suddenly whispered to me that a goat was coming down the slide at its edge, near the woods. I was in a most uncomfortable position for a shot. Twisting my head round, I could see the goat waddling downhill, looking just like a handsome tame billy, especially when at times he stood upon a stone to glance around, with all four feet close together. I cautiously tried to shift my position, and at once dislodged some pebbles at the sound of which the goat sprang promptly up on the bank, his whole mien changing into one of alert, alarmed curiosity. He was less than a hundred yards off, so I risked a shot, all cramped and twisted though I was. My bullet went low, breaking his left fore leg, and he disappeared over the bank like a flash. We raced and scrambled after him, and Willis, an excellent tracker, took up the bloody trail. It went along the hillside for nearly a mile, and then turned straight up the mountain, Willis leading with his long free gait, while I toiled after him at a dogged trot. The trail went up the sharpest and steepest places, skirting the cliffs and precipices. At one spot I nearly came to grief for good and all, for in running along a shelving ledge, covered with loose slates, one of these slipped as I stepped on it, throwing me clear over the brink.

The first drop was at least sixty feet. When Willis saw Theodore disappear over the edge he gave him up for dead.

However the force of the fall was broken by the top of a tall pine through which Theodore went. He bounded into the outstretched limbs of a tree under it, then into another one, and finally landed on a bunch of moss that was as thick as a feather bed. All around this series of trees were jagged rocks that would have shredded the falling man. As it was he still had his rifle in his hand.

"Not a bit hurt," he shouted gaily up to Willis. "Wait until I find my glasses and I'll be with you."

He found his glasses—unbroken—and raced up the side of the mountain to rejoin Willis in the chase of the goat.

The trail came into a regular game path and grew fresher, the goat having stopped to roll and wallow in the dust now and then. Suddenly, on the top of the mountain, we came upon him close to us. He had just risen from rolling and stood behind a huge fallen log, his back barely showing above it as he turned his head to look at us. I was completely winded, and had lost my strength as well as my breath, while great bead drops of sweat stood in my eyes. I steadied myself as well as I could and aimed to break the backbone, the only shot open to me, and not a difficult one at such a short distance. However, my bullet went just too high, cutting the skin above the long spinal bones over the shoulders, and the speed with which that three-legged goat went down the precipitous side of the mountain would have done credit to an antelope on the level.

Weary and disgusted, we again took up the trail. It led straight downhill, and we followed it at a smart pace. Down and down it went, into the valley and straight to the edge of the stream, but half a mile above camp. The goat crossed the water on a fallen tree trunk, and we took the same path. Once across, it went right up the mountain. We followed it as fast as we could, although pretty nearly done out, until it was too dark to see the blood stains any longer. We returned to camp, dispirited and so tired that we could hardly drag ourselves along, for we had been going at top speed for five hours, up and down the roughest and steepest ground.

Next morning at daybreak we again climbed the mountain and took up the trail. Soon it led into others and we lost it, but we kept up the hunt nevertheless for hour after hour, making continually wider and wider circles. About midday our perseverance was rewarded, for coming silently out on a great bare cliff shoulder, I spied the goat lying on a ledge below me some seventy yards off. This time I shot true, and he rose only to fall back dead. A minute afterward we were standing over him, handling the glossy black horns and admiring the snow-white coat.

After this we shifted camp some thirty miles to a wide valley through whose pine-clad bottom flowed a river, hurrying on to the Pacific between unending forests. On one side the valley was hemmed in by an unbroken line of frowning cliffs, and on the other by chains of lofty mountains in whose sides the ravines cut deep gashes.

The weather had grown colder. At night the frost skimmed with thin ice the edges of the ponds and small lakes that at long intervals dotted the vast reaches of woodland. But we were very comfortable, and hardly needed our furs, for as evening fell we kindled huge fires, to give us both light and warmth. The clear, cold water of the swift streams too was a welcome change from the tepid and muddy currents of the rivers of the plains. We heartily enjoyed the baths, a plunge into one of the icy pools making us gasp for breath and causing the blood to tingle in our veins with the shock.

Our tent was pitched in a little glade, which was but a few yards across, and carpeted thickly with the red kinnikinnick berries, in their season beloved of bears, and from the leaves of which bush the Indians make a substitute for tobacco. Little three-toed woodpeckers with yellow crests scrambled about over the trees near by, while the great logcocks hammered and rattled on the tall dead trunks. Jays that were dark blue all over came familiarly round camp in company with the ever-present moose-birds and whiskeyjacks.

Although we saw no game it was very pleasant to sit out, on the still evenings, among the tall pines or on the edge of a great gorge, until the afterglow of the sunset was dispelled by the beams of the frosty moon. Now and again the hush would be suddenly broken by the long howling of a wolf, that echoed and rang under the hollow woods and deep chasms until they resounded again, while it made our hearts bound and the blood leap in our veins. Then there would be silence once more, broken only by the rush of the river and the low moaning and creaking of the pines, or the strange calling of the owls might be answered by the far-off, unearthly laughter of a loon, its voice carried through the stillness a marvelous distance from the little lake on which it was swimming.

Near where they were camped there was a beautiful water-fall Theodore wanted to photograph. It was not possible to get the exact shots that he wanted from the banks of the river. He persuaded Willis and Merrifield, in spite of their arguments, to lower him over a precipice with a two-hundred foot rope. Willis warned him that they might not be able to drag him back up. His prediction proved accurate.

"Cut the rope and let me fall into the stream," Theodore called up to them.

Willis worked his way down to the foot of the falls and discovered that the drop would be at least sixty feet into water filled with whirlpools and jagged rocks. Finally, he remembered there was an additional twenty-five foot piece of rope back at camp. He returned with this to find Theodore, who had been swinging with the rope under his arms for two hours, still enjoying himself hugely. This second rope reduced the drop to about thirty-five feet. Willis quickly constructed a small raft, pushed out into the water, had Theodore drop his camera which he caught without getting it wet, and then Merrifield cut the rope. The fall, luckily in good water, stunned Theodore but after Willis had pulled him aboard the raft, he quickly recovered.

"By Jove," he cried, "that was great fun, and that was a great catch you made of the camera."

A few days later, after Theodore had secured two more white goats in an unexciting hunt, they broke camp and set off for the settlement. By now Theodore and Willis had developed a warm friendship which lasted for life.

On this trip Theodore talked constantly to Willis, who made his living by slaughtering game for their hides, about the necessity for conserving wildlife. Although he would not admit it at the time, Theodore had made of him a staunch believer in conservation and he thereafter not only ceased to be a game butcher but became a strong worker for its preservation.

Chapter 12

The Great Blizzard of 1886-1887: A Moose Hunt

By THE summer of 1886 two things about the Bad Lands were evident to Theodore. The first was that the country was being overgrazed; the second that the time had come for law-and-order in the region. He spent a great deal of his time working for this second but could do very little about the first.

In his Roosevelt in the Bad Lands Hermann Hagedorn tells about one of the first elections held at Little Missouri. "Hell-Roaring" Bill Jones, who became one of Theodore's best friends, was a watcher at the polls to see that no unauthorized persons voted. Theodore found a group of his friends near the polls.

"Has there been any disorder?" he asked.

"Disorder, hell!" said one of the men in the group. "Bill Jones just stood there with one hand on his gun and the other pointing over toward the new jail whenever any man who didn't have a right to vote come near the polls. There was only one of them tried to vote, and Bill knocked him down. Lord!" he concluded meditatively, "the way that man fell."

"Well," said "Hell-Roaring" Bill, "if he hadn't fell, I'd of walked round behind him to see what was proppin' him up!"

By this summer both Sewall and Dow were extremely doubtful about the success of their venture. Even the arguments of Theodore, who made such a good Fourth of July speech at Dickinson that the editor of The Badlands Cowboy told him he would someday be President of the United States, did not convince them. After Theodore's return from the white goat hunt with John Willis they told him that they had decided to return to Maine. "I never want to fool away anybody else's money," Sewall said, "and I never had any of my own to fool away."

Theodore himself had an additional pull back east. He and Edith Carow, a childhood sweetheart, were again going together. Theodore wondered about his future as a lawyer and asked Sewall his opinion. "You'd be a good lawyer," Bill said, "but I think you ought to go into politics. Good men like you ought to go into politics. If you do, and if you live, I think you'll be President."

After squaring with Sewall and Dow, Theodore turned all of his cattle over to Ferris and Merrifield on a new contract. Then he went east where, against his better judgment, he entered the election as Republican candidate for Mayor of New York. Abraham S. Hewitt, the Democratic candidate, was elected, Henry George, the United Labor Party candidate, ran second, and Theodore finished third. He went abroad immediately after the election and in December, in London, he married Edith Carow.

That winter, still talked about by old timers, death and destruction swept across the Bad Lands. Blizzard followed blizzard.

"You cannot imagine anything more dreary than the look of the Bad Lands," Theodore wrote Sewall when he got back there in late spring. "Everything was cropped as bare as a bone. The sagebrush was just fed out by the starving cattle. . . . You boys were lucky to get out when you did; if you had waited until Spring, I guess it would have been a case of walking."

There was not a single cow left of Theodore's stock— "only a few hundred sick-looking steers."

The first impulse was to try to recoup the losses. But, eventually, Theodore decided that he could not risk any more money.

He spent most of the summer at the Elkhorn Ranch. It would have been lonesome with Sewall and Dow and their families gone, but Merrifield, newly married, moved into the Elkhorn ranchhouse. But the old glow, the pull, of the region, the great dreams that had been built around it, had vanished and lay in the ruin and desolation which the past winter had brought. The pull now was back to the house on Oyster Bay, which had been started for Alice Lee, and which was now occupied by Edith Carow.

To keep up his spirits, Theodore, in September, 1887, went hunting for an animal he had not yet killed—moose.

It was on this hunt one night that Theodore left his pants

—his only pair—too near the fire. The next morning they were completely burnt up. There was no clothing stores in two hundred miles. Willis found an old prospector who sold him a pair of disreputable old overalls for a dollar. Theodore held up the muddy, dirty and frayed garment and examined it admiringly.

"Boss of the Road," he read from a label that was barely distinguishable. "That's us. We're bosses of the road, or the trail, anyway. Just made to my order. That's bully."

The overalls were three inches too short and lacked many inches in meeting around the waist. This did not bother Theodore. He tied them on with string and pronounced them a perfect fit.

"I'm a prospector now, as well as a hunter," he announced with boyish glee. "We must dig for gold, somewhere. Even if we don't find any, we won't be any worse off than the original owner of these beautiful pants."

He wore them for the next three weeks while trying to find moose.

Although we found a country where there was moose, we tried to kill them by hunting in the same manner that we hunted elk—by choosing a place where there was sign, and going carefully through it against or across the wind. Unfortunately, this plan failed.

However, a few days after the hunt I met a crabbed old trapper named Hank Griffin who was going after beaver in the mountains, and who told me that if I would go along he would show me moose. I jumped at the chance.

We went to a high, marshy valley stretched for several

miles between two rows of stony mountains, clad with a forest of rather small fir trees. This valley was covered with reeds, alders, and rank grass, and studded with little willow-bordered ponds and island-like clumps of spruce and graceful tamaracks.

Having surveyed the ground and found moose sign the preceding afternoon, we were up in the cool morning to begin our hunt. Before sunrise we posted ourselves on a rocky spur of the foothills, behind a mask of evergreen where unseen we overlooked all the valley, and we knew we could see any animal which might be either feeding away from cover or on its journey homeward from its feeding-ground to its day-bed.

As it grew lighter we scanned the valley with increasing care and eagerness. Almost as soon as the sun rose behind us, we made out some large beast moving among the dwarf willows beside a little lake half a mile in our front. In a few minutes the thing walked out where the bushes were thinner, and we saw that it was a young bull moose browsing on the willow tops. He had evidently nearly finished his breakfast, and he stood idly for some moments, now and then lazily cropping a mouthful of twig tips. Then he walked off with great strides in a straight line across the marsh, splashing among the wet water-plants, and ploughing through boggy spaces with the indifference begotten of vast strength and legs longer than those of any other animal on this continent. At times he entered beds of reeds which hid him from view, though their surging and bending showed the wake of his passage; at other times he walked through meadows of tall grass, the withered yellow stalks rising to his flanks, while his body loomed above them, glistening black and wet in the level sunbeams. Once he stopped for a few moments on a rise of dry ground, seemingly to enjoy the heat of the young sun. He stood there motionless, save that his ears were continually pricked, and his head sometimes slightly turned, showing that even in this remote land he was on the alert. Once, with a somewhat awkward motion, he reached his hind leg forward to scratch his neck. Then he walked forward again into the marsh. At places where the water was quite deep he broke into the long, stretching, springy trot, which forms the characteristic gait of his kind, churning the marsh water into foam. He held his head straight forward, the antlers resting on his shoulders.

After a while he reached a spruce island, through which he walked to and fro, but evidently could find therein no resting-place quite to his mind, for he soon left and went on to another. Here, after a little wandering he chose a point where there was some thick young growth which hid him from view when he lay down, though not when he stood. After some turning he settled himself in his bed just as a steer would.

He could not have chosen a spot better suited for us. He was nearly at the edge of the morass, the open space between the spruce clump where he was lying and the rocky foot-hills being comparatively dry and not much over a couple of hundred yards broad, while some sixty yards from it, and between it and the hills, was a little hummock, tufted with firs, so as to afford us just the cover we needed. Keeping back from the edge of the morass we were able to walk upright through the forest, until we got to the point where he was lying in a line with this little hummock. We then dropped on our hands and knees, and crept over the soft, wet sward, where there was nothing to make a noise. Wherever the ground rose at all we crawled flat on our bellies. The air was still, for it was a very calm morning.

At last we reached the hummock, and I got into position for a shot, taking a final look at my faithful Winchester to see that all was in order. Peering cautiously through the shielding evergreens, I at first could not make out where the moose was lying, until my eye was caught by the motion of his big ears, as he occasionally flapped them lazily forward. Even though I could not see his outline, I knew where he was, and having pushed my rifle forward on the moss, I snapped a dry twig to make him rise. My veins were thrilling and my heart beating with that eager, fierce excitement known only to the hunter of big game, and forming one of the keenest and strongest of the many pleasures which go to make up "the wild joy of living."

As the sound of the snapping twig smote his ears the moose rose nimbly to his feet, with a lightness on which one would not have reckoned in a beast so heavy of body. He stood broadside to me for a moment, his ungainly head slightly turned, while his ears twitched and his nostrils snuffed the air. Drawing a fine bead against his black hide, behind his shoulder and two-thirds of his body's depth below his shaggy withers, I pressed the trigger. Although he neither flinched nor reeled, but started with his regular ground-covering trot through the spruces, I knew he was mine, for the light blood sprang from both of his nostrils, and he fell dying on his side before he had gone thirty rods.

Getting this trophy was the result of a number of fruitless trips, weary walking, patient waiting and infinite patience. For that reason I prized it all the more.

John Willis in his Roosevelt in the Rough *tells about an experience which happened after this hunt was over. Late one afternoon they stopped for the night at a roadhouse kept by "Jenny," a famous character who had kept a "resort" at Virginia City. She was now over eighty years old but still sprightly. She and her husband, also an old-timer, entertained Theodore for several hours.*

Just before supper six burly bruisers and an old man, obviously their boss, came in. They were cutting railroad ties in the neighborhood. After a few drinks they began making remarks about that "four-eyed gink" and aiming other pointed allusions to Theodore. He ignored them.

At supper they all sat at a long table. The lumberjacks continued their insulting remarks which John saw were making Theodore madder and madder. There was some boiled rice on the table out of Theodore's reach.

"Please pass the porridge," he said to the man opposite him.

"What do you suppose the four-eyed gink means by porridge?" one of them said.

John knew what was going to happen. He threw a cup of coffee into the face of the man opposite him, turned the table over, and went out into the hall for his rifle. Before he reached the door he saw Theodore drive a terrific smash into the face of the man sitting beside him and John knew that one was out of commission. When he reappeared, with his rifle, a second man was lying on the floor, and Theodore was in the act of putting a third one out of the fight.

"Don't shoot, Jack," he called, "I can take care of them if they don't break my glasses."

With this he let the third one have it with a blow to the pit of the stomach, and with his lips drawn back from his teeth in a tigerish smile, moved toward the fourth one. This one did not want any more.

"That's enough," he muttered as he joined those still on their feet.

Before they were allowed to leave Theodore and Jack made them pay Jenny for their food in spite of their protests that they had not eaten it.

Later in the fall, while in the Bitter Root Mountains, between Idaho and Montana, Theodore again hunted for moose. While camping in an alpine meadow, with a companion, Theodore awoke early, crawled out of his buffalo bag, shivering and yawning, and, leaving his companion sleeping soundly, went to a meadow where he had seen moose sign the night before. Before leaving shelter, he halted to listen and, almost immediately "heard a curious splashing sound from the middle of the meadow, where the brook broadened into small willow-bordered pools."

Crouching, I stole noiselessly along the edge of the willow thicket. The stream twisted through it from side to side in zigzags, so that every few rods I got a glimpse down a lane of black water. In a minute I heard a slight splashing near me and, on passing the next point of bushes, I saw the shadowy outline of the moose's hind quarters, standing in a bend of the water. In a moment, he walked onward, disappearing. I ran forward a couple of rods, and then turned in among the willows, to reach the brook where it again bent back toward me. The splashing in the water, and the rustling of the moose's body against the frozen twigs, drowned the noise made by my moccasined feet.

I strode out on the bank at the lower end of a long, narrow pool of water, dark and half-frozen. In this pool, halfway down and facing me, but a score of yards off, stood the mighty marsh beast, strange and uncouth in look as some monster surviving over from the Pliocene. His vast bulk loomed black and vague in the dim gray dawn; his huge antlers stood out sharply; columns of steam rose from his nostrils. For several seconds he fronted me motionless; then he began to turn, slowly, as if he had a stiff neck. When a quarter-way round I fired into his shoulder. He reared and bounded on the bank with a great leap, vanishing in the willows. Through these I heard him crash like a whirlwind for a dozen rods, then down he fell, and when I reached the spot he had ceased to struggle. The ball had gone through his heart.

When a moose is thus surprised at close quarters, it will often stand and gaze for a moment or two, and then turn stiffly around until headed in the right direction. Once headed aright it starts off with extraordinary speed.

The moose is the giant of all deer and many hunters esteem it the noblest of American game. Beyond question there are few trophies more prized than the huge shovel horns of this strange dweller in the cold northland forest.

Chapter 13

A Caribou Hunt in the Selkirks

WHEN THEODORE returned to New York in the fall of 1887 he was never to return to his Bad Lands ranch except for short hunts. A year later he stayed there a few days and then joined his old hunting partner, John Willis, on a caribou hunt in the Selkirk Mountains in southeast British Columbia. After a fruitless try they came down out of the mountains and camped a few days on the shores of Kootenai Lake, from which flows Columbia River. With them was their hunting companion, "an impassive Indian named Ammal." While there, several parties of Indians passed down the lake in strangely shaped bark canoes with peaked, projecting prows and sterns.

After a rest, early one morning, they started back up into the mountains for another try for caribou. They traveled light, leaving almost all they had with the tent and boat at the lake.

We walked in single file, Willis first, I followed, and the Indian pigeon-toed along behind, carrying his pack, not as we did ours, but by help of a forehead band, which he sometimes shifted across his breast. The traveling through the tangled, brush-choked forest, and along the boulder-strewn and precipitous mountainsides, was inconceivably rough and difficult. Every step was severe toil. Up the almost perpendicular hillsides we in many places went practically on all fours. Most difficult of all were the dry water-courses, choked with alders, where the intertwined tangle of tough stems formed an almost impenetrable barrier.

At noon we halted beside a little brook for a bite of lunch—a chunk of cold frying-pan bread, which was all we had. I sat on a great stone by the edge of the brook, idly gazing at a water wren. It flew by me to a little rapids close at hand, lighting on a round stone and then slipping unconcernedly into the swift water. Soon it emerged, stood on another stone, and trilled a few bars, then dived again into the stream.

This strange, pretty water-thrush was to me one of the most attractive and interesting birds to be found in the gorges of the great Rockies. Its haunts are romantically beautiful, for it always dwells beside and in the swift-flowing mountain brooks. It spends half of its time under the water, walking along the bottom, swimming and diving, and flitting through as well as over the cataracts.

When this interlude was over we resumed our march, toiling silently onward through the wild and rugged country. Toward evening the valley widened a little, and we were able to walk in bottoms.

An hour or two before sunset, as we were traveling through an open wood of great hemlock trees, Willis suddenly dropped down in his tracks, pointing forward. Some fifty feet beyond I saw the head and shoulders of a bear as he rose to make a sweep at some berries. I fired, meaning to shoot through the shoulders, but instead, in the hurry, taking him in the neck. Down he went but whether hurt or not we could not see, for the second he was on all fours he was no longer visible. To my surprise he uttered no sound, so I raced forward, the hunter close behind me, while Ammal danced about in the rear, very much excited, as Indians always are in the presence of big game. We saw by the swaying of tall plants that the bear was coming our way. Willis was some ten feet distant, a hemlock trunk between us. The next moment the bear sprang clean up a bank the other side of the hemlock and almost within arm's length of my companion. For a moment it looked as if he stood a fair chance of being hurt. However, as the beast sprang out of the hollow he poised for a second on the edge of the bank to recover his balance, giving me a beautiful shot. The bullet struck between the eye and ear, and he fell as if hit with a poleaxe.

Immediately the Indian began jumping about the body, uttering wild yells, his impassive face lighted up with excitement, while Willis and I stood at rest, leaning on our rifles and laughing. It was a strange scene, the dead bear lying in the shade of the giant hemlocks, while the fantastic-looking savage danced round him with shrill whoops, and the frontiersman looked quietly on.

Our prize was a large black bear with two curious brown

streaks down his back, one on each side of the spine. We
skinned him and camped by the carcass. We built a huge
fire to one side of which we made our beds of balsam and
hemlock boughs. Then we supped on sugarless tea, frying-
pan bread and quantities of bear meat, fried or roasted. After
eating our fill we stretched ourselves around the fire. The
leaping sheets of flame lighted the tree-trunks round about,
causing them to stand out against the cavernous blackness
beyond, and reddened the interlacing branches that formed
a canopy overhead. The Indian sat on his haunches, gazing
steadily and silently into the pile of blazing logs, while
Willis and I talked.

The next morning the hunters took up their march, heading upstream, to its source amid the mountains where the
snowfields fed its springs. Their progress was slow as they
stopped to hunt along the way. White goats were plentiful
but since they were too musky to eat they did not kill them.
In addition to the troubles which the mountains offered,
as they went higher and higher Ammal became more and
more morose. It turned out that he feared "little bad Indians" by which he meant hobgoblins. "Indeed," wrote
Theodore, "the night sounds of these great stretches of
mountain woodlands were very weird and strange. After
nightfall, around the camp fire, or if awakened after sleeping
a little while, I would often lie silently for many minutes,
listening to the noises of the wilderness. At times the wind
moaned harshly through the tops of the tall pines and hemlocks; at times the branches were still. The splashing murmur of the torrent never ceased. The clatter of huge rocks

falling down the cliffs, the dashing of cataracts in far off ravines, the hooting of the owls. . . . If I listened long enough, it would almost seem that I heard thunderous voices laughing and calling to one another, and as if at any moment some shape might stalk out of the darkness into the dim light of the embers."

The first day after reaching their final camp, they hunted across a set of spurs and hollows but saw nothing. They began to fear that they might have to return without seeing the game they came after because their shoes were cut to ribbons on the sharp rocks and they were out of flour and had little to eat.

It was find caribou or else. The next day, "Willis struck such a brisk pace, plunging through thickets and leaping from log to log, and from boulder to boulder" that Theodore could hardly keep up with him. Each of them had several bad falls, barely saving their rifles. After two or three hours they came to a spur of open hemlock forest. Willis stopped and pointed exultingly to a well-marked game trail in which appeared the great round footprints of the caribou. But they were not to be found. They had wandered all over the bogs and through shallow pools, but evidently only at night or in the dusk, when feeding or coming to drink. But the hunters kept after them. Soon the timber disappeared entirely, and thick brushwood took its place. They were in a high, bare alpine valley, the snow lying in drifts along its side. After going through this valley for several miles, they reached a forest, which widened out and "crept up the mountainsides." Another stream entered the one they were following. They descended the steep incline with care, scanning every object, and using every caution not to slip on the hemlock needles, nor to strike a stone or break a stick with their feet. The sign was very fresh, and when still half a mile or so from the bottom they came on three bull caribou.

Instantly Willis crouched down, while I ran noiselessly forward behind the shelter of a big hemlock trunk until within fifty yards of the grazing and unconscious quarry. They were feeding with their heads uphill, but so greedily that they had not seen us. They were rather difficult to see themselves, for their bodies harmonized well with the brown tree trunks and lichen-covered boulders. The largest, a big bull with a good head, was nearest. As he stood fronting me with his head down I fired into his neck, breaking the bone, and he turned a tremendous back somersault. The other two halted a second in stunned terror, then one, a yearling, rushed past us up the valley down which we had come. The other, a large bull with small antlers, crossed right in front of me, at a canter, his neck thrust out, and his head turned toward me. There was a spur a little beyond, and up this he went at a swinging trot, halting when he reached the top, and turning to look at me once more. He was only a hundred yards away and, though I had not intended to shoot him, the temptation was sore. I was glad when, in another second, the stupid beast turned again and went off up the valley at a slashing run.

We hurried down to examine with pride and pleasure the dead bull. His massive form, sleek coat, and fine antlers made it one of those moments that repay the hunter for days of toil and hardship.

It was getting late so we halted only long enough to dress the caribou, take a steak with us, then went back to camp very fast, too much elated to heed scratches and tumbles. It was growing dark when we came opposite our camp, crossed the river on a fallen hemlock, and walked up to the moody Indian as he sat crouched by the fire. He lost his sullenness when he heard what we had done. The next day we all went up and skinned and butchered the caribou, returning to camp and making ready to start back to the lake the following morning. That night we feasted royally.

We were off by dawn, the Indian joyfully leading, carrying the caribou's skull and antlers on his head. At the end of the day he confessed to me that it had made his head "heap sick"—as well it might. Coming up it had taken four days. Returning, we knew how to take the shortest route and were going down hill, so we made the whole distance in twelve hours' travel. At sunset we came out on the last range of steep foothills, overlooking the cove where we had pitched our permanent camp, and from a bare cliff shoulder we saw our boat on the beach and our white tent among the trees, just as we had left them, while the glassy mirror of the lake reflected the outlines of the mountains opposite.

On our way out of the woods, there was a slight warm spell, followed by rain and then by freezing weather, so as to bring about what is known as a silver thaw. Every twig was sheathed in glittering ice, and in the moonlight the forest gleamed as if carved out of frosted silver.

Chapter 14

The Guide Who Betrayed Theodore

IN 1889 Theodore was appointed to the Civil Service Commission by President Harrison. By now there were four children besides Alice—Theodore, Jr., Kermit, Ethel and Quentin. He taught each of them, as they grew old enough, how to camp out, swim, ride and shoot. They were a happy family no matter where they were.

Before moving to Washington, Theodore went back to the Bad Lands for a hunt. He heard that a very few bison were still left around the head of Wisdom River. He went there and hunted them faithfully, but found no trace of them. A few days later that same year, he came across "these great wild cattle" at a time when he had no idea of seeing them. It was as nearly as he could tell, in Idaho, just south of the Montana boundary-line, and some twenty-five miles west of the line of Wyoming. He had an old hunter with him who, because of rheumatism, carried a long staff instead of a rifle.

Toward the middle of one afternoon they crossed a low, rocky ridge above timber line, and saw at their feet a round valley of singular beauty. Its walls were formed by steep mountains. At its upper end lay a small lake, bordered on one side by a meadow of emerald green. Frowning pine forests came down to the edge of the lake on the other side and at its outlet.

Beyond the lake the ground rose in a pass evidently much frequented by game in bygone days, their trails lying along it in thick zigzags, each gradually fading out after a few hundred yards, and then starting again in a little different place, as game trails so often seem to do.

We bent our steps toward these trails, and no sooner had we reached the first than the old hunter bent over it with a sharp exclamation of wonder. There in the dust were the unmistakable hoof-marks of a small band of bison, apparently but a few hours old. They were headed toward the lake. There had been half a dozen animals in the party, one a big bull, and two calves.

We immediately turned and followed the trail. It led down to the little lake, where the beasts had spread and grazed on the tender, green blades, and had drunk their fill. The footprints then came together again, showing where the animals had gathered and walked off in single file to the forest. Evidently they had come to the pool in the early morning, walking over the game pass from some neighboring valley, and after drinking and feeding had moved into the pine forest to find some spot for their noon-tide rest.

It was a very still day, and there were nearly three hours of daylight left. Without a word my silent companion, who had been scanning the whole country with hawk-eyed eagerness, besides scrutinizing the sign on his hands and knees, took the trail, motioning me to follow. In a moment we entered the woods, breathing a sigh of relief as we did so, for while in the meadow we could never tell that the buffalo might not see us, if they happened to be lying in some place with a commanding lookout.

The old hunter was thoroughly roused, and he showed himself a very skillful tracker. We were much favored by the character of the forest, which was rather open, and in most places free from undergrowth and down timber. As in most Rocky Mountain forests the timber was small, not only as compared to the giant trees of the groves of the Pacific coast, but as compared to the forests of the Northeast. The ground was covered with pine-needles and soft moss, so that it was not difficult to walk noiselessly. Once or twice when I trod on a small dry twig, or let the nails in my shoes clink slightly against a stone, the hunter turned to me with a frown of angry impatience. As he walked slowly, continually halting to look ahead, as well as stooping over to examine the trail, I did not find it very difficult to move silently. I kept a little behind him and to one side, save when he crouched to take advantage of some piece of cover, and I crept in his footsteps. I did not look at the trail at all, but kept watching ahead, hoping at any moment to see the game.

It was not very long before we struck their day-beds, which were made on a knoll, where the forest was open and where there was much down timber. After leaving the day-beds the animals had at first fed separately around the grassy base and sides of the knoll, and had then made off in their usual single file, going straight to a small pool in the forest. After drinking they had left this pool, and traveled down toward the gorge at the mouth of the basin, the trail leading along the sides of the steep hill, which were dotted by open glades. Here we moved with redoubled caution, for the sign had grown very fresh and the animals had once more scattered and begun feeding. When the trail led across the glades we usually skirted them so as to keep in the timber.

At last, on nearing the edge of one of these glades we saw a movement among the young trees on the other side, not fifty yards away. Peering through the safe shelter yielded by some thick evergreen bushes, we speedily made out three bison, a cow, a calf, and a yearling, grazing greedily on the other side of the glade, under the fringing timber, all with their heads uphill. Soon another cow and calf stepped out after them. I did not wish to shoot, waiting for the ap-pearance of the big bull which I knew was accompanying them.

So for several minutes I watched the great, clumsy, shaggy beasts, as all unconscious they grazed in the open glade. Mixed with the eager excitement of the hunter was a cer-tain half-melancholy feeling as I gazed on these bison, them-selves part of the last remnant of a doomed and nearly vanished race. Few, indeed, are the men who now have, or ever more shall have, the chance of seeing the mightiest of American beasts, in all his wild vigor, surrounded by the tremendous desolation of his far-off mountain home.

At last, when I had begun to grow very anxious lest the others should take alarm, the bull likewise appeared on the edge of the glade, and stood with outstretched head, scratching his throat against a young tree, which shook violently. I aimed low, behind his shoulder, and pulled trigger. At the crack of the rifle all the bison, without the momentary halt of terror-struck surprise so common among game, turned and raced off at headlong speed. The fringe of young pines beyond and below the glade cracked and swayed as if a whirlwind were passing, and in another moment they reached the top of a very steep incline, thickly strewn with boulders and dead timber. Down this they plunged with reckless speed. Their surefootedness was a marvel in such seemingly unwieldy beasts. A column of dust obscured their passage, and under its cover they disappeared in the forest. The trail of the bull was marked by splashes of frothy blood, and we followed it at a trot. Fifty yards beyond the border of the forest we found the stark black body stretched motionless. He was a splendid old bull, still in his full vigor, with large, sharp horns, and heavy mane and glossy coat. I felt the most exulting pride as I handled and examined him, for I had procured a trophy such as can fall henceforth to few hunters indeed.

It was too late to dress the beast that evening so, after taking out the tongue and cutting off enough meat for supper and breakfast, we scrambled down to near the torrent, and after some search found a good spot for camping. Hot and dusty from the day's hard tramp, I undressed and took a plunge in the stream, the icy water making me gasp. Then, after having built a slight lean-to of brush, and dragged together enough dead timber to burn all night, we cut long alder twigs, sat down before some embers raked apart, and grilled and ate our buffalo meat with the utmost relish. Night had fallen; a cold wind blew up the valley; the torrent roared as it leaped past us and drowned our words as we strove to talk over our adventures and success; while the flame of the fire flickered and danced, lighting up with continual vivid flashes the gloom of the forest round about.

Theodore and his guide continued the hunt to the headwaters of the Salmon and Snake Rivers in Idaho, and along the Montana boundary line from the Big Hole Basin and the head of the Wisdom River to the neighborhood of the Red Rock Pass and to the north and west of Henry's Lake. His guide became surlier, complaining that he did not like the idea of "trundling a tenderfoot." He liked to lie abed late, and so Theodore usually had to get breakfast and because of the old man's rheumatism, do most of the work around the camp. Finally, one day he declined to go out with him at all, saying that he had a pain. When Theodore got back to camp, he speedily found what the "pain" was. They had been traveling very light, having practically nothing but a sleeping bag, and necessary clothing. Theodore had also taken along a flask of whiskey for emergencies.

The old fellow was sitting on a tree trunk, very erect, with his rifle across his knees, and in response to my nod of greeting he merely leered at me. I leaned my rifle against a tree, walked over to where my bed was lying, and, happening to rummage in it for something, I found the whiskey flask was empty. I turned to him at once and accused him of

having drunk it, to which he merely responded by asking
what I was going to do about it. There did not seem much
to do, so I said that we would part company—we were only
four or five days from a settlement, and I would go in alone,
taking one of the horses. He responded by cocking his rifle
and saying that I could go alone and be damned to me, but
I could not take a horse. I answered "all right," that if I
could not I could not, and began to move around to get
some flour and salt pork. He was misled by my quietness
and by the fact that I had not in any way resented either his
actions or his language during the days we had been together, and did not watch me as closely as he ought to have
done. He was sitting with the cocked rifle across his knees,
the muzzle to the left. My rifle was leaning against a tree
near the cooking things to his right. Managing to get near
it, I whipped it up and threw the bead on him, calling,
"Hands up!" He of course put up his hands, and then said,
"Oh, come, I was only joking"; to which I answered, "Well,
I am not. Now straighten your legs and let your rifle go to
the ground." He remonstrated, saying the rifle would go
off, and I told him to let it go off. However, he straightened
his legs in such fashion that it came to the ground without
a jar. I then made him move back, and picked up the rifle.
By this time he was quite sober, and really did not seem
angry, looking at me quizzically. He told me that if I would
give him back his rifle, he would call it quits and we could
go on together. I did not think it best to trust him, so I
told him that our hunt was pretty well through, anyway,
and that I would go home. There was a blasted pine on the
trail, in plain view of the camp, about a mile off, and I told

him that I would leave his rifle at that blasted pine if I could see him in camp, but that he must not come after me, for if he did I should assume that it was with hostile intent and would shoot. He said he had no intention of coming after me and, as he was very much crippled with rheumatism, I did not believe he would do so.

Accordingly, I took the little mare, with nothing but some flour, bacon, and tea, and my bed roll, and started off. At the blasted pine I looked round, and as I could see him in camp, I left his rifle there. I then traveled till dark, and that night, for the only time in my experience, I used in camping a trick of the old-time trappers in the Indian days. I did not believe I would be followed, but still it was not possible to be sure, so, after getting supper, while my pony fed round, I left the fire burning, repacked the mare, and pushed ahead until it literally became so dark that I could not see. Then I picketed the mare, slept where I was without a fire until the first streak of dawn, and then pushed on for a couple of hours before halting to take breakfast and to let the little mare have a good feed. No plainsman needs to be told that a man should not lie near a fire if there was danger of an enemy creeping up on him, and that above all a man should not put himself in a position where he could be ambushed at dawn. On this second day I lost the trail, and towards nightfall gave up the effort to find it, camped where I was, and went out to shoot a grouse for supper.

On the third day, after getting lost a couple of times, Theodore camped in a little open spot by the side of a small, noisy brook, with crystal water. "The place was carpeted with soft, wet, green moss, dotted red with the kinnikinnic berries, and at its edge, under the trees where the ground was dry," he threw down the buffalo bed on the mat of sweet-smelling pine needles. Making camp took but a moment. He opened the pack, tossed the bedding on a smooth spot, knee-haltered the little mare, dragged up a few dry logs, and then strolled off, rifle on shoulder, through the frosty gloaming, to see if he could pick up a grouse for supper. For half a mile he walked quickly and silently over the pine-needles, across a succession of slight ridges separated by narrow, shallow valleys. Though the sun was behind the mountains there was yet plenty of light by which to shoot, but it was fading rapidly.

At last, as I was thinking of turning toward camp, I stole up to the crest of one of the ridges, and looked over into the valley some sixty yards off. Immediately I caught the loom of some large, dark object and, another glance showed me a big grizzly walking slowly off with his head down. He was quartering to me, and I fired into his flank, the bullet, as I afterward found, ranging forward and piercing one lung. At the shot he uttered a loud, moaning grunt, and plunged forward at a heavy gallop, while I raced obliquely down the hill to cut him off. After going a few hundred feet he reached a laurel thicket, some thirty yards broad, and two or three times as long, which he did not leave. I ran up to the edge and there halted, not liking to venture into the mass of twisted, close-growing stems and glossy foliage. More-over, as I halted, I heard him utter a peculiar, savage kind of whine from the heart of the brush. Accordingly, I began to skirt the edge, standing on tiptoe and gazing earnestly to see if I could not catch a glimpse of his hide. When I was at the narrowest part of the thicket, he suddenly left it directly opposite, and then wheeled and stood broadside to me on the hillside, a little above. He turned his head stiffly toward me, scarlet strings of froth hung from his lips, his eyes burned like embers in the gloom.

I held true, aiming behind the shoulder, and my bullet shattered the point or lower end of his heart, taking out a big nick. Instantly the great bear turned with a harsh roar of fury and challenge, blowing the bloody foam from his mouth, so that I saw the gleam of his white fangs, and then he charged straight at me, crashing and bounding through the laurel bushes, so that it was hard to aim. I waited till he came to a fallen tree, raking him as he topped it, with a ball which entered his chest and went through the cavity of his body, but he neither swerved nor flinched, and at the moment I did not know that I had struck him. He came steadily on, and in another second was almost upon me. I fired for his forehead, but my bullet went low, entering his open mouth, smashing his lower jaw and going into the neck. I leaped to one side almost as I pulled the trigger and, through the hanging smoke, the first thing I saw was his paw as he made a vicious side blow at me. The rush of his charge carried him past. As he struck he lurched forward, leaving a pool of bright blood where his muzzle hit the ground. He recovered himself and made two or three jumps onward, while I hurriedly jammed a couple of cartridges into the magazine, my rifle holding only four, all of which I had fired. Then he tried to pull up, but as he did so his muscles seemed suddenly to give way, his head drooped, and he rolled over and over like a shot rabbit. Each of my first three bullets had inflicted a mortal wound.

It was already twilight, and I merely opened the carcass, and then trotted back to camp. Next morning I returned and with much labor took off the skin. The fur was very fine, the animal being in excellent trim, and unusually bright-colored.

I had a most exasperating time trying to bring in the skin. The little mare cared nothing for bears or anything else, so there was no difficulty in packing her. But the man without experience can hardly realize the work it was to get that bearskin off the carcass and then to pack it, wet, slippery, and heavy, so that it would ride evenly on the pony.

The next few days, while he was working his way back to civilization, were some of the worst that Theodore had spent up to then. With infinite labor he would get the skin on the pony and run the ropes over it until it seemed fastened properly. Then he would start, and after he had gone a hundred yards or so, the hide would begin to bulge somewhere. He would shift it, and then it would bulge somewhere else. "The feat of killing the bear sank into nothing," he wrote, "compared with the feat of making the bearskin ride properly as a pack on the following three days." But when he finally did get back to civilization he had, as a trophy, the finest bearskin that he had secured, as well as the memory of a most exciting hunt.

Chapter 15

A Hunt at Two-Ocean Pass: An Elk Fight

In September, 1891, *Theodore made one of his last big hunts in the West. He went to northwestern Wyoming among the Shoshone Mountains where they join the Hoodoo and Absaroka ranges.*

This was one of the pleasantest hunts I ever made. As always in the mountains, save where the country was so rough and so deeply wooded that one had to go afoot, we had a pack-train. We took a more complete outfit than we had ever before taken on such a hunt, and so traveled in much comfort. We had with us two hunters, Tazewell Woody and Elwood Hofer, a packer who acted as cook, and a boy to herd the horses. There were twenty of these—six saddle animals and fourteen for the packs. Like most pack-animals, they were either half-broken, or else broken down—tough, unkempt, jaded-looking beasts of every color

170

—sorrel, buckskin, pinto, white, bay, roan. After the day's work was over, they were turned loose to shift for themselves and, about once a week, they strayed and all hands had to spend the better part of the day hunting for them.

There were two sleeping tents, another for the provisions —in which we ate during bad weather—and a canvas teepee, which was put up with lodge-poles, Indian fashion. A teepee is more difficult to put up than an ordinary tent but is very convenient when there is rain or snow. A small fire kindled in the middle kept it warm, the smoke escaping through the open top—that is when it escaped at all.

We had a very good camp-kit, including plenty of cooking and eating utensils. We even had canned goods and sweetmeats to give relish to our meals of meat and bread. Our fur coats and warm clothing was chiefly needed at night, including plenty of bedding among which was a couple of caribou-hide sleeping bags procured from the survivors of a party of Arctic explorers.

As our way was so rough, we had to halt at least once every hour to fix the packs. First it would be "that white-eyed cayuse; one side of its pack's down!" Then we would be notified that the saddle-blanket of the "lop-eared Indian buckskin" had slipped back. Then a shout, "Look out for the pinto!" which would be followed by that pleasing beast's appearance, bucking and squealing, smashing dead timber, and scattering its load to the four winds.

For two days our journey was uneventful, save that we came on the camp of a squaw man—one Beaver Dick, an old mountain hunter, living in a skin teepee, where dwelt his comely Indian wife and half-breed children.

The morning of the third day was gray and lowering. Gusts of rain blew in my face. It still lacked an hour of noon, as we were plodding up a valley beside a rapid brook running through narrow willow flats, the dark forest crowding down on either hand from the low foothills of the mountains. Suddenly the call of a bull elk came echoing down through the wet woodland on our right, beyond the brook, seemingly less than half a mile off, to be answered by a faint, far-off call from a rival on the mountain beyond. Instantly halting the train, Woody and I slipped off our horses, crossed the brook, and started to still hunt the first bull.

The forest was composed of the Western tamarack— large, tall trees stood well apart—and there was much down timber, but the ground was covered with deep wet moss, over which we trod noiselessly. The elk was traveling slowly upwind, stopping continually to paw the ground and thrash the bushes with his antlers. He was very noisy, challenging every minute or two, being doubtless much excited by the neighborhood of his rival on the mountain. We followed, Woody leading, guided by the incessant calling.

It was very exciting as we crept toward the great bull, and the challenge sounded nearer and nearer. While we were still at some distance the pealing notes were like those of a bugle, delivered in two bars, first rising, then abruptly falling. As we drew nearer they took on a harsh squealing sound.

Each call made our veins thrill; it sounded like the cry of some huge beast of prey. At last we heard the roar of the challenge not eighty yards off. Stealing forward three or four yards, I saw the tips of the horns through a mass of dead timber and young growth, and I slipped to one side to get a clean shot.

Seeing us but not making out what we were, and full of fierce and insolent excitement, the wapiti bull stepped boldly toward us with a stately swinging gait. Then he stood motionless, facing us, barely fifty yards away, his handsome twelve-tined antlers tossed aloft, as he held his head with the lordly grace of his kind. I fired into his chest, and as he turned I raced forward and shot him in the flank, but the second bullet was not needed, for the first wound was mortal and he fell before going fifty yards.

The huge, shapely body of the dead elk was set on legs that were as strong as steel rods, and yet slender, clean, and smooth. They were a beautiful dark brown color, contrasting well with the yellowish of the body. The neck and throat were garnished with a mane of long hair and the symmetry of the great horns set off the fine, delicate lines of the noble head.

We cut off the head, and bore it down to the train. The horses crowded together, snorting, with their ears pricked forward, as they smelt the blood. We also took the loins with us, as we were out of meat, though bull elk in the rutting season is not very good.

The rain had changed to a steady downpour when we again got under way. Two or three miles farther we pitched camp, in a clump of pines on a hillock in the bottom of a valley, starting hot fires of pitchy stumps before the tents, to dry our wet things. Next day opened with fog and cold rain. The drenched pack-animals, when driven into camp, stood mopingly, with drooping heads and arched backs,

groaning and grunting as the loads were placed on their
backs and the cinches tightened, the packers bracing one
foot against the pack to get a purchase as they hauled in on
the lash rope. By ten we broke camp. My hunting-shoes,
though comfortable, were old and thin, and let the water
through like a sieve. On the top of the first plateau, where
black-spruce groves were strewn across the grassy surface, we
saw a band of elk, cows and calves, trotting off through the
rain. Then we plunged down into a deep valley, and, crossing it, a hard climb took us to the top of a great bare table-
land, bleak and wind swept. A cutting wind blew the icy
rain in our faces. For two or three hours we traveled toward
the farther edge of the table-land.

As we neared the edge the storm lulled, and pale, watery
sunshine gleamed through the rifts in the low scudding
clouds. At last our horses stood on the brink of a bold cliff.
Deep down beneath our feet lay the wild and lonely valley
of Two-Ocean Pass, walled in on either hand by rugged
mountain chains, their flanks scarred and gashed by precipice and chasm. Beyond, in a wilderness of jagged and
barren peaks, stretched the Shoshones. At the middle point
of the pass, two streams welled down from either side. At
first each flowed in but one bed, but soon divided into two,
each of the twin branches then joined the like branch of the
brook opposite, and swept one to the east and one to the
west, on their long journey to the two great oceans. They
ran as rapid brooks, through wet meadows and willow flats,
the eastern to the Yellowstone, the western to the Snake.

It was getting late, and after some search we failed to find
any trail leading down, so we plunged over the brink as a

venture. It was very rough scrambling, dropping from bench to bench, and in places it was not only difficult but dangerous for the loaded pack-animals. Here and there we were helped by well-beaten elk trails, which we could follow for several hundred yards at a time. On one narrow pine-clad ledge, we met a spike-bull face to face, and in scrambling down a very steep, bare, rock-strewn shoulder, the loose stones started by the horses' hoofs, bounding in great leaps to the forest below, dislodged two cows.

As evening fell, we reached the bottom, and pitched camp in a beautiful point of open pine forest, thrust out into the meadow. There was good shelter, and plenty of wood, water, and grass. We built a huge fire and put up our tents, scattering them in likely places among the pines, which grew far apart and without undergrowth. We dried our steaming clothes, and ate a hearty supper of elk meat, then we turned into our beds, warm and dry, and slept soundly under the canvas, while all night long the storm roared without. Next morning it still stormed fitfully. The high peaks and ridges round about were all capped with snow.

Woody and I started on foot for an all-day tramp. For three hours we walked across the forest-clad spurs of the foothills. We roused a small band of elk in thick timber, but they rushed off before we saw them, with much smashing of dead branches. Then we climbed to the summit of the range. The wind was light and baffling, blowing from all points, veering every few minutes. Occasional rain squalls soaked our feet and legs and we became chilled through whenever we sat down to listen. We caught a glimpse of a big bull feeding uphill, and followed him. Finally we got within a hundred twenty-five yards, but in very thick timber, and all I could see plainly was the hip and the after-part of the flank. I waited for a chance at the shoulder, but the bull got my wind and was off before I could pull trigger. It was just one of those occasions when there were two courses to pursue, neither very good, and when one was apt to regret whichever decision was made.

At noon we came to the edge of a deep and wide gorge, and sat down shivering to await what might turn up, our fingers numb, and our wet feet icy. Suddenly the love-challenge of an elk came pealing across the gorge, through the fine, cold rain, from the heart of the forest opposite. An hour's stiff climb, down and up, brought us nearly to him. The wind forced me to advance from below through a series of open glades. He was lying on a point of the cliff shoulder, surrounded by his cows, and he saw us and made off. An hour afterward, as we were trudging up a steep hillside dotted with groves of fir and spruce, a young bull roused from his day-bed by our approach, galloped across us some sixty yards off. We were in need of better venison than could be furnished by an old rutting bull, so I instantly took a shot at the fat and tender young ten-pointer. Aiming well ahead I pulled trigger just as he came to a small gully. He fell into it in a heap with a resounding crash. This was the birthday of my eldest small son, so I took him home the horns, "for his very own."

Next morning dawned clear and cold, the sky a glorious blue. Woody and I started to hunt over the great tableland, and led our stout horses up the mountainside, by elk trails so bad that they had to climb like goats. Some grouse rose from beside our path; Clark's crows flew past us, with a hollow, flapping sound, or lit in the pine-tops, calling and flirting their tails; snow-shoe rabbits scuttled away, the big-furry feet which gave them their name already turning white. At last we came out on the great plateau, seamed with deep, narrow ravines. Almost immediately we heard the bugle of a bull elk, and saw a big band of cows and calves on the other side of a valley. There were three bulls with them, one very large, and we tried to creep up on them but the wind was baffling and spoiled our stalk. So we returned to our horses, mounted them, and rode a mile farther, toward a large open wood on a hillside. When within two hundred yards we heard directly ahead the bugle of a bull, and pulled up short. In a moment I saw him walking through an open glade. The slight breeze brought us down his scent. Elk have a strong characteristic smell. It is usually sweet, like that of a herd of Alderney cows, but in old bulls, while rutting, it is rank, pungent, and lasting. We stood motionless till the bull was out of sight, then stole to the wood, tied our horses, and trotted after him. He was traveling fast, occasionally calling. Evidently he had been driven out of some herd by the master-bull.

He went faster than we did, and while we were vainly trying to overtake him we heard another very loud and sonorous challenge to our left. It came from a ridge crest at the edge of the woods, among some scattered clumps of pinon. We at once walked up-wind toward the ridge. In a minute or two, to our chagrin, we stumbled on an out-lying spike-bull, evidently kept on the outskirts of the herd by the master-bull. I thought he would alarm all the rest but, as we stood motionless, he could not see clearly what we were. He stood, ran, stood again, gazed at us, and trotted slowly off. We hurried forward with too little care, for we suddenly came in view of two cows. As they raised their heads to look, Woody squatted down where he was, to keep their attention fixed, while I cautiously tried to slip off to one side unobserved. Favored by the neutral tint of my buckskin hunting shirt, with which my shoes, leggings, and soft hat matched, I succeeded. As soon as I was out of sight I ran hard and came up to a hillock crested with pinons, behind which I judged I should find the herd. As I approached the crest, their strong, sweet smell smote my nostrils. In another moment I saw the tips of a pair of mighty antlers, and I peered over the crest with my rifle at the ready. Thirty yards off, behind a clump of pinons, stood a huge bull, his head thrown back as he rubbed his shoulders with his horns. There were several cows around him, and one saw me immediately, and took alarm. I fired into the bull's shoulder, inflicting a mortal wound, although he went off. I raced after him at top speed, firing twice into his flank. He stopped very sick, and I broke his neck with a fourth bullet.

The elk was a giant. His body was the size of a steer's and his antlers, though not unusually long, were very massive and heavy. He lay in a glade, on the edge of a great cliff. Standing on its brink we overlooked a most beautiful country, the home of all homes for the elk—a wilderness of mountains, the immense evergreen forest broken by park and glade, by meadow and pasture, by bare hillside and barren table-land. Some five miles off lay the sheet of water known to the old hunters as Spotted Lake. Two or three shallow, sedgy places, and spots of geyser formation, made pale green blotches on its wind-rippled surface. Far to the southwest, in daring beauty and majesty, the grand domes and lofty spire of the Tetons shot into the blue sky. Too sheer for the snow to rest on their sides, it yet filled the rents in their rough flanks, and lay deep between the towering pinnacles of the dark rock.

After a week at Two-Ocean Pass, the hunting party moved across to the summit of Wolverine Pass, near Pinon Peak, beside a little mountain lake. A few days later, after several hunts, they shifted to Wolverine Creek. It was here that Theodore killed two of his finest elk:

The next morning Woody and I went up the steep, forest-clad mountainside, and before we had walked an hour heard two elk whistling ahead of us. As we crept stealthily forward, the calling grew louder and louder, until we could hear the grunting sounds with which the challenge of the nearest ended. He was in a large wallow, which was also a lick. When we were still sixty yards off, he heard us, and rushed out, but wheeled and stood a moment to gaze, puzzled by my buckskin suit. I fired into his throat, breaking his neck, and down he went in a heap. Rushing in and turning, I called to Woody, "He's a twelve-pointer, but the horns are small!" As I spoke I heard the roar of the challenge of the other bull not two hundred yards ahead, as if in a defiant answer to my shot.

Running quietly forward, I speedily caught a glimpse of his body. He was behind some fir trees about seventy yards off, and I could not see which way he was standing, and so fired into the patch of flank which was visible, aiming high, to break the back. My aim was true, and the huge beast crashed downhill through the evergreens. Racing forward, I broke his neck. His antlers were the finest I ever got.

A year later, in 1892, on a trip with his old hunting partner, John Willis, to the Bitter Root Range, Theodore and his companion saw a thrilling sight. At the first faint streak of dawn they set out to a place where much elk sign had been seen the afternoon before. As they trod noiselessly over the dense moss and pine needles, under scattering trees, they heard a sharp clang and clatter up the valley ahead of them. They knew this meant game of some sort and, stealing lightly and cautiously forward, they soon saw before them the cause of the noise.

In a little glade, a hundred and twenty-five yards from us, two bull elk were engaged in deadly combat, while two others were looking on. It was a splendid sight. The great beasts faced each other with lowered horns, the manes that covered their thick necks and the hair on their shoulders bristling and erect. Then they charged furiously, the crash of the meeting antlers resounding through the valley. The shock threw them both on their haunches, then with locked horns and glaring eyes they strove against each other, getting their hind legs well under them, straining every muscle in their huge bodies, and squealing savagely. They were evenly matched in weight, strength and courage and, push as they might, neither got the upper hand, first one yielding a few inches, then the other, while they swayed to and fro in their struggles, smashing the bushes and ploughing up the soil.

Finally they separated and stood some little distance apart, under the great pines, their sides heaving, and columns of steam rising from their nostrils through the frosty air of the brightening morning. Again they rushed together with a crash, and each strove mightily to overthrow the other, or get past his guard, but the branching antlers caught every vicious lunge and thrust. This set-to was stopped rather curiously. One of the onlooking elk was a yearling; the other, though scarcely as heavy-bodied as either of the fighters, had a finer head. He was evidently much excited by the battle, and he now began to walk toward the two combatants, nodding his head and uttering a queer, whistling noise. They dared not leave their flanks uncovered to his assault and, as he approached, they promptly separated, and walked off side by side a few yards apart. In a moment, however, one spun round and jumped at his old adversary, seeking to stab him in his unprotected flank. The latter was just as quick, and as before caught the rush on his horns. Although they closed as furiously as ever, the utmost either could do was to inflict one or two punches on the neck and shoulders of his foe, where the thick hide served as a shield. Again the peacemaker approached, nodding his head, whistling, and threatening; and again they separated.

As this was repeated once or twice, I began to be afraid

lest the breeze, which was light and puffy, should shift and give them my wind. So, resting my rifle on my knee I fired twice, putting one bullet behind the shoulder of the peace-maker, and the other behind the shoulder of one of the combatants. Both were deadly shots, but, as so often with wapiti, neither of the wounded animals at the moment showed any signs of being hit. The yearling ran off un-scathed. The other three crowded together and trotted behind some spruce on the left, while we ran forward for another shot. In a moment one fell, whereupon the re-maining two turned and came back across the glade, trotting to the right. As we opened fire they broke into a lumbering gallop, but were both downed before they got out of sight in the timber.

As soon as the three bulls were down we busied ourselves taking off their heads and hides, and cutting off the best portions of the meat—from the saddles and hams—to take back to camp, where we smoked it. But first we had break-fast. We kindled a fire beside a little spring of clear water and raked out the coals. Then we cut two willow twigs as spits, ran on each a number of small pieces of elk loin, and roasted them over the fire. We had salt; we were very hungry; and I never ate anything that tasted better.

Chapter 16

Farewell to the Bad Lands

PERHAPS IT was inevitable from the beginning that the East would win out over the West. Few men have been more strongly drawn to a region than Theodore was to the fantastic Bad Lands and the awe-inspiring Rockies. Yet there was the far deeper call of his family, which could never have fitted into the environment of Elkhorn Ranch, and of his future as a national figure. For a while at least, the outdoors would have to take a minor place. He ended his days in the Bad Lands appropriately:

In 1894, on the last day I spent at the ranch, and with the last bullet I fired from my rifle, I killed a fine whitetail buck. I left the ranchhouse early in the afternoon on my favorite pony, Muley, my foreman, Sylvane Ferris, riding with me. We forded the shallow river and rode up a long winding coulee, with belts of timber running down its bottom. After going a couple of miles, by sheer good luck we stumbled on three whitetail—a buck, a doe, and a fawn. When we saw them they were trying to sneak off, and immediately my foreman galloped toward one end of the belt of timber in which they were, and started to ride down through it, while I ran Muley to the other end to intercept them. They were, of course, quite likely to break off to one side but this happened to be one of the occasions when everything went right. When I reached the spot from which I covered the exits from the timber, I leaped off, and immediately afterward heard a shout from my foreman that told me the deer were on foot. Muley was a pet horse, and enjoyed immensely the gallop after game, but his nerves invariably failed him at the shot. On this occasion he stood snorting beside me, and finally, as the deer came in sight, away he tore—only to go about two hundred yards, however, and stand and watch us, snorting, with his ears pricked forward until, when I needed him, I went for him. At this moment, however, I paid no heed to Muley, for a cracking in the brush told me the game was close, and I caught the shadowy outlines of the doe and fawn as they scudded through the timber. By good luck, the buck, evidently flurried, came right on the edge of woods next to me, and as he passed, running like a quarter-horse, I held well ahead of him and pulled trigger. The bullet broke his neck and down he went—a fine fellow with a handsome ten-point head, and fat as a prize sheep—for it was just before the rut. Then we rode home, and I sat in a rocking-chair on the ranchhouse veranda, looking across the wide, sandy river bed at the strangely shaped buttes and the groves of shim-

mering cottonwoods until the sun went down and the frosty
air bade me go in.

Theodore Roosevelt's ranching experiences in the Bad
Lands had been a heavy financial loss—probably eighty
thousand dollars. But money to him had never had the real-
ity of a rifle, a horse, an elk, or even a social or an economic
problem. The money spent, wherever it had gone, had given
to him glorious fun and adventure. It had brought him a
companionship that was genuine and vital, and friends
that remained loyal to his death. It had taught him lessons
in practical democracy that he could have learned nowhere
else. It had given him a firsthand knowledge of men, tutored
his judgment, and tempered him so that he could thereafter
answer most challenges and fit himself into most situations.
It had given him "the outreaching spirit, the spirit that re-
fuses to take things for granted or ready made, that insists
on the constructing of life direct from the raw materials, on
the facing of life without interpositions, on the manifesta-
tion of life without other aid than knowledge, faculties and
native genius."

Theodore's ranching and hunting experiences in many
ways constituted the most important post-graduate courses a
statesman ever took.

"The West owes a lot to you," Charles F. Lummis once
said to him. "You've helped to translate it to the tender-
foots."

"What?" Theodore boomed. "I owe everything to the
West! It made me! I found myself there!"

The West that Lummis talked about had no geography

to it. "Anywhere is West," he said, "if it is far enough from the East to be out from under."

Theodore certainly learned about men from his ranching experience. "I regard my experience during those years, when I lived and worked with my own fellow ranchmen on what was the frontier," he said in a speech at Sioux Falls in 1910, "as the most important educational asset of all my life. It is a mighty good thing to know men, not from looking at them, but from having been one of them. When you have worked with them, when you have lived with them, you do not have to wonder how they feel, because you feel it yourself. I know how the man that works with his hands and the man on the ranch are thinking, because I have been there and I am thinking that way myself. It is not that I divine the way they are thinking, but that I think the same way."

It was a raw and vivid experience. "We knew toil and hardship and hunger and thirst, and we saw men die violent deaths as they worked among the horses and cattle, or fought in evil feuds with one another. But we felt the beat of hardy life in our veins, and ours was the glory of work and the joy of living."

Then there was hunting. "The hunter's instinct," wrote Stewart Edward White, "was in [Theodore] strongly developed; and as was his habit he faced fairly and squarely all the questions involved in that instinct. It was noble because, rightly followed, it was a vehicle for the development of the manly qualities. . . . He must do an immense amount of work of all sorts. He must develop an iron hardihood; an indifference to discomforts great and small; a single-minded determination in face of apparent impossibility; great physical endurance, accurate nerve and muscular coordination; nice judgment; a vast lore of woodcraft; wide knowledge of the varying habits under all conditions of the game he pursues; close observation and the power of synthetic correlation of what he sees; an immense and philosophic patience; a certain ability to enter into and understand the mental processes of his quarry; indifference to profound fatigue; an unquenchable optimism; and an indomitable resistance to circumstance."

In his preface to Wilderness Hunter, 1893, the last of his three books on ranching and hunting in the West, Theodore wrote, "No one, but he who has partaken thereof, can understand the keen delight of hunting in lonely lands. For him is the joy of the horse well ridden and the rifle well held; for him the long days of toil and hardship, resolutely endured, and crowned at the end with triumph. In after-years there shall come forever to his mind the memory of endless prairies shimmering in the bright sun; of vast snow-clad wastes lying desolate under gray skies; of the melancholy marshes; of the rush of mighty rivers; of the breath of the evergreen forest in summer; of the crooning of ice-armored pines at the couch of the winds of winter; of cataracts roaring between hoary mountain masses; of all the innumerable sights and sounds of the wilderness; of its immensity and mystery; and of the silences that brood in its still depths."

No wonder Theodore became interested in the conservation of wildlife in America; no wonder he stated emphatically, "I should much regret to see grow up in this country a system of large private game preserves kept for the enjoyment of the very rich. One of the chief attractions of the life of the wilderness is its rugged and stalwart democracy. There every man stands for what he actually is and can show himself to be."

The end of the Bad Lands chapter, in a way, marked the end of Theodore's youth. But nothing—fatigue, disappointment, grief, illness—could take away the youthful spirit that the West had crystallized in him.

He was now ready for the Glory Road.

PART THREE

The Glory Road

Chapter 1

A Man to Trust and a Trust-Buster

UNTIL THEODORE ROOSEVELT was appointed to the Civil Service Commission its work had been of minor importance. He brought it national attention. Its annual report, before this little more than statistical nonsense, now became controversial pamphlets plugging for efficiency in government. When Congress would not give him the necessary money he took his case to the people through the newspapers. During the time he was on the Commission more than twenty thousand positions were taken out of the realm of political appointment and placed on the merit basis.

His next step toward popular recognition came in 1895 when he resigned from the Civil Service Commission to become President of the Board of Police Commissioners for the City of New York. After his reforms in the Police Department attracted national attention he was, in 1897,

appointed Assistant Secretary of the Navy by President Mc-
Kinley. Under his aggressive leadership the navy was made
ready for what he considered inevitable—war with Spain.
When this war broke out he resigned his position and raised
a volunteer regiment known as the "Rough Riders" because so many members were cowboys and ranchmen from
the West. He warned the men who joined that there would
be action, danger and death.

There was. The Rough Riders gained eternal fame on
their charge up San Juan Hill in which the Spaniards were
driven from their trenches and the way opened for the
eventual surrender of Santiago. Theodore's fame skyrocketed.
On his return to this country he joined in the "round
robin" of protest against the way in which the War Department had handled the conduct of the war.

Soon after being mustered out of the service, in September 1898, Theodore was nominated by the Republican
Party as its candidate for the governorship of New York,
and was elected after making a spirited campaign. In 1900
he was practically forced into being a candidate for Vice-
President by the Republican boss of New York, Senator
Thomas C. Platt, who wanted him side-tracked.

Although Theodore did not relish the idea of the Vice-
Presidency, he campaigned as vigorously as he would have
done for the top spot. Early in September, 1901, he visited
Dakota, although he did not go to his old ranch. Joe Ferris
was the first to greet him.*

"Joe, old boy," cried Roosevelt exuberantly, "will you
ever forget the first time we met?"

* Reported by Hermann Hagedorn in his *Roosevelt in the Bad Lands*
as being taken verbatim from contemporary newspapers.

"No," Joe admitted.

"You nearly murdered me. It seemed as if all the ill-luck in the world pursued us."

Joe grinned and nodded.

"Do you remember too, Joe," exclaimed Roosevelt, "how I swam the swollen stream and you stood on the bank and kept your eyes on me?"

"I wouldn't have taken that swim for all of Dakota," said Joe.

Joe got on the train with Theodore and rode to Medora. They sat by the window looking out and talking as each butte, each crag reminded them of something.

"The romance of my life began here," Theodore said, as the train neared Medora.

At Medora he was greeted by many of his old friends among them an old cowboy, George Myers, who had worked for him.

"George used to cook for me," Theodore said.

"Do you remember the time I made green biscuits for you?" asked George with a grin.

"I do, George, I do. And I remember the time you fried the beans with rosin instead of lard. The best proof in the world, George, that I have a good constitution is that I ate your cooking and survived."

"Well, now, Governor," exclaimed George, "I was thinking it would be a good idea to get that man Bryan up here and see what that kind of biscuit would do for him."

Theodore glanced around. "It does not seem right," he exclaimed, "that I should come here and not stay."

Theodore rode on a bronco eastward toward the trail to the bluff that rose a thousand feet behind Medora. "Over

there is Square Butte," he cried eagerly, "and over there is
Sentinel Butte. There is the church erected for the use of the
wife of the Marquis de Mores. His old house is beyond.
You can see it."

This house and the location where Theodore ranched
are now National Parks.

"Looking back to my old days here," Theodore said, "I
can paraphrase Kipling and say, 'Whatever may happen, I
can thank God I have lived and toiled with men.'"

Chapter 2

A Cougar Hunt in Colorado

In January, 1901 Vice-President elect Roosevelt went on a cougar hunt in Colorado. His companions were Philip B. Stewart and Doctor Gerald Webb of Colorado Springs. When they reached Meeker, Colorado, on January 11, after a forty-mile drive from the railroad through bitter weather, it was eighteen below zero. They were met there by John H. Goff, a hunter, and they left the next morning on horseback for his ranch. Altogether Roosevelt stayed out for five weeks in which he hunted north of the White River, most of the time in the neighborhood of Coyote Basin and Colorow Mountain. His clothing consisted of heavy flannels, jackets lined with sheepskin, caps which covered the ears entirely, and in addition to ordinary socks, German woolen socks and overshoes. For galloping through the underbrush he found that overalls were better than ordinary trousers. He continued to wear his old

195

buckskin jacket of Bad Lands days. The game that they were after was cougars.

Success in cougar hunting depends absolutely upon the hounds. If not properly trained they are worse than useless. Goff, in addition to being one of the best hunters in the country, had a pack of hounds trained to perfection for this special sort of hunting. His pack ran only bear, cougar and bobcat.

As the dogs did all the work, we naturally became extremely interested in them, and rapidly grew to know the voice, peculiarities, and special abilities of each. There were eight hounds and four fighting dogs. The hounds were of the ordinary Eastern type, used from the Adirondacks to the Mississippi and the Gulf in the chase of deer and fox. Six of them were black-and-tan and two were mottled. They differed widely in size and voice. The biggest, and, on the whole, the most useful, was Jim, a very fast, powerful, and true dog with a great voice. Among the cliffs and precipices the pack usually ran out of sight and hearing if the chase lasted any length of time. Their business was to bring the quarry to bay, or put it up a tree and then to stay with it and make a noise until the hunters came up. On several occasions Goff had known them to keep a cougar up a tree overnight and to be still barking around the tree when the hunters at last found them the following morning.

Jim was a great bully with the other dogs, robbing them of their food, and yielding only to Turk.

On the whole the most useful dog next to Jim was old Boxer. Age had made Boxer slow, and in addition to this, the first cougar we tackled bit him through one hind leg, so that for the remainder of the trip he went on three legs, but this seemed not to interfere with his appetite, his endurance, or his desire for the chase. Of all the dogs, he was the best to puzzle out a cold trail on a bare hillside or in any difficult place.

Next in size to Jim was Tree'em. He was not a noisy dog, and when "barking treed" he had a meditative way of giving single barks, separated by intervals of several seconds, all the time gazing stolidly up at the big, sinister cat which he was baying.

Lil and Nell were two very stanch and fast bitches, the only two dogs that could keep up to Jim in a quick burst. They had shrill voices. Their only failing was a tendency to let the other members of the pack cow them, so that they did not get their full share of the food. It was not a pack in which a slow or timid dog had much chance for existence. They would all unite in the chase and the fierce struggle which usually closed it; but the instant the quarry was killed each dog resumed his normal attitude of greedy anger or greedy fear toward the others. Another bitch rejoiced in the not very appropriate name of Pete. She was a most ardent huntress. In the middle of our trip she gave birth to a litter of puppies, but before they were two weeks old she would slip away after us and join with the utmost ardor in the hunting and fighting.

The fighting dogs always trotted at the heels of the horses, which had become entirely accustomed to them and made no objection when they literally rubbed against their heels. The fighters never left us until we came to where we could hear the hounds "barking treed," or with their quarry at bay. Then they tore in a straight line to the sound. They were the ones who were expected to do the seizing and take the punishment, though the minute they actually had hold of the cougar, the hounds all piled on, too, and did their share of the killing. The fighters or seizers fought the head while the hounds generally took hold behind.

All of them, fighters and hounds alike, were exceedingly good-natured with their human friends, though short-tempered to a degree with one another.

The best of the fighters was old Turk, who was by blood half hound and half "Siberian" bloodhound. Turk's head and body were seamed with scars. He had lost his lower fangs, but he was still a most formidable dog. Three dogs like Turk, in their prime and with their teeth intact, could, I believe, kill an ordinary female cougar, and could hold even a big male so as to allow it to be killed with the knife.

Next to Turk were two half-breeds between bull and shepherd, named Tony and Baldy. They were exceedingly game, knowing-looking little dogs, with a certain alert swagger that reminded one of the walk of some light-weight prize-fighters. They too had been badly mauled and had lost a good many of their teeth.

The pack had many interesting peculiarities, but none more so than the fact that four of them climbed trees. Only one of the hounds, little Jimmie, ever tried the feat. Of the fighters, not only Tony and Baldy, but big Turk, climbed every tree that gave them any chance. A photograph of Turk and a bobcat in a pinon showed them at an altitude of about thirty feet above the ground. They could not fight well while in a tree, and were often scratched or knocked to the

ground by a cougar. When the quarry was shot out of its
perch and seized by the expectant throng below, the dogs
in the tree, yelping with eager excitement, dived headlong
down through the branches, regardless of consequences.

We started out on our hunt on January 14. We made
our way slowly up the snow-covered, pinon-clad side of the
mountain back of the house, and found a very old cougar
trail which it was useless to try to run. After crisscrossing
over the shoulder of the mountain for two or three hours,
and scrambling in and out of the ravines, we finally struck
another cougar trail, much more recent. The hounds had
been hunting free to one side or the other of the path. They
were now summoned by a blast of the horn, and with a
wave of Goff's hand away they went on the trail. Had it
been fresh they would have run out of hearing at once, for
it was fearfully rough country. But they were able to work
but slowly along the loops and zigzags of the trail, where it
led across bare spaces, and we could keep well in sight and
hearing of them. Finally they came to where it descended
the sheer side of the mountain and crossed the snow-covered
valley beneath. Jim and the three bitches were in the lead,
while Boxer fell behind, as he always did when the pace was
fast.

While we were working our way to the other side of a
divide, the sudden increase in the baying told Goff that they
had struck the fresh trail of the beast, and in two or three
minutes we heard Jim's deep voice "barking treed." The
three fighters, who had been trotting at our heels, recognized
the difference in the sound, and plunged at full speed
toward it down the steep hillside, throwing up the snow

like so many snow-ploughs. In a minute or two the chorus told us that all the dogs were around the tree.

While we were still some distance off we could see the cougar in a low pinon moving about as the dogs tried to get up, and finally knocking one clean out of the top. Not liking the sight of the reinforcements, the cougar jumped out and ran uphill. So quick was she that the dogs failed to seize her, and for the first fifty yards she went a great deal faster than they did. Both in the jump and the run she held her tail straight out behind her.

In a minute the cougar went up another tree, but, as we approached, again jumped down, and, after running a couple of hundred yards, the dogs seized it. The growling, snarling, and yelling rang among the rocks, and leaving our horses, we plunged at full speed through the snow down the rugged ravine in which the fight was going on. It was a small though old female and the dogs would have killed it, but as it was doing some damage to the pack, I ended the struggle by a knife-thrust behind the shoulder.

The next day, after two hours' ride, we came upon an old trail. It led among low hills, covered with pinon and cedar, and broken by washouts and gullies, in whose sharp sides of clay the water had made holes and caves. Suddenly the dogs began to show great excitement, and then one gave furious tongue at the mouth of a hole in some sunken and broken ground not thirty yards to our right. The whole pack rushed toward the challenge, the fighters leaped into the hole, and in another moment the row inside told us that they had found a cougar at home. We jumped off and ran down to see if we could be of assistance. To get into the hole was impossible, for two or three hounds had jumped down to join the fighters, and we could see nothing but their sterns. Then we saw Turk backing out with a dead kitten in his mouth. I had supposed that a cougar would defend her young to the last, but such was not the case in this instance. For some minutes she kept the dogs at bay, but then gradually gave ground, leaving her three kittens. Of course the dogs killed them instantly, much to our regret, as we would have given a good deal to have kept them alive. As soon as she had abandoned them, away she went completely through the low cave, leaped out at the other end, which was thirty yards off, scaled the bank, and galloped into the woods, the pack getting after her at once. She did not run more than a couple of hundred yards, and as we tore up on our horses we saw her standing in the lower branches of a pinon only six or eight feet from the ground. She was not snarling or grinning, and looked at us as quietly as if nothing had happened. As we leaped out of the saddles she jumped down from the tree and ran off through the pack. They were after her at once, however, and a few yards farther on she started up another tree. Either Tony or Baldy grabbed her by the tip of the tail, she lost her footing for a moment, and the whole pack seized her.

She was a powerful female of about average size, and made a tremendous fight. Savage enough she looked, her ears tight back against her head, her yellow eyes flashing, and her great teeth showing as she grinned. For a moment the dogs had her down, but biting and striking, she freed her head and fore quarters from the fighters, and faced us as we ran up, the hounds still having her from behind.

This was another chance for the knife, and I cheered on the fighters. Again they seized her by the head, but though absolutely staunch dogs, their teeth had begun to suffer, and they were no longer always able to make their holds good. Just as I was about to strike her she knocked Turk loose with a blow, bit Baldy, and then, her head being free, turned on me. Fortunately, Tony caught her free paw on that side, while I jammed the gun-butt into her jaws with my left hand and struck home with the right, the knife driving straight to the heart. The deep fang marks she left in the stock, biting the corner of the shoulder clean off, gave an idea of the power of her jaws.

The dogs were pretty well damaged, and all retired and lay down under the trees, where they licked their wounds and went to sleep, growling savagely at one another when they waked, but greeting us with demonstrative affection, and trotting eagerly out to share our lunch as soon as we began to eat it.

A few days later, in mid-afternoon, we struck the tracks of two cougars, one a very large one, an old male. They had evidently been playing and frolicking together, for they were evidently mating. For three hours the pack followed the cold trail through an exceedingly rugged and difficult country in which Goff helped them out again and again.

Just at sunset the cougars were jumped and ran straight into and through a tangle of spurs and foothills, broken by precipices and riven by long deep ravines. In the gathering gloom we galloped along the main divide, my horse once falling on a slippery hillside as I followed headlong after

Goff. The last vestige of sunlight disappeared, but the full moon was well up in the heaven when we came to a long spur, leading off to the right for two or three miles beyond which we did not think the chase could have gone. Making our way down the rough and broken crest of this spur, we heard far off the clamorous baying which told us that the hounds had their quarry at bay. We did not have the fighters with us, as they were still under the weather from the results of another encounter in a cave.

A couple of hundred yards from the spot, we left the horses and scrambled along on foot, guided by the furious clamor of the pack. When we reached them the cougar had gone along the face of the cliff. It was some time before we could make him out. Then I got up close. Although the moonlight was bright I could not see the sights of my rifle and fired a little too far back. The bullet, however, inflicted a bad wound, and the cougar ran along a ledge, disappearing around the cliff shoulder.

The conduct of the dogs showed that he had not left the cliff. It was about a hundred feet high and the top overhung the bottom, while from above the ground sloped down to the brink at a rather steep angle, so that we had to be cautious about our footing. There was a large projecting rock on the brink to which I clambered down, and, holding it with one hand, peeped over the edge. After a minute I made out first the tail and then the head of the cougar, who was lying on a narrow ledge only some ten feet below me. Because of the steepness of the incline I could not let go of the rock with my left hand because I would have rolled over. I got Goff to come down, brace his feet against the projection and grasp me by my legs. He then lowered me gently down until my head and shoulders were over the edge and my arms free. I shot the cougar right between the ears, he being in a straight line beneath me.

The dogs were confident that he was going to be shot, for they had gathered below the cliff to wait for him to fall, and, sure enough, down he came with a crash, luckily not hitting any of them.

The dogs were a source of unceasing amusement, not merely while hunting, but because of their relations to one another when off duty. Queen's temper was of the shortest toward the rest of the pack, although, like Turk, she was fond of crawling into my lap, when we sat down to rest after the worry which closed the chase. As soon as I began to eat my lunch, all the dogs clustered close around and I distributed small morsels to each in turn. Once Jimmie, Queen, and Boxer were sitting side by side, tightly wedged together. I treated them with entire impartiality, and soon Queen's feelings overcame her, and she unostentatiously but firmly bit Jimmie in the jaw. Jimmie howled tremendously and Boxer literally turned a back somersault, evidently fearing lest his turn should come next.

A few days later, when my hunt was about to end, near the mouth of a gorge we encountered the hounds, who had worked the trail down and across the gorge, and were now hunting up the steep shoulder to our left. Evidently the cougar had wandered to and fro over this shoulder, and the dogs were much puzzled and worked in zigzags and circles around it, gradually getting clear to the top. Then old Boxer suddenly gave tongue with renewed zest and started off at a run almost on top of the ridge, the other dogs following. Immediately afterward they jumped the cougar.

We galloped up a hillside to get a better view of what was happening. In a minute the cougar jumped out of a tree among the hounds, who made no attempt to seize him, but followed him as soon as he had cleared their circle. He came downhill at a great rate and jumped over a low cliff, bringing after him such an avalanche of snow that it was a moment before I caught sight of him again, this time crouched on a narrow ledge some fifteen or twenty feet below the brink from which he had jumped, and about as far above the foot of the cliff, where the steep hill slope again began. The hounds soon found him and came along the ledge barking loudly, but not venturing near where he lay facing them, with his back arched like a great cat. Turk and Queen were meanwhile working their way uphill. Turk got directly under the ledge and could not find a way up. Queen went to the left, and in a minute we saw her white form as she made her way through the dark-colored hounds straight for the cougar.

"That's the end of Queen," said Goff, "he'll kill her now, sure."

In another moment she had made her rush, and the cougar, bounding forward, had seized her and driven his great fangs right through the side of her head, fortunately missing the brain. In the struggle he lost his footing and both rolled off the ledge, and when they struck the ground below he let go of the bitch. Turk, who was near where they struck, was not able to spring for the hold he desired, and in another moment the cougar was coming downhill like a quarter horse. We stayed perfectly still, as he was traveling in our direction. Queen was on her feet almost as quick as the cougar, and she and Turk tore after him, the hounds following in a few seconds, being delayed in getting off the ledge.

It was astonishing to see the speed of the cougar. He ran considerably more than a quarter of a mile downhill, and at the end of it had left the dogs more than a hundred yards behind. But his bolt was shot, and after going perhaps a hundred yards up the hill on the other side and below us, he climbed a tree, under which the dogs began to bay frantically, while we scrambled toward them. When I got down I found him standing half upright on a big branch, his fore paws hung over another higher branch, his sides puffing like bellows, and evidently completely winded. I shot him through the heart. At the shot he sprang clean into the top of the tree, head and tail up, and his face fairly demoniac with rage, but before he struck the ground he was dead.

The only dog hurt was Queen, and very miserable indeed she looked. She stood in the trail, refusing to lie down or join the other dogs, as, with prodigious snarls at one another, they ate the pieces of the carcass we cut out for them. I gave most of my lunch to Queen, who evidently felt that it was a delicacy, for she ate it, and then trotted home behind us with the rest of the dogs. Rather to my astonishment, next day she was all right, and as eager to go with us as ever. Though one side of her head was much swollen, in her work she showed no signs of her injuries.

On this trip Theodore often ate the meat of the cougar and pronounced it extremely good. When the hunt was over, reinvigorated, brown and healthly looking, he journeyed back east again soon to take the oath of office as Vice-President.

Six months after Theodore was inaugurated as Vice-President, he became President when McKinley was assassinated. The word went forth that his old cowboy friends, as well as his companions in the Rough Riders, were wanted in the White House for visits. And they came. But Sylvane Ferris had to spend two days convincing the doorkeeper before he could get in.

"Next time they don't let you in, Sylvane," Theodore said indignantly, "just shoot through the window."

John Willis came to see him about a reclamation project, but he would not dine at the White House. "If you are taking any horseback rides out on the trail here tomorrow, I'm your man," he said, "but I guess I will get my grub downtown at the hashery where I'm bunking."

In 1903 Theodore went back to Medora for the last time. He wrote to John Hay:

As soon as I got west of the Missouri I came into my own former stamping-ground. At every station there was somebody who remembered my riding in there when the Little Missouri roundup went down to the Indian reservation and then worked north across Cannon Ball and up Knife and Green Rivers; or who had been an interested and possibly malevolent spectator when I had ridden east with other rep-

resentatives of the cowmen to hold a solemn council with
the leading rangers on the vexed subject of mavericks; or
who had been hired as a train-hand when I had been taking
a load of cattle to Chicago, and who remembered how he
and I at the stoppages had run frantically down the line
of the cars and with poles jabbed the unfortunate cattle
who had lain down until they again stood up, and thereby
gave themselves a chance for their lives; and who remembered how when the train started we had to clamber hurriedly aboard and make our way back to the caboose along
the tops of the cattle cars.

At Mandan two of my old cowhands, Sylvane and Joe
Ferris, joined me. At Dickinson all of the older people had
known me and the whole town turned out with wild and
not entirely sober enthusiasm. It was difficult to make them
much of a speech, as there were dozens of men each earnestly desirous of recalling to my mind some special incident. One man told how he helped me bring in my cattle
to ship, and how a blue roan steer broke away leading a
bunch which it took him and me three hours to round up
and bring back; another, how seventeen years before I had
come in a freight train from Medora to deliver the Fourth
of July oration; another, a gray-haired individual, who
during my early years at Medora had shot and killed an
equally objectionable individual, reminded me how, just
twenty years before, when I was on my first buffalo hunt,
he loaned me the hammer off his Sharp's rifle to replace the
broken hammer of mine; another recalled the time when he
and I worked on the roundup as partners, going with the
Little Missouri "outfit" from the head of the Box Alder to

the mouth of the Big Beaver, and then striking over to represent the Little Missouri brands on the Yellowstone roundup; yet another recalled the time when I, as deputy sheriff of Billings County, had brought in three cattle thieves, he then being sheriff in Dickinson. . . .

At Medora, which we reached after dark, the entire population of the Bad Lands down to the smallest baby had gathered to meet me. This was formerly my home station. The older men and women I knew well; the younger ones had been wild tow-headed children when I lived and worked along the Little Missouri. I had spent nights in their ranches. I still remembered meals which the women had given me when I had come from some hard expedition, half famished and sharp-set as a wolf. I had killed buffalo and elk, deer and antelope with some of the men. With others I had worked on the trail, on the calf roundup, on the beef roundup. They all felt I was their man, their old friend; and even if they had been hostile to me in the old days, when we were divided by the sinister bickering and jealousies and hatreds of all frontier communities, they now firmly believed they had always been my staunch friends and admirers. They all gathered in the town hall, which was draped for a dance—young children, babies, everybody being present. I shook hands with them all, and almost each one had some memory of special association with me he or she wished to discuss. I only regretted that I could not spend three hours with them.

When Theodore visited Butte, Montana, John Willis was there to greet him.

"My God, Theodore," he blurted out, forgetting his etiquette, "where in the hell did you get that pot belly?"

The members of the entertainment committee gasped at this familiarity with the President. But Theodore did not. He threw back his head, showing his famous teeth, and roared.

"You know I made a man of you," Willis went on, ignoring the discomfiture of the committee, "and now you are spoiling all of my work."

"Yes, and I made a Christian of you," Theodore came back, "and don't spoil my work."

Truly the yeast that the West had put into Theodore's blood never ceased to work.

Chapter 3

Presidential Hunts

IN APRIL, 1905, Theodore, now President, went to Colorado again with John Goff, this time to hunt bear with dogs. Another hunter, Jake Borah, combined his pack with that of Goff's.

Three of Goff's dogs—Jim, Tree'em, and Bruno—which had been on the cougar hunt were still with him. There were four terriers one of which was a heavy, liver-colored half-breed bulldog, "a preposterous animal who looked as if his ancestry had included a toadfish" and who was a terrible fighter. There was also "a funny little black-and-tan" terrier named Skip, "a most friendly little fellow, especially fond of riding in front or behind the saddle of any one of us who would take him up, although perfectly able to travel forty miles a day on his own sturdy legs if he had to, and then to join in the worry of the quarry when once it had been shot."

After breakfast each morning the party left for a ten to twelve hour hunt in the saddle, without eating again until dinner that evening. The little terrier, Skip, adopted the president as his special master, rode with him when permitted, and slept on the foot of his bed at night, growling defiance at anyone or anything that came near. Theodore grew so attached to him that at the end of the hunt he sent him back to the White House as a playmate for his children.

It was a great, wild country. In the creek bottoms there were a good many ranches but we only occasionally passed by these, on our way to our hunting grounds in the wilderness along the snow line. The mountains crowded close together in chain, peak, and table land. All the higher ones were wrapped in an unrent shroud of snow. The high peaks were bare of trees. Cottonwoods, and occasionally dwarfed birch or maple and willows, fringed the streams, aspens grew in groves higher up.

Bears and cougars had once been very plentiful throughout this region, but during the last three or four years the cougars had greatly diminished in number. The great grizzlies were now rare.

This Colorado trip was the first on which I hunted bears with hounds. The black bear could not, save under exceptional circumstances, escape from such a pack as we had with us, and the real merit of the chase was confined to the hounds and to Jake and Johnny for their skill in handling them. As for the rest of us, we needed to do little more than to sit ten or twelve hours in the saddle and occasionally lead the horses up or down the most precipitous and cliff-like of the mountainsides. But it was great fun, nevertheless, and usually a chase lasted long enough to be interesting.

On one hunt some twenty good-natured, hard-riding young fellows from the ranches within a radius of a dozen miles had joined our party to "see the President kill a bear." They were a cheerful and friendly crowd, as hardy as so many young moose, and utterly fearless horsemen. One of them rode his wild nervous horse bareback, because it had bucked so when he tried to put the saddle on it that morning that he feared he would get left behind, and so abandoned the saddle outright. Whenever they had a chance they rode at headlong speed, paying no heed to the slope of the mountainside or the character of the ground. In the deep snow they did me a real service, for of course they had to ride their horses single file through the drifts, and by the time my turn came we had a good trail.

The pack finally put up a bear. We had an interesting glimpse of the chase as the bear quartered up across an open spot of the hillside. The hounds were but a short distance behind him, strung out in a long string, the more powerful, those which could do best in the snow-bucking, taking the lead. We pushed up the mountainside after them, horse after horse getting down in the snow, and speedily heard the redoubled clamor which told us that something had been treed.

They had treed the bear far up the mountainside in the thick spruce timber, and a short experiment showed us that the horses could not possibly get through the snow. Accordingly, off we jumped and went toward the sound on foot, all the young ranchmen and cowboys rushing ahead,

and thereby again making me an easy trail. On the way to
the tree the rider of the bareback horse pounced on a snow-
shoe rabbit which was crouched under a bush and caught
it with his hands.

It was half an hour before we reached the tree, a big
spruce, up which the bear had gone to a height of some
forty feet. I broke her neck with a single bullet.

*On the way back to Washington Theodore stopped in
Oklahoma for a coyote-coursing hunt with "Catch-'em-
alive" Jack Abernathy, a professional wolf-hunter. The end
of a chase after a coyote was quite exciting:*

Abernathy was far ahead, his white horse loping along
without showing any signs of distress. As we began to go
downhill I let the horse fairly race, for by Abernathy's mo-
tions I could tell that he was close to the wolf and that it
was no longer running in a straight line, so there was a
chance of my overtaking them. In a couple of miles I was
close enough to see what was going on. But one greyhound
was left with Abernathy. The coyote was obviously tired,
and Abernathy, with the aid of his perfectly trained horse,
was helping the greyhound catch it. Twice he headed it,
and thus enabled me to gain rapidly. They had reached a
small unwooded creek by the time I was within fifty yards.
The little wolf tried to break back to the left but Abernathy
headed it and rode almost over it, and it gave a wicked
snap at his foot, cutting the boot. Then he wheeled and
came toward it. Again it galloped back, and just as it crossed
the creek the greyhound made a rush, pinned it by the

hind leg and threw it. There was a scuffle, then a yell from the greyhound as the wolf bit it. At the bite the hound let go and jumped back a few feet, and at the same moment Abernathy, who had ridden his horse right on them as they struggled, leaped off and sprang on top of the wolf. He held the reins of the horse with one hand and thrust the other, with a rapidity and precision even greater than the rapidity of the wolf's snap, into the wolf's mouth, jamming his hand down crosswise between the jaws, seizing the lower jaw and bending it down so that the wolf could not bite him. He had a stout glove on his hand, but this would have been of no avail whatever had he not seized the animal just as he did.

When he leaped on and captured the coyote it was entirely free, the dog having let go of it, and he was obliged to keep hold of the reins of his horse with one hand. I was not twenty yards distant at the time, and as I leaped off the horse he was sitting placidly on the live wolf, his hand between its jaws, the greyhound standing beside him, and his horse standing by as placid as he was. It was as remarkable a feat of the kind as I have ever seen.

Through some oversight we had no straps with us, and Abernathy had lost the wire which he usually carried in order to tie up the wolves' muzzles—for he habitually captured his wolves in this fashion. However, Abernathy regarded the lack of straps as nothing more than a slight bother. Asking one of us to hold his horse, he threw the wolf across in front of the saddle, still keeping his grip on the lower jaw, then mounted and rode off with us on the back track. The wolf was not tied in any way. It was unhurt, and the hold he had was on its lower jaw. I was surprised that it did not strive to fight with its legs, but after becoming satisfied that it could not bite, it seemed to resign itself to its fate, was fairly quiet, and looked about with its ears pricked forward.

Two years later, in October, 1907, Theodore hunted for bear in the canebrakes of northern Louisiana, after the fashion of the old Southern planters, as he had for years wanted to do. Their first camp was on Tensas Bayou, in the heart of a great alluvial bottomland "created during the countless ages through which the mighty Mississippi has poured out of the heart of the continent."

This was a country of cultivated fields that had been hacked out of towering forests, many of the scarred and battered trunks of dead trees still standing. Beside lakes and bayous giant cypress rivalled in size the red gums and white oaks farther back. The canebrakes stretched along the slight rises of ground, often extending for miles, forming one of the most striking and interesting features of the country, their feathery, graceful stalks standing in ranks, tall, slender, serried, each one only a few inches away from its neighbors, and often fifteen or twenty feet tall.

It was most difficult to walk through them and impossible to see more than a few feet. Bears made their lairs in them. "In the lakes and larger bayous we saw alligators, garfish, and monstrous snapping turtles, fearsome brutes of the slime, as heavy as a man, and with huge horny beaks that with a single snap could take off a man's hand or foot." Water moccasins kept near the water and farther back the

*party killed a number of rattlesnakes and copperheads.
Coons and possums were quite plentiful. Birds sang everywhere.*

The most notable birds and those which most interested
me were the great ivory-billed woodpeckers. Of these I saw
three, all of them in groves of giant cypress, their brilliant
white bills contrasting finely with the black of their general
plumage. They were noisy but wary, and they seemed to
me to set off the wildness of the swamp as much as any
of the beasts of chase. Among the birds of prey the commonest were the barred owls, which I had never elsewhere
found so plentiful. Their hooting and yelling were heard
all around us throughout the night, and once one of them
hooted at intervals for several minutes at midday. One of
these owls had caught and was devouring a snake in the
late afternoon, while it was still daylight. In the dark nights
and still mornings and evenings their cries seemed strange
and unearthly, the long hoots varied by screeches, and by
all kinds of uncanny noises.

At our first camp our tents were pitched by the bayou.
For four days the weather was hot, with steaming rains.
After that it grew cool and clear. Huge biting flies, bigger
than bees, attacked our horses, but the insect plagues, so
veritable a scourge in the country during the months of
warm weather, had well-nigh vanished in the first weeks of
the Fall.

The morning after we reached camp we were joined by
Ben Lilly, the hunter, a spare, full-bearded man, with mild,
gentle, blue eyes and a frame of steel and whipcord. I never

met any other man so indifferent to fatigue and hardship.
He equalled Cooper's Deerslayer in woodcraft, in hardihood, in simplicity—and also in loquacity. He had trapped
and hunted throughout almost all the half-century of his
life, and on trail of game he was as sure as his own hounds.
His observations on wild creatures was singularly close and
accurate. He was particularly fond of the chase of the bear,
which he followed by himself, with one or two dogs. Often
he would be on the trail of his quarry for days at a time,
lying down to sleep wherever night overtook him, and he
had killed over a hundred and twenty bears.

Late in the evening of the same day we were joined by
Clive and Harley Metcalf, planters from Mississippi, skilled
marksmen, and utterly fearless horsemen. For a quarter of
a century they had hunted bear and deer with horse and
hound, and were masters of the art. They brought with
them their pack of bearhounds, only one, however, being a
thoroughly stanch and seasoned veteran. The pack was
under the immediate control of a Negro hunter, Holt Collier, in his own way as remarkable a character as Ben Lilly.
He was a man of sixty and could neither read nor write, but
he had all the dignity of an African chief, and for half a
century he had been a bear hunter, having killed or assisted in killing over three thousand bears.

*For several days, in spite of having the best hunters in
the country, they found no bears around Tensas Bayou, although there were plenty of deer which kept them in fresh
meat. Theodore was fascinated with the skill of the hunters
in using the horn to summon and control the hounds and*

for signalling among the hunters themselves. "The tones of
many of the horns were full and musical, and it was pleasant
to hear them as they wailed to one another, backwards and
forward, across the great stretches of lonely swamp and
forest."

After a few days they shifted their camp to Bear Lake,
fifteen or twenty miles away. This was a tranquil stretch of
water, a part of an old river bed, a couple of hundred yards
broad, with a winding length of several miles.

Giant cypress grew at the edge of the water, the singular
cypress knees rising in every direction round about, while at
the bottoms of the trunks themselves were often cavernous
hollows opening beneath the surface of the water, some of
them serving as dens for alligators. There was a waxing
moon, so the nights were as beautiful as the days.

From our new camp we hunted as steadily as from the
old. We saw bear sign, but not much of it, and only one
or two fresh tracks. One day the hounds jumped a bear,
probably a yearling from the way it ran. After a three hours'
run it managed to get clear without one of the hunters ever
seeing it, and it ran until the dogs were tired out.

We had seen the tracks of an old she in the neighborhood, and the next morning we started to hunt her out.
On reaching the cypress slough near which the tracks of
the old she had been seen the day before, Clive Metcalf and
I separated from the others and rode off at a lively pace between two of the canebrakes. After an hour or two's wait
we heard, very far off, the notes of one of the loudest-

mouthed hounds, and instantly rode toward it, until we
could make out the babel of the pack. Some hard galloping
brought us opposite the point toward which they were
heading—for experienced hunters can often tell the probable line of a bear's flight, and the spots at which it will
break cover. But on this occasion the bear shied off from
leaving the thick cane and doubled back and, soon, the
hounds were once more out of hearing, while we galloped
desperately around the edge of the cane. The tough woods
horses kept their feet like cats as they leaped logs, plunged
through bushes, and dodged in and out among the tree
trunks. We had all we could do to prevent the vines from
lifting us out of the saddle, while the thorns tore our hands
and faces. Hither and thither we went, now at a trot, now
at a run, now stopping to listen for the pack. Occasionally
we could hear the hounds, and then off we would go racing
through the forest toward the point for which we thought
they were heading. Finally, after a couple of hours of this,
we came up on one side of a canebrake on the other side
of which we could hear not only the pack but the yelling
and cheering of Harley Metcalf and one or two of the Negro
hunters, all of whom were trying to keep the dogs up to
their work in the thick cane. Again we rode ahead, and now
in a few minutes were rewarded by hearing the leading
dogs come to bay in the thickest of the cover. Having galloped as near to the spot as we could, we threw ourselves
off the horses and plunged into the cane, trying to cause as
little disturbance as possible, but of course utterly unable
to avoid making some noise. Before we were within gun-
shot, however, we could tell by the sounds that the bear

had once again started, making what is called a "walking bay." Clive Metcalf, a finished bear hunter, was speedily able to determine what the bear's probable course would be, and we stole through the cane until we came to a spot near which he thought the quarry would pass. Then we crouched down, I with my rifle at the ready. Nor did we have long to wait. Peering through the thick-growing stalks I suddenly made out the dim outline of the bear coming straight toward us. Noiselessly, I cocked and half raised my rifle, waiting for a clearer chance. In a few seconds it came. The bear turned almost broadside to me, and walked forward very stiff-legged, almost as if on tiptoe, now and then looking back at the nearest dogs. These were Rowdy, a very deep-voiced hound, in the lead, and Queen, a shrill-tongued brindled bitch, a little behind. Once or twice the bear paused as she looked back at them, evidently hoping that they would come so near that by a sudden race she could catch one of them. But they were too wary.

All of this took but a few moments, and as I saw the bear quite distinctly some twenty yards off, I fired for behind the shoulder. Although I could see her outline, yet the cane was so thick that my sight was on it and not on the bear itself. But I knew my bullet would go true and, sure enough, at the crack of the rifle the bear stumbled and fell forward, the bullet having passed through both lungs and out at the opposite side. Immediately the dogs came running forward at full speed, and we raced forward likewise lest the pack should receive damage. The bear had but a minute or two to live, yet even in that time more than one valuable hound might lose its life, so when within half a dozen steps of the black, angered beast, I fired again, breaking the spine at the root of the neck. Down went the bear stark dead, slain in the canebrake in true hunter fashion.

One by one the hounds struggled up and fell on their dead quarry, the noise of the worry filling the air. Then we dragged the bear out to the edge of the cane, and my companion wound his horn to summon the other hunters.

This was a big she bear, very lean, and weighing two hundred and two pounds. In her stomach were palmetto berries, beetles, and a little mutton cane, but chiefly acorns chewed up in a fine brown mass.

After the death of my bear I had only a couple of days left. We spent them a long distance from camp, having to cross two bayous before we got to the hunting grounds. I missed a shot at a deer, seeing little more than the flicker of its white tail through the dense bushes, and the pack caught and killed a very lean two-year-old bear weighing eighty pounds. On the trip, all told, we killed and brought into camp three bears, six deer, a wildcat, a turkey, a possum, and a dozen squirrels, and we ate everything except the wildcat.

In the evenings we sat around the blazing camp fires, and, as always on such occasions, each hunter told tales of his adventures and of the strange feats and habits of the beasts of the wilderness.

Chapter 4

Little Adventures at Sagamore Hill and the White House

FEW MEN enjoyed his children more than Theodore Roosevelt. In addition to Alice, he had four sons —Theodore, Jr., Kermit, Archie and Quentin—and another daughter, Ethel. He inculcated all of them with his love for the outdoors, and both at Sagamore Hill and at the White House, taught them to love wildlife, particularly birds. "One flicker became possessed of a mania to dig its hole in one corner of the house, just under the roof," he wrote, in discussing the birdlife at Sagamore Hill. "It hammered lustily at boards and shingles, and returned whenever driven away, until at last we were reluctantly forced to decree its death." He was particularly concerned about the little-eared owl which is called screech-owl. "Its tremulous, quavering cry is not a screech at all," he protested. "These little owls came up to the house after dark, and were fond of sitting on the elk-antlers over the gable. When the moon

*was up, by choosing one's position, the little owl appeared
in sharp outline against the bright disk, seated on his many-
tined perch."*

At Sagamore Hill we liked to have the wood-folk and
field-folk familiar. Yet there were necessary bounds to such
familiarity where chickens were kept for use and where the
dogs were valued family friends. The rabbits and gray squirrels were as plenty as ever. The flying squirrels and chipmunks still held their own, as did the muskrats in the
marshes. The woodchucks, which we used to watch as we
sat in rocking-chairs on the broad veranda, had disappeared.
Recently one made himself a home under the old barn,
where we were doing our best to protect him. A mink which
lived by the edge of the bay under a great pile of lumber
had to be killed. Its lair showed the remains not only of
chickens and ducks, but of two muskrats, and what was
rather curious, of two skates or flatfish. A fox which lived
in the big wood-lot evidently disliked our companionship
and abandoned his home.

Of recent years I actually saw but one fox near Sagamore Hill. This was early one morning, when I had spent
the night camping on the wooded shores near the mouth
of Huntington Harbor. The younger children were with
me, this being one of the camping-out trips, in the rowboat,
on the Sound, taken especially for their benefit. We had
camped the previous evening in a glade by the edge of a
low sea bluff, far away from any house and, while the children were intently watching me as I fried strips of beefsteak
and thin slices of potatoes in bacon fat, we heard a fox
barking in the woods. This gave them a delightfully wild

feeling, and with refreshing confidence they discussed the likelihood of seeing it next morning and, to my astonishment, see it we did, on the shore, soon after we started to row home.

One pleasant fall morning I was writing in the gun-room, on the top floor of the house, from the windows of which one can see far over the Sound. Suddenly my small boy of five bustled up in great excitement to tell me that the hired man had come back from the wood-pile pond—a muddy pool in a beech and hickory grove a few hundred yards from the house—to say that he had seen a coon and that I should come down at once with my rifle. The gardener had been complaining much about the loss of his chickens and did not know whether the malefactor was a coon or a mink. Accordingly, I picked up a rifle and trotted down to the pond, holding it in one hand, while the little boy trotted after me, affectionately clasping the butt. Sure enough, in a big blasted chestnut close to the pond was the coon, asleep in a shallow hollow of the trunk, some forty feet from the ground. It was a very exposed place for a coon to lie during the daytime, but this was a bold fellow and seemed entirely undisturbed by our voices. He was altogether too near the house, or rather the chicken coops, to be permitted to stay where he was—especially as but a short time before I had, with mistaken soft-heartedness, spared a possum I found on the place. Accordingly I raised my rifle, then I remembered for the first time that the rear sight was off, as I had taken it out for some reason. In consequence I underwent the humiliation of firing two or three shots in vain before I got the coon. As he fell out of the tree the little boy pounced gleefully on him. Fortunately, he was dead, and we walked back to the house in triumph, each holding a hind leg of the quarry.

The possum I had spared was found in a dogwood tree, not more than eighty yards from the house, one afternoon when we were returning from a walk in the woods. As something had been killing the hens, I felt that it was at least under suspicion and that I ought to kill it. But a possum is such an absurd creature that I could not resist playing with it for some time. After that I felt that to kill it in cold blood would be too much like murder, and let it go. The tender-heartedness was regarded as much misplaced both by farmer and gardener, hence the coon suffered.

A couple of years later, on a clear, cold Thanksgiving Day, we had walked off some five miles to chop out a bridlepath which had become choked with down timber. The two elder of our little boys were with us. The sun had set long ere our return. We were walking home on a road through our own woods and were near the house. We had with us a stanch friend, a large yellow dog, which one of the children, with fine disregard for considerations of sex, had named Susan. Suddenly Susan gave tongue off in the woods to one side and we found he had treed a possum. This time I was hardhearted and the possum fell a victim. The five-year-old boy explained to the seven-year-old that "it was the first time he had ever seen a fellow killed."

Susan was one of many dogs whose lives were a joy and whose deaths were a real grief to the family. Among them were Sailor Boy, the Chesapeake Bay dog, who not only loved guns but also fireworks and rockets, and who exercised a close and delighted supervision over every detail of each Fourth of July celebration. There were two Scotch terriers, Alan and Jessie, and Jack, the most loved of all, a black, smooth-haired Manchester terrier. Jack lived in the house while the others lived outside and were ever on the lookout to join the family in rambles through the woods. Jack was human in his intelligence and affection. He learned all kinds of tricks, was a high-bred gentleman, never brawled, and was a dauntless fighter. Besides the family, his especial friend, playfellow, and teacher was colored Charles, the footman at Washington. Skip, the little black-and-tan terrier that I brought back from the Colorado bear-hunt, changed at once into a real little-boy's dog. He never let his small master out of his sight, and rode on every horse that would let him—by preference on Algonquin, the sheltie, whose nerves were of iron.

In the spring of 1903, while in Western Kansas, a little girl gave me a baby badger, captured by her brother, and named after him, Josiah. I took Josiah home to Sagamore Hill, where the children received him literally with open arms, while even the dogs finally came to tolerate him. He grew apace, and was a quaint and on the whole a friendly—though occasionally short-tempered—pet. He played tag with us with inexhaustible energy, looking much like a small mattress with a leg at each corner. He dug holes with marvelous rapidity, and when he grew snappish we lifted him up by the back of the neck, which rendered him harmless. He ate bread and milk, dead mice and birds, and eggs. He would take a hen's egg in his mouth, break it, and avoid spilling any of the contents. When angered, he hissed, and at other times he made low guttural sounds. The nine-year-old boy became his especial friend. Now and then he nipped the little boy's legs, but this never seemed to interrupt the amicable relations between the two. As the little boy normally wore neither shoes nor stockings, and his blue overalls were thin, Josiah probably found the temptation at times irresistible. If on such occasions the boy was in Josiah's wire-fenced enclosure, he sat on the box with his legs tucked under him. If the play was taking place outside he usually climbed into the hammock, while Josiah pranced and capered clumsily beneath, tail up and head thrown back. But Josiah never bit when picked up, although he hissed like a tea-kettle as the little boy carried him about, usually tightly clasped round where his waist would have been if he had had one.

One of my boys—the special friend of Josiah the badger —once discovered a flying squirrel's nest, in connection with which a rather curious incident occurred. The little boy had climbed a tree which was hollow at the top and in this hollow he discovered a flying squirrel mother with six young ones. She seemed so tame and friendly that the little boy for a moment hardly realized that she was a wild thing, and called down that he had "found a guinea pig up the tree." Finally the mother made up her mind to remove her family. She took each one in turn in her mouth and flew or sailed down from the top of the tree to the foot of another tree near by, ran up this, holding the little squirrel in her mouth, and again sailed down to the foot of another tree some distance off. Here she deposited her young one on the grass, and then, reversing the process, climbed and sailed back to the tree where the nest was. Then she took out another young one and returned with it, in exactly the same fashion as with the first. She repeated this until all six of the young ones were laid on the bank, side by side in a row, all with their heads the same way. Finding that she was not molested she ultimately took all six of the little fellows back to her nest, where she reared her brood undisturbed.

Among the small mammals at Sagamore Hill the chipmunks were the most familiar and the most in evidence, for they readily became tame and confiding. For three or four years a chipmunk—I suppose the same chipmunk—lived near the tennis court and it developed the rather puzzling custom of sometimes scampering across the court while we were in the middle of a game. This happened two or three times every year, and was rather difficult to explain, for the chipmunk could just as well have gone round the court, and there seemed no possible reason why he should suddenly run out on it while the game was in full swing. If he was seen, everyone stopped to watch him, and then he might stop and sit up to look about, but we might not see him until just as he was finishing a frantic scurry across, in imminent danger of being stepped on.

At different times I was given a fairly appalling number of animals, from known and unknown friends. In one year the list included—besides a lion, a hyena, and a zebra from the Emperor of Ethiopia—five bears, a wildcat, a coyote, two macaws, an eagle, a barn-owl, and several snakes and lizards. Most of these went to the Zoo, but a few were kept by the children. Those thus kept numbered at one end of the scale

gentle, trustful, pretty things, like kangaroo-rats and flying
squirrels, and at the other end a queer-tempered young black
bear, which the children named Jonathan Edwards, partly
because of certain well-marked Calvinistic tendencies in his
disposition, partly out of compliment to their mother,
whose ancestors included that Puritan divine. The kangaroo-rats and flying squirrels slept in their pockets and
blouses, went to school with them, and sometimes unexpectedly appeared at breakfast or dinner. The bear added
zest to life in more ways than one. When we took him to
walk, it was always with a chain and a club, and when at
last he went to the Zoo, the entire household breathed a
sigh of relief, although I think the dogs missed him, as he
had occasionally yielded them the pleasure of the chase in
its strongest form.

As a steady thing, the children found rabbits and guinea
pigs the most satisfactory pets. The guinea pigs usually rejoiced in the names of the local or national celebrities of the
moment. At one time there were five, which were named
after naval heroes and friendly ecclesiastical dignitaries—
An Episcopalian Bishop, a Catholic Priest, and my own
Dutch Reformed Pastor—Bishop Doane, Father O'Grady,
Doctor Johnson, Fighting Bob Evans and Admiral Dewey.
Father O'Grady, by the way, proved to be of the softer sex
—a fact definitely established when two of his joint owners,
rushing breathless into the room, announced to a mixed
company, "Oh, oh, Father O'Grady has had some children!"

Of course there are no pets like horses and horsemanship
is a test of prowess. As with everything else, so with riding,

some take to it naturally, others never can become even fairly good horsemen. All the children rode, with varying skill. While young, a Shetland pony served—the present pony, Algonquin, a calico or pinto, was as knowing and friendly as possible. His first small owner simply adored him, treating him as a twin brother, and having implicit faith in his mental powers. On one occasion, when a naval officer of whom the children were fond, came to call, in full dress, Algonquin's master, who was much impressed by the sight, led up Algonquin to enjoy it too, and was shocked by the entire indifference with which the greedy pony persisted in eating grass. One favorite polo-pony, old Diamond, long after he became a pensioner, served for whichever child had just graduated from the sheltie. Next in order was a little mare named Yagenka, after the heroine of one of Sienkiewicz's blood-curdling romances of medieval Poland. When every ridable animal was impressed, all the children sometimes went out with their mother and me.

Of recent years I had not been able to ride to hounds but, when opportunity offered, I kept as saddle-horses one or two hunters, so that instead of riding the road I could strike off across country, the hunters scrambling handily through rough places and jumping an occasional fence if necessary. While in Washington this was often, except for an occasional long walk down Rock Creek or along the Virginia side of the Potomac, the only exercise I could get.

Francis Leupp in the book, The Man Roosevelt, *has an interesting anecdote that happened when Theodore was in the White House. A man had been commissioned to buy*

some saddle horses and had selected two solely on the basis
of their pedigree and deportment. The first horse caracoled
about with the grace and precision of a show animal; the
second took little mincing steps, and it took a lot of goad-
ing to get it into a gallop. When tried at a three-foot jump,
it meekly stopped, smelled the obstruction, and soon lost
its Presidential rider.

"Well, Sir?" asked the man inquiringly.

"Oh, for goodness sake, send them back," exclaimed
Theodore. "I ordered horses—not rabbits."

The Roosevelts had a little place in Albemarle County,
Virginia, to which they went, taking the children, for a
three or four days outing. It was called Pine Knot, and was
near the big stock farm "Plain Dealing," which belonged
to an old friend, Mr. Joseph Wilmer.

There were plenty of quail and rabbits in the fields and
woods near by, so we lived partly on what our guns brought
in, and there were also wild turkeys. I spent the first three
days of November, 1906, in an effort to kill a wild turkey.
Each morning I left the house between three and five
o'clock, under a cold, brilliant moon. The frost was heavy
and my horse shuffled over the frozen ruts. I was on the
turkey grounds before the faintest streak of dawn had appeared in the east and I worked as long as daylight lasted. It
was interesting and attractive in spite of the cold. In the
night we heard the quavering screech owls and, occasionally,
the hooting of one of their bigger brothers. At dawn we
listened to the lusty hammering of the big logcocks, or to

the curious coughing or croaking sound of a hawk before it left its roost. Now and then loose flocks of small birds straggled by us as we sat in the blinds or rested to eat our lunch. Once a shrike pounced on a field-mouse by a haystack; once we came on a ruffed grouse sitting motionless in the road.

The last day I had with me Jim Bishop, a man who had hunted turkeys by profession, a hard-working farmer, whose ancestors had for generations been farmers and woodsmen, an excellent hunter, tireless, resourceful, with an eye that nothing escaped—just the kind of man one likes to regard as typical of what is best in American life. Until this day, and indeed until the very end of this day, chance did not favor us. We tried to get up to the turkeys on the roosts before daybreak, but they roosted in pines. Before day though it was, they were evidently on the lookout, for they always saw us long before we could make them out, and then we could hear them fly out of the treetops. Turkeys are quite as wary as deer, and we never got a sight of them while we were walking through the woods. But two or three times we flushed gangs, and my companion then at once built a little blind of pine boughs, in which we sat while he tried to call the scattered birds up to us by imitating, with marvelous fidelity, their cries. Twice a turkey started toward us, but on each occasion the old hen began calling some distance off and all the scattered birds went toward her. At other times I slipped around to one side of the wood while my companion walked through it, but either there were no turkeys or they went out somewhere far far away from us.

Finally, late in the afternoon, after being out thirteen

hours, Jim Bishop marked a turkey into a point of pines, which stretched from a line of wooded hills down into a narrow open valley on the other side of which again rose wooded hills. I ran down to the end of the point and stood behind a small oak, while Bishop and Dick walked down through the trees to drive the turkeys toward me. This time the turkey came out of the cover not too far off and sprang into the air, heading across the valley and offering me a side shot at forty yards as he sailed by. It was just the distance for the close-shooting ten-bore duck gun I carried and, at the report, down came the turkey in a heap, not so much as a leg or wing moving. I was well pleased when Dick lifted the fine young gobbler, his bronze plumage iridescent in the light of the westering sun.

PART FOUR

African Adventures

Chapter 1

Heading Adventureward Again

As HIS second term as President drew to an end, Theodore Roosevelt faced tremendous adjustments. The Roosevelts had enjoyed the White House; they had made of this official residence a home, and a lusty, enjoyable home at that. There is no doubt that Theodore loved the power, loved the excitement and the associations which the Presidency brought to him. Furthermore, he fervently wished for the continuation of the progressive program he had started. But who would continue it? John Willis sternly warned Theodore against William Howard Taft. Willis the frontiersman, with his ability to see through outward trappings, told him that Taft, though he had integrity, was both easy-going and ambitious—a combination which might make Taft a good judge: he could make decisions slowly and on the basis of precedent. But he would not make a good President. *Still Theodore, as a matter of pride, wanted to pick his successor, and turned his influence to Taft who was elected.*

With politics out of the way (at least temporarily), Theodore plunged into his plans for an African trip with characteristic enthusiasm—and a little plus. He decided to take the older boys. Ted did not want to go—girl trouble—but Kermit did.

Without a doubt Carl Akeley had talked Theodore into making this hunting trip at a White House dinner several years before. Akeley tells about it:

"My back yard was Africa, but there was also present at that White House dinner-party a man whose back yard was Alaska. Before dinner Roosevelt had been making him talk about the natural resources and the animal life of the territory, and as we entered the dining-room the President remarked, 'When I am through with this job, I am going to Alaska for a good hunt.'

"I have reason to believe that we were served a most excellent dinner but this belief is not based upon gustatory observation, for the President fired questions at me so rapidly that I had little time for anything but talking.

"Among the stories that I told was one of sixteen lions that were seen emerging from a cave on Juja Farm. At the time certain congressmen were irritating the President considerably and, when I had finished my tale, he turned to Congressman Mann, who sat at his right and said, 'Congressman, I wish I had those sixteen lions to turn loose on Congress.'

" 'But, Mr. President,' queried the congressman after

some hesitation, 'aren't you afraid that they might make a mistake?'

"With a snap of his teeth Roosevelt replied, 'Not if they stayed long enough.'

"So he really originated the cry with which the Senate crowd retaliated when he departed for Africa, 'America expects every lion to do his duty.'

"When the last course appeared, I had not exhausted my repertoire, but apparently I had said enough to influence the President to change his plan. As he rose from the table, he remarked emphatically, 'When I am through with this job, I am going to Africa.'

" 'But what about Alaska?' interposed the man from the North.

" 'Alaska will have to wait.' "

Akeley goes on to say, "that the lions failed to do the duty that certain elements in the United States Senate expected of them was not because Roosevelt refused to give them opportunity. As a hunter, he completely disregarded his own bodily welfare. While President of the United States he had to accept a bodyguard; but on the trail in Africa his bodyguard—that is, his companions—very thoroughly understood that they were not to interfere with any attacking animal until Roosevelt was down. I recall an incident of a lion-hunt, recounted to me by one of his men. This man saw a lioness at very close quarters in the high grass, crouched to spring at Roosevelt. He was about to shoot, when fortunately Roosevelt saw the beast, fired, and killed her. His companion was very grateful for the outcome, for Roosevelt

told him afterward that they would have parted company
had he shot the beast for Roosevelt's protection."

The expedition headed by Roosevelt was sent out by the
Smithsonian Institution to collect birds, reptiles, plants and
big game for the National Museum at Washington.

In addition to myself and my son Kermit, the party consisted of three naturalists: Surgeon Lieutenant-Colonel
Edgar A. Mearns, U.S.A., retired; Mr. Edmund Heller, of
California, and Mr. J. Alden Loring, of Owego, N.Y. My
arrangements for the trip had been chiefly made through
two valued English friends, Mr. Frederick Courteney Selous, the greatest of the world's big-game hunters, and Mr.
Edward North Buxton, also a mighty hunter. On landing
we were to be met by Messrs. R. J. Cuninghame and Leslie
Tarlton, both famous hunters.

On the ship, at Naples, we found Selous, also bound for
East Africa on a hunting trip. A veteran whose first hunting in Africa was nearly forty years ago, he cared only for
exceptional trophies of a very few animals, while we desired
specimens of both sexes of all the species of big game that
Kermit and I could shoot, as well as complete series of all
the smaller mammals.

Most of the hunting was done in British East Africa,
chiefly in the province of Kenia. The starting point was
the East Indian Ocean port of Mombasa from which place
the party went by railroad (which extends from Mombasa
northwestward to Lake Victoria) to Kapiti Plains where the
safari was organized. For several months they hunted in

this region, known as the Southern Game Preserve, mostly to the north and east. Then they traveled through "the thirst," a waterless region west of the railroad, to the Sotik. From here the safari moved northward to Lake Naivasha, still south and west of the railroad. The next big hunt, primarily after elephants, was northeast and north, in Kenia Province and the Northern Game Preserve, a trip which skirted along the western slope of Mount Kenia, an 18,620 foot peak. After this hunt the safari returned to the railroad and moved in the general direction of Lake Victoria, with a side excursion deep into the Uasin Basin, northeast of Lake Victoria and in the western portion of the Northern Game Preserve. After this hunt the safari broke up, with most of the native porters, gun bearers and guards remaining behind. The rest of the party went by rail to Lake Victoria, across it by steamer to Entebbe, at its northwesternmost tip, and then by land to Lake Albert, hunting on the way. From here their course was north by boat, with a rhinoceros hunt in the Congo forests, until they got to the Nile River. They disembarked at Khartoum with a hunt or so on the way, on March 14, 1910, after a year of glorious adventure for Theodore and Kermit.

On April 21 the party steamed into the beautiful and picturesque harbor of Mombasa which lies just south of the equator. After official welcoming by British officials, they went, by the Uganda Railway, through the great game preserve on what Theodore called "the most interesting railway journey in the world." The locomotive was fitted "with *a comfortable seat across the cowcatcher"* on which, except at meal times, Theodore sat for most of the journey.

The first afternoon we did not see many wild animals, but birds abounded, and the scenery was both beautiful and interesting. A black-and-white hornbill, feeding on the track, rose so late that we nearly caught it with our hands; guinea-fowl and francolin, and occasionally bustard, rose near by; brilliant rollers, sunbirds, bee-eaters, and weaver-birds flew beside us, or sat unmoved among the trees as the train passed. In the dusk we nearly ran over a hyena. Mishaps were continually taking place on the line. The night we went up there was an interruption in the telegraph service due to giraffes having knocked down some of the wires and a pole in crossing the track. Two or three times, at night, giraffes had been run into and killed; once a rhinoceros was killed, the engine being damaged in the encounter.

Some of the savages we saw wore red blankets, and in deference to white prejudice draped them so as to hide their nakedness. But others appeared—men and women— with literally not one stitch of clothing, although they might have rather elaborate hairdresses, and masses of metal ornaments on their arms and legs. In the region where one tribe dwelt, all the people had their front teeth filed to sharp points. It was strange to see a group of these savages, stark naked, with oddly shaved heads and filed teeth, armed with primitive bows and arrows, stand gravely gazing at the train as it rolled into some station. One group of women, nearly nude, had their upper arms so tightly bound with masses of bronze or copper wire that their muscles were completely malformed. So tightly was the wire wrapped round the upper third of the arm, that it was reduced to about one half of its normal size.

Next morning we were in the game country, and as we sat on the seat over the cowcatcher it was literally like passing through a vast zoological garden. At one time we passed a herd of a dozen or so of great giraffes, cows and calves, cantering along through the open woods a couple of hundred yards to the right of the train. Again, still closer, four waterbuck cows, their big ears thrown forward, stared at us without moving. Hartebeests [antelope] were everywhere. A long-tailed straw-colored monkey ran from one tree to another. Huge black ostriches appeared from time to time. Once a troop of impala, [large antelope] close by the track, took fright, and as the beautiful creatures fled we saw now one and then another bound clear over the high bushes. A herd of zebra clattered across a cutting of the line not a hundred yards ahead of the train.

Soon after lunch we drew up at the little station of Kapiti Plains, where our safari was awaiting us—"safari" being the term employed throughout East Africa to denote both the caravan with which one makes an expedition and the expedition itself.

As a compliment, which I much appreciated, a large American flag was floating over my own tent, and in the front line, flanking this tent on either hand, were other big tents for the members of the party, with a dining tent and skinning tent. Behind were the tents of the two hundred porters, the gunbearers, the tent boys, the *askaris* or native soldiers, and the horse boys or *saises*. In front of the tents stood the men in two lines, the first containing fifteen *askaris*, the second line porters. The *askaris* were uniformed, each in a red fez, a blue blouse, and white knickerbockers, and each carrying his rifle and belt. The porters were chosen from several different tribes or races to minimize the danger of combination in the event of mutiny.

Equatorial Africa was in most places none too healthy a place for the white man, and he had to care for himself as he would have scorned to in the lands of pine and birch and frosty weather. Camping in the Rockies or the North woods could be combined with "roughing it." The early pioneers of the West, the explorers, prospectors, and hunters, who always roughed it, were as hardy as bears, and lived to a hale old age, if Indians and accidents permitted. But in tropic Africa a lamentable proportion of the early explorers paid in health or life for the hardships they endured. Throughout most of the country no man could long rough it, in the Western and Northern sense, with impunity.

Our tents, our accommodations generally, seemed almost too comfortable for men who knew camp life only on the great plains, in the Rockies, and in the North woods. My tent had a fly which was to protect it from the great heat. There was a little rear extension in which I bathed—a hot bath, never a cold bath, was a tropic necessity. There was a ground canvas, of vital moment in a land of ticks, jiggers and scorpions, and a cot to sleep on, so as to be raised from the ground. Then I had two tent boys to see after my belongings, and to wait at table as well as in the tent. Ali, a Mohammedan mulatto (Arab and Negro) was the chief of the two, and spoke some English, while under him was

"Bill," a speechless black boy. Two other Mohammedan Negroes, clad like the *askaris*, reported to me as my gun bearers. My two *saises*, were both pagans. The two horses for which these men cared were stout, quiet little beasts, one a sorrel, I named Tranquillity, and the other, a brown, had so much the cob-like build of a zebra that we christened him Zebra-shape.

For forty-eight hours we were busy arranging our outfit. The provisions were those usually included in an African hunting or exploring trip, save that, in memory of my days in the West, I included in each provision box a few cans of Boston baked beans, California peaches, and tomatoes. We had plenty of warm bedding, for the nights were cold at high altitudes, even under the equator. While hunting I wore heavy shoes, with hobnails or rubber soles, khaki trousers, the knees faced with leather, and the legs buttoning tight from the knee to below the ankle, to avoid the need of leggins, a khaki-colored army shirt, and a sun helmet, which I wore in deference to local advice, instead of my beloved and far more convenient slouch-hat. My rifles were an army Springfield, 30-caliber, stocked and sighted to suit myself, a Winchester 405, and a double-barrelled 500-450 Holland, a beautiful weapon presented to me by some English friends. Kermit's battery was of the same type, except that instead of a Springfield he had another Winchester shooting the army ammunition, and his double-barrel was a Rigby. In addition I had a Fox No. 12 shotgun; no better gun was ever made.

There was one other bit of impedimenta, less usual for African travel, but perhaps almost as essential for real enjoyment even on a hunting trip, if it is to be of any length. This was the "Pigskin's Library," so called because most of the books were bound in pigskin. They were carried in a light aluminum and oil-cloth case, which, with its contents, weighed a little less than sixty pounds, making a load for one porter.

In his The Happy Hunting-Ground *Kermit Roosevelt gives an interesting note on this Pigskin Library. "One of the most careful preparations that father made for the African expedition was the choosing of the library. He selected as wide a range as possible, getting the smallest copy of each book that was obtainable with decent reading type. He wanted a certain number of volumes mainly for the contrast to the daily life. He told me that he had particularly enjoyed Swinburne and Shelley in ranching days in the Bad Lands, because they were so totally foreign to the life and the country—and supplied an excellent antidote to the daily round. Father read so rapidly that he had to plan very carefully in order to have enough books to last him through a trip."*

Theodore continues:

I used my Whitman tree army saddle and my army field glasses. In addition, for studying the habits of the game, I carried a telescope. I had a slicker for wet weather, an army overcoat, and a mackinaw jacket for cold, if I had to stay out overnight in the mountains. In my pockets I carried a knife, a compass, and a water-proof match-box. Finally, just before leaving home, I had been sent, for good luck, a gold-

mounted rabbit's foot, by Mr. John L. Sullivan, at one time
ring champion of the world.

*By mid-afternoon of the third day they were ready to
hunt. They first saw hartbeest, wildebeest and gazelles.
What Theodore first wanted were two good specimens, bull
and cow, of the wildebeest—a variety of the brindled gnu
somewhat like the American bison.*

I first tried to get up to a solitary old bull, and after a
good deal of maneuvering, and by taking advantage of a rain
squall, I got a standing shot at him at four hundred yards,
and hit him, but too far back. Although keeping a good
distance away, he tacked and veered so, as he ran, that by
much running myself I got various other shots at him, at
very long range, but missed them all. He had run into view
of Kermit who took up the chase with enthusiasm. Yet it
was sunset, after a run of six or eight miles, when he finally
ran into and killed the tough old bull, which had turned to
bay, snorting and tossing its horns.

Meanwhile I managed to get within three hundred and
fifty yards of a herd, and picked out a large cow which was
unaccompanied by a calf. Again my bullet went too far
back. After going a mile it lay down, and would have been
secured without difficulty if a wretched dog had not run
forward and put it up. One of the hunters followed it on
horseback for some miles and when I overtook him he was
standing by the dead cow.

It was long after nightfall before we reached camp, ready
for a hot bath and a good supper. As always thereafter with

anything we shot, we used the meat for food and preserved the skins for the National Museum. Both the cow and the bull were fat and in fine condition, though covered with ticks.

The next day we rode some sixteen miles to the beautiful hills of Kitanga and, for over a fortnight, were the guests of the owner of a farm (or ranch as we would call it in the West), an Englishman, Sir Alfred Pease.

The house was one story high, clean and comfortable, with a veranda running round three sides. From the house we looked over hills and wide lonely plains. The green valley below, with its flat-topped acacias, was very lovely. In the evening we could see, scores of miles away, the snowy summit of mighty Kilimanjaro turn crimson in the setting sun. The twilights were not long and when night fell, stars new to Northern eyes flashed glorious in the sky. Above the horizon hung the Southern Cross, and directly opposite in the heavens was our old familiar friend the Wain, the Great Bear, upside down and pointing to a North Star so low behind a hill that we could not see it.

This was a dry country which reminded Theodore of the great plains of the West, where they slope upward to the foothills of the Rockies. "As my horse shuffled forward, under the bright, hot sunlight, across the endless flats or gently rolling slopes of brown and withered grass, I might have been on the plains anywhere, from Texas to Montana." The trees were different however. Most of them were mimosas, or a similar kind, usually thorny. There were bushes of the color and size of sagebrush covered with flowers like morning glories. "There were also wild sweet

peas, on which the ostriches fed, as they did on another
plant with a lilac flower of a faint heliotrope fragrance."

In my hunting, unless there was something special on,
like a lion or rhinoceros hunt, I usually rode off followed
only by my sais and gun bearers. I could not describe the
beauty and unceasing interest of these rides, through the
teeming herds of game. The rides through the wild, lonely
country, with only my silent black followers, had a peculiar
charm. When the sky was overcast it was cool and pleasant,
for it was a high country, but as soon as the sun appeared
the vertical tropical rays made the air quiver above the
scorched land. As we passed down a hillside we brushed
through aromatic shrubs and the hot, pleasant fragrance
enveloped us. When we came to a nearly dry watercourse,
there would be beds of rushes, beautiful lilies and lush green
plants with staring flowers, and great deep-green fig-trees,
or flat-topped mimosas. In many of these trees there were
sure to be native beehives—sections of hollow logs hung
from the branches—which formed striking and characteristic
features of the landscape.

When we left the hills and the wooded watercourses we
might ride for hour after hour across the barren desolation
of the flats, while herds of zebra and hartbeest stared at us
through the heat haze. Then the zebra, with shrill, barking
neighs, would file off across the horizon, or the high-
withered hartbeests, snorting and bucking, would rush off
in a confused mass, as unreasoning panic succeeded foolish
confidence. If I shot anything, vultures of several kinds,
and the tall, hideous marabou storks, gathered before the
skinners were through with their work. They usually re-

mained at a wary distance, but the handsome ravens, glossy-hued with white napes, big-billed, long-winged, and short-tailed, came round more familiarly.

I rarely had to take the trouble to stalk anything. The shooting was necessarily at rather long range, but, by ma-neuvering a little, and never walking straight toward a beast, I was usually able to get whatever the naturalists wanted.

Occasionally we drove a ravine or a range of hills by means of beaters. On such occasions all kinds of things were put up. Most of the beaters, especially if they were wild savages impressed for the purpose from some neighbor-ing tribe, carried throwing-sticks, with which they were very expert. The beats, with the noise and laughter of the good-humored excitable savages, and the alert interest as to what would turn up next, were great fun. But the days that I enjoyed most were those spent alone with my horse and gun bearers. We might be off by dawn, and see the tropic sun flame splendid over the brink of the world. Strange creatures rustled through the bush or fled dimly through the long grass, before the light grew bright. The air was fresh and sweet as it blew in our faces. When the still heat of noon drew near I would stop under a tree, with my water canteen and my lunch. The men lay in the shade, and the hobbled pony grazed close by, while I either dozed or else watched through my telescope the herds of game lying down or standing drowsily in the distance. As the shadows lengthened, I would again mount, and finally ride home-ward as the red sunset paled to amber and opal, and all the vast, mysterious African landscape grew to wonderful beauty in the dying twilight.

Chapter 2

Lion Hunting on the Kapiti Plains

THE MOST dangerous game of Africa are the lion, buffalo, elephant, rhinoceros and leopard. The hunter who follows any of these does so at great risk to life or limb. In addition there are others like the crocodile, the hyena and poisonous snakes that entail some risk, as does the hippopotamus. Various hunters have differed on which of the dangerous ones is "the most dangerous." Theodore gave his vote to the lion.

Everywhere throughout the country we were crossing there were many lions, for the game on which they feed was extraordinarily abundant. Their favorite food was yielded by the swarming herds of hartbeests and zebras, on which they could prey at will. In this region they rarely preyed on buffalo, although elsewhere they habitually do so. But where zebras and hartbeests could be obtained without effort, it was evidently not worth their while to challenge such formidable quarry. Every "kill" I saw was a hartbeest or a zebra.

One day we started from the ranch-house in good season for an all-day lion-hunt. We began to beat down a long *donga*, or dry watercourse—a creek, as we should call it in the Western plains country. The watercourse with low, steep banks wound in curves, and here and there were patches of brush, which might contain anything in the shape of lion, cheetah, hyena, or wild dog. Soon we came upon lion spoor in the sandy bed; first the footprints of a big male, then those of a lioness. We walked cautiously along each side of the *donga*, the horses following close behind so that if the lion were missed we could gallop after him and round him up on the plain. The dogs began to show signs of scenting the lion and we beat out each patch of brush, the natives shouting and throwing in stones, while we stood with the rifles where we could best command any probable exit. After a couple of false alarms the dogs drew toward one patch, their hair bristling, and showing such eager excitement that it was evident something big was inside and, in a moment, one of the boys called, "simba" (lion), and pointed with his finger. It was just across the little ravine, there about four yards wide and as many feet deep. I shifted my position, peering eagerly into the bushes for some moments before I caught a glimpse of tawny hide. As it moved, there was a call to me to "shoot," for at that distance, if the lion charged, there would be scant time to stop it. I fired into what I saw. There was a commotion in the bushes, and Kermit fired. Immediately afterward there broke out on the other side, not the hoped-for big lion, but two cubs the size of mastiffs. Each was badly wounded and we finished them off, for even if unwounded they were too big to take alive.

A couple of miles away was another *donga*, and toward this we cantered. Almost as soon as we reached it our leader found the spoor of two big lions. With every sense acock, we dismounted and approached the first patch of tall bushes. We shouted and threw in stones, but nothing came out. Another small patch showed the same result. Then we mounted our horses again, and rode toward another patch a quarter of a mile off. I was mounted on Tranquillity, the stout and quiet sorrel. We rode up to the patch and shouted loudly. The response was immediate, in the shape of loud gruntings, and crashings through the thick brush. We were off our horses in an instant, I throwing the reins over the head of mine, and without delay the good old fellow began placidly grazing, quite unmoved by the ominous sounds immediately in front.

I sprang to one side and, for a second or two, we waited, uncertain whether we should see the lions charging out ten yards distant or running away. Fortunately, they adopted the latter course. Right in front of me, thirty yards off, there appeared, from behind the bushes which had first screened him from my eyes, the tawny, galloping form of a big mane-less lion. Crack! the Winchester spoke and, as the soft-nosed bullet ploughed forward through his flank, the lion swerved so that I missed him with the second shot. My third bullet went through the spine and forward into his chest. Down he came, sixty yards off, his hind quarters dragging, his head

up, his ears back, his jaws open and lips drawn up in a
prodigious snarl, as he endeavored to turn to face us. His
back was broken but of this we could not at the moment
be sure, so Kermit and I fired, almost together, into his
chest. His head sank, and he died.

This lion had come out on the left of the bushes; the
other, to the right of them, had not been hit, and we saw
him galloping off across the plain, six or eight hundred yards
away. A couple more shots missed, and we mounted our
horses to try to ride him down. The plain sloped gently
upward for three-quarters of a mile to a low crest or divide,
and long before we got near him he disappeared over this.

Sir Alfred and Kermit were tearing along in front and
to the right, while Tranquillity carried me, as fast as he
could, on the left. On topping the divide I saw the lion,
loping along close behind some kongoni [hartbeest] and this
enabled me to gain rapidly, and, finding out this, the lion
suddenly halted and came to bay in a slight hollow, where
the grass was rather long. The plain seemed flat, and we
could see the lion well from horseback but it was most
difficult to make him out on foot, and impossible to do so
when kneeling.

We were about a hundred and fifty yards from the lion.
Kermit and I tried shooting from the horses but, at such a
distance, this was not effective. Then Kermit got off. But
his horse would not let him shoot and, when I got off, I
could not make out the animal through the grass with sufficient distinctness to enable me to take aim. At this moment my black *sais*, Simba, came running up to me and took
hold of the bridle. He had seen the chase from the line of

march and had cut across to join me. There was no other *sais* or gun-bearer anywhere near, and his action was plucky for he was the only man afoot, with the lion at bay.

Now, an elderly man with a varied past which includes rheumatism does not vault lightly into the saddle. I had already made up my mind that in the event of the lion's charging it would be wise for me to trust to straight powder rather than to try to scramble into the saddle and get under way in time. Simba was on foot and it was of course out of the question for me to leave him. So I said, "Good, Simba, now we'll see this thing through," and gentle-mannered Simba smiled a shy appreciation of my tone, though he could not understand the words. I was still unable to see the lion when I knelt, but he was now standing up, looking first at one group of horses and then at the other, his tail lashing to and fro, his head held low, and his lips dropped over his mouth in peculiar fashion, while his harsh and savage growling rolled thunderously over the plain. Seeing Simba and me on foot, he turned toward us, his tail lashing quicker and quicker. Resting my elbow on Simba's bent shoulder, I took steady aim and pressed the trigger. The bullet went in between the neck and shoulder, and the lion fell over on his side, one fore leg in the air. He recovered in a moment and stood up, evidently very sick, and once more faced me, growling hoarsely. I think he was on the eve of charging. I fired again at once, and this bullet broke his back just behind the shoulders and, with the next, I killed him outright.

These were two good-sized maneless lions, and very proud of them I was.

It was late before we got the lions skinned. Then we set off toward the ranch, two porters carrying each lion-skin, strapped to a pole, and two others carrying the cub-skins. Night fell long before we were near the ranch but the brilliant tropic moon lighted the trail. The stalwart savages who carried the bloody lion-skins, as the sun went down, began to chant in unison, one uttering a single word or sentence, and the others joining in a deep-toned, musical chorus. The men on a safari, and indeed African natives generally, were always excited over the death of a lion, and the hunting tribes then chanted their rough hunting-songs, or victory songs, until the monotonous, rhythmical repetitions made them grow almost frenzied. The ride home through the moonlight, the vast barren landscape shining like silver on either hand, was one to be remembered.

Three days later we had another successful lion-hunt. As the safari was stationary, we took fifty or sixty porters as beaters.

There was a long, wide valley, or rather a slight depression in the ground—for it was only three or four feet below the general level—in which the grass grew tall, as the soil was quite wet. The beaters were put in at the lower end, formed a line across the valley, and beat slowly toward us, making a great noise.

They were still some distance away when three lions slunk stealthily off ahead of them through the grass. I overshot. However, the bullet must have passed very close—indeed, I think it just grazed one—for he jumped up and faced us, growling savagely. Then, his head lowered, he threw his tail straight into the air and began to charge. The first few steps he took at a trot, and before he could start into a gallop I put the soft-nosed Winchester bullet in between the neck and shoulder. Down he went with a roar. The wound was fatal, but I was taking no chances, and I put two more bullets in him. Then we walked toward another lion—the lioness, as it proved—I could not kneel to shoot in grass so tall. At sixty yards I could make her out clearly, snarling at me as she faced me, and I shot her full in the chest. She at once performed a series of extraordinary antics, tumbling about on her head, just as if she were throwing somersaults, first to one side and then to the other. I fired again, but managed to shoot between the somersaults, so to speak, and missed her. The shot seemed to bring her to herself, and away she tore but, instead of charging us, she charged the line of beaters. She was dying fast, however, and in her weakness failed to catch any one. We advanced to look her up, our rifles at full cock, and the gun-bearers close behind. It is ticklish work to follow a wounded lion in tall grass, and we walked carefully, every sense on the alert. A beater came running up and pointed toward where he had seen her, and we walked toward the place. At thirty yards' distance, I made out the form of the lioness showing indistinctly through the grass. She was half crouching, half sitting, her head bent down, but she still had strength to do mischief. She saw us, but before she could turn I sent a bullet through her shoulders. Down she went, and was dead when we walked up.

We were a long way from camp, and, after beating in vain for the other lion, we started back. It was after nightfall before we saw the camp-fires. It was two hours later before the porters appeared, bearing on poles the skin of the dead lion, and the lioness entire. The moon was nearly full, and it was interesting to see them come swinging down the trail in the bright silver light, chanting in deep tones, over and over again, a line or phrase that sounded like:

"Zou-zou-boule ma ja guntai; zou-zou-boule ma ja guntai." Occasionally they would interrupt it by the repetition in unison, at short intervals, of a guttural ejaculation, sounding like "huzlem." They marched into camp, then up and down the lines, before the rows of small fires; then, accompanied by all the rest of the porters, they paraded up to the big fire where I was standing. Here they stopped and ended the ceremony by a minute or two's vigorous dancing amid singing and wild shouting. The firelight gleamed and flickered across the grim dead beasts, and the shining eyes and black features of the excited savages, while all around the moon flooded the landscape with her white light.

Chapter 3

On Safari: Rhino and Giraffe

WHEN WE killed the last lions we were already on safari, and the camp was pitched by a water-hole on the Potha, a half-dried stream, little more than a string of pools and reed beds, winding down through the sun-scorched plain. Next morning we started for another water-hole at the rocky hill of Bondoni, about eight miles distant.

Safari life was very pleasant, and also very picturesque. The porters were strong, patient, good-humored savages, with something childlike about them that made one really fond of them. When we were to march, camp was broken as early in the day as possible. Each man had his allotted task, and the tents, bedding, provisions, and all else were expeditiously made into suitable packages. Each porter was supposed to carry from fifty-five to sixty pounds, which might all be in one bundle or in two or three. The American flag, which flew over my tent, was a matter of much

259

pride to the porters, and was always carried at the head or near the head of the line of march.

As they started, some of them would blow on horns or whistles and others beat little tom-toms and, at intervals, this would be renewed again and again throughout the march. The men might suddenly begin to chant, or merely to keep repeating in unison some one word or one phrase which, when we asked to have it translated, might or might not prove to be entirely meaningless.

The head men carried no burdens, and the tent-boys hardly anything, while the *saises* walked with the spare horses. In addition to the canonical and required costume of blouse or jersey and drawers, each porter wore a blanket, and usually something else to which his soul inclined. It might be an exceedingly shabby coat; it might be, of all things in the world, an umbrella, an article for which they had a special attachment. Often I would see a porter, who thought nothing whatever of walking for hours at midday under the equatorial sun with his head bare, trudging along with solemn pride either under an open umbrella, or carrying the umbrella in one hand, as a wand of dignity. Then their headgear varied according to the fancy of the individual. Normally it was a red fez, a kind of cap only used in hot climates, and exquisitely designed to be useless therein because it gave absolutely no protection from the sun. But one would wear a skin cap; another would suddenly put one or more long feathers in his fez; and another discarding the fez, would revert to some purely savage head-dress which he would wear with equal gravity whether it were, in our eyes, really decorative or merely comic. One such head-dress consisted of the skin of the top of a zebra's head, with the two ears. Another was made of the skins of squirrels, with the tails both sticking up and hanging down. Another consisted of a bunch of feathers woven into the hair, which itself was pulled out into strings that were stiffened with clay. Another included the man's natural hair, some strips of skin, and an empty tin can.

If it were a long journey and we broke it by a noon-day halt, or if it were a short journey and we reached camp ahead of the safari, it was interesting to see the long file of men approach. Here and there, leading the porters, scattered through the line, or walking alongside, were the *askaris*, the rifle-bearing soldiers. They were not marksmen, to put it mildly, and I should not have regarded them as particularly efficient allies in a serious fight; but they were excellent for police duty in camp, and were also of use in preventing collisions with the natives. After the leading *askaris* might come one of the head men. Then would come the man with the flag, followed by another blowing on an antelope horn, or perhaps beating an empty can as a drum; and then the long line of men, some carrying their loads on their heads, others on their shoulders, others, in a very few cases, on their backs. As they approached the halting place their spirits rose, the whistles and horns were blown, and the improvised drums beaten, and perhaps the whole line would burst into a chant.

On reaching the camping-ground each man at once set about his allotted task, and the tents were quickly pitched and the camp put in order, while water and firewood were fetched. The tents were pitched in long lines, in the first of which stood my tent, flanked by those of the other white men and by the dining tent. In the next line were the cook tent, the provision tent, the store tent, the skinning tent, and then came the lines of small white tents for the porters. Between each row of tents was a broad street. In front of our own tents in the first line an *askari* was always pacing to and fro. When night fell we would kindle a camp-fire and sit around it under the stars. Before each of the porters' tents was a little fire, and beside it stood the pots and pans in which the porters did their cooking. Here and there were larger fires, around which the gun-bearers or a group of *askaris* or *saises* might gather. After nightfall the multitude of fires lit up the darkness and showed the tents in shadowy outline and, around them, squatted the porters, their faces flickering from dusk to ruddy light, as they chatted together or suddenly started some snatch of wild African melody in which all their neighbors might join. After a while the talk and laughter and singing would gradually die away, and as we white men sat around our fire, the silence would be unbroken except by the queer cry of a hyena, or much more rarely by a sound that always demanded attention—the yawning grunt of a questing lion.

A few days later they were guests of Captain Slatter who had an ostrich farm. The next day Theodore and the Captain went for a hunt. In the morning they came upon a herd of eland—the largest of the antelopes, being quite as heavy as fattened ox.

As I crept toward them I was struck by their likeness to great, clean, handsome cattle. They were grazing or resting, switching their long tails at the flies that hung in attendance upon them and lit on their flanks, just as if they were Jerseys in a field at home. My bullet fell short, their size causing me to underestimate the distance, and away they went at a run, one or two of the cows in the first hurry and confusion skipping clean over the backs of others that got in their way—a most unexpected example of agility in such large and ponderous animals. After a few hundred yards they settled down to the slashing trot which is their natural gait, and disappeared over the brow of a hill.

Early in the afternoon we saw the eland-herd again. They were around a tree in an open space, and we could not get near them. But instead of going straight away they struck off to the right and described almost a semicircle, and though they were over four hundred yards distant, they were such big creatures and their gait was so steady that I felt warranted in shooting. On the dry plain I could mark where my bullets fell, and though I could not get a good chance at the bull I finally downed a fine cow and, by pacing, I found it to be a little over a quarter of a mile from where I stood when shooting.

It was about nine miles from camp, and I dared not leave the eland alone, so I stationed one of the gun-bearers by the great carcass and sent a messenger in to Heller, on whom we depended for preserving the skins of the big game. Hardly had this been done when a Wakamba man came running up to tell us that there was a rhinoceros on the hillside three-quarters of a mile away, and that he had left a companion to watch it while he carried us the news. Slatter and I immediately rode in the direction given, following our wild-looking guide; the other gun-bearer trotting after us.

In five minutes we had reached the opposite hill crest, where the watcher stood, and he at once pointed out the rhino. The huge beast was standing in entirely open country, although there were a few scattered trees of no great size at some little distance from him. We left our horses in a dip of the ground and began the approach. The wind blew from him to us, and a rhino's eyesight is dull. Thirty yards from where he stood was a bush four or five feet high, and though it was so thin that we could distinctly see him through the leaves, it shielded us from the vision of his small, pig-like eyes as we advanced toward it, stooping and in single file, I leading. The big beast stood like an uncouth statue, his hide black in the sunlight, a monster surviving over from the world's past, from the days when the beasts of the prime ran riot in their strength, before man grew so cunning of brain and hand as to master them. So little did he dream of our presence that when we were a hundred yards off he actually lay down.

Walking lightly, and with every sense keyed up, we at last reached the bush, and I pushed forward the safety of the double-barrelled Holland rifle which I was now to use for the first time on big game. As I stepped to one side of the bush so as to get a clear aim, with Slatter following, the rhino saw me and jumped to his feet with the agility of a polo-pony. As he rose I put in the right barrel, the bullet going through both lungs. At the same moment he wheeled, the blood spouting from his nostrils, and galloped full on us. Before he could get quite all the way round in his head-long rush to reach us, I struck him with my left-hand barrel, the bullet entering between the neck and shoulder and piercing his heart. At the same instant Captain Slatter fired, his bullet entering the neck vertebrae. Ploughing up the ground with horn and feet, the great bull rhino, still headed toward us, dropped just thirteen paces from where we stood.

This was a wicked charge, for the rhino meant mischief and came on with the utmost determination.

Leaving a couple of men with the dead rhino, to protect it from the Wakamba by day and the lions by night, we rode straight to camp, which we reached at sunset. It was necessary to get to work on the two dead beasts as soon as possible in order to be sure of preserving their skins.

On hearing of our success, Heller at once said that we ought to march out to the game that night so as to get to work by daylight. Moreover, we were not comfortable at leaving only two men with each carcass, for lions were both bold and plentiful.

The moon rose at eight and we started as soon as she was above the horizon. We did not take the horses, because there was no water where we were going, and furthermore we did not like to expose them to a possible attack by lions.

The march out by moonlight was good fun, for though I had been out all day, I had been riding, not walking, and so was not tired. A hundred porters went with us so as to enable us to do the work quickly and bring back to camp the skins and all the meat needed, and these porters carried water, food for breakfast, and what little was necessary for a one-night camp. We tramped along in single file under the moonlight, up and down the hills, and through the scattered thorn forest. Kermit went first, and struck such a

pace that after an hour we had to halt him so as to let the
tail end of the file of porters catch up. Then Captain Slatter
and I set a more decorous pace, keeping the porters close
up in line behind us. In another hour we began to go down
a long slope toward a pin-point of light in the distance which
we knew was the fire by the rhinoceros. The porters, like
the big children they were, felt in high feather, and began to
chant to an accompaniment of whistling and horn-blowing
as we tramped through the dry grass which was flooded with
silver by the moon, now high in the heavens.

As soon as we reached the rhino, Heller with his Wakamba skinners pushed forward the three-quarters of a mile
to the eland, returning after midnight with the skin and
all the best parts of the meat.

Around the dead rhino the scene was lit up both by the
moon and by the flicker of the fires. The porters made their
camp under a small tree a dozen rods to one side of the
carcass, building a low circular fence of branches on which
they hung their bright-colored blankets, two or three big
fires blazing to keep off possible lions. Half as far on the
other side of the rhino a party of naked savages had established their camp, if camp it could be called, for really
all they did was to squat down round a couple of fires with
a few small bushes disposed round about. The rhino had
been opened, and they had already taken out of the carcass
what they regarded as tidbits and what we certainly did not
grudge them. Between the two camps lay the huge dead
beast, his hide glistening in the moonlight. In each camp the
men squatted around the fires chatting and laughing as they
roasted strips of meat on long sticks, the fitful blaze play-

ing over them, now leaving them in darkness, now bringing them out into a red relief. Our own tent was pitched under another tree a hundred yards off, and when I went to sleep, I could still hear the drumming and chanting of our feasting porters; the savages were less at ease, and their revel was quiet.

The following day I again rode out with Captain Slatter. During the morning we saw nothing except the ordinary game. After lunch we scanned the country round about with our glasses and made out three giraffes a mile and a half in our front. We mounted our horses and rode toward where the three tall beasts stood, on an open hillside with trees thinly scattered over it. Half a mile from them we left the horses in a thick belt of timber beside a dry watercourse, and went forward on foot.

I was carrying the Winchester loaded with full metal-patched bullets. I wished to get for the museum both a bull and a cow. One of the three giraffes was much larger than the other two, and as he was evidently a bull I thought the two others were cows.

As we reached the tree the giraffes showed symptoms of uneasiness. One of the smaller ones began to make off, and both the others shifted their positions slightly, curling their tails. I instantly dropped on my knee, and getting the bead just behind the big bull's shoulder, I fired with the three-hundred-yard sight. I heard the "pack" of the bullet as it struck just where I aimed, and away went all three giraffes at their queer rocking-horse canter. Running forward, I emptied my magazine, firing at the big bull and also at one of his smaller companions, and then, slipping into the barrel what proved to be a soft-nosed bullet, I fired at the latter again. The giraffe was going straightaway and it was a long shot, at four or five hundred yards but, by good luck, the bullet broke its back and down it came. The others were now getting over the crest of the hill, but the big one was evidently sick, and we called and beckoned to the two saises to hurry up with the horses. The moment they arrived we jumped on, and Captain Slatter cantered up a neighboring hill so as to mark the direction in which the giraffes went if I lost sight of them. Meanwhile I rode full speed after the giant quarry. I was on the tranquil sorrel, the horse I much preferred in riding down game of any kind, because he had a fair turn of speed, and yet was good about letting me get on and off. As soon as I reached the hill crest I saw the giraffes ahead of me, not as far off as I had feared, and I raced toward them without regard to rotten ground and wart-hog holes. The wounded one lagged behind, but when I got near he put on a spurt, and as I thought I was close enough I leaped off, throwing the reins over the sorrel's head, and opened fire. Down went the big bull, and I thought my task was done. But as I went back to mount the sorrel he struggled to his feet again and disappeared after his companion among the trees, which were thicker here, as we had reached the bottom of the valley. So I tore after him again, and in a minute came to a dry watercourse. Scrambling into and out of this I saw the giraffes ahead of me just beginning the ascent of the opposite slope and, touching the horse with the spur, we flew after the wounded bull. This time I made up my mind I would get up close enough but Tranquillity did not quite like the look of the thing ahead of him. He did not refuse to come up to the giraffe, but he evidently felt that, with such an object close by and evident in the landscape, it behooved him to be careful as to what might be hidden therein, and he shied so at each bush we passed that we progressed in a series of loops. So off I jumped, throwing the reins over his head, and opened fire once more; and this time the great bull went down for good.

Tranquillity recovered his nerve at once and grazed contentedly while I admired the huge proportions and beautiful coloring of my prize. In a few minutes Captain Slatter loped up, and the gun-bearers and saises followed. As if by magic, three or four Wakamba turned up immediately afterward, their eyes glistening at the thought of the feast ahead for the whole tribe. It was mid-afternoon, and there was no time to waste. My sais, Simba, an excellent long-distance runner, was sent straight to camp to get Heller and pilot him back to the dead giraffes. Beside each of the latter, for they had fallen a mile apart, we left a couple of men to build fires. Then we rode toward camp. To my regret, the smaller giraffe turned out to be a young bull and not a cow.

Chapter 4

Hippo and Leopard Hunting

THE SAFARI next went to Juja Farm, which lay on the edge of the Athi Plains northeast of the Kapiti Plains. The farmhouse (or ranchhouse) was near the junction of two small rivers, the Nairobi and Rewero. It was a one-story building with a vine-shaded veranda all around it. This was a large ranch with many outbuildings, large flocks and herds, a cornfield, a vegetable garden, and immediately in front of the house "a very pretty flower garden carefully tended by unsmiling Kikuyu savages. Their ears were slit to enable them to stretch the lobes to an almost unbelievable extent, and in these apertures they wore fantastically carved native ornaments. One of them, whose arms and legs were massive with copper and iron bracelets, had been given a blanket because he had no other garment. He got along quite well with the blanket excepting when he had to use the lawnmower, and then he would usually wrap the blanket around his neck and handle the lawn-mower with the evident feeling that he had done all that the most exacting conventionalism could require."

The host and hostess at Juja Farm were Mr. and Mrs. W. N. McMillan. McMillan and Selous were to go on a safari in a few days and in the meantime they let Roosevelt and his party use a professional hunter, Mr. W. Judd, who was going to accompany them.

Game came right around the house. Hartebeests, wilde-beests, and zebras grazed in sight on the open plain. The hippopotami that lived close by in the river came out at night into the garden. A couple of years before a rhino had come down into the same garden in broad daylight, and quite wantonly attacked one of the Kikuyu laborers, tossing him and breaking his thigh. It had then passed by the house out to the plain, where it saw an ox-cart, which it immedi-ately attacked and upset, cannoning off after its charge and passing up through the span of oxen, breaking all the yokes but fortunately not killing an animal. Then it met one of the men of the house on horseback, immediately assailed him, and was killed for its pains.

In the open woods which marked the border between the barren plains and the forested valley of the Athi, Kermit and I shot water-buck and impala. The water-buck is a stately antelope with long, coarse gray hair and fine carriage of the head and neck; the male alone carries horns. The impala were found in exactly the same kind of country as the water-buck, and often associated with them. To my mind they are among the most beautiful of all antelope.

They are about the size of a white-tailed deer, their beautiful annulated horns making a single spiral, and their coat is
like satin with its contrasting shades of red and white. They
have the most graceful movements of any animal I know,
and it is extraordinary to see a herd start off when frightened, both bucks and does bounding clear over the tops
of the tall bushes, with a peculiar bird-like motion and lightness.

In one case I had just killed a water-buck cow, hitting
it at a considerable distance and by a lucky fluke, after a
good deal of bad shooting. We started the porters in with
the water-buck, and then rode west through an open country, dotted here and there with trees and with occasional
ant-hills. In a few minutes we saw an impala buck, and I
crept up behind an ant-hill and obtained a shot at about
two hundred and fifty yards. The buck dropped, and as I
was putting in another cartridge I said to Judd that I didn't
like to see an animal drop like that, so instantaneously, as
there was always the possibility that it might only be creased,
and that if an animal so hurt got up, it always went off
exactly as if unhurt. When we raised our eyes again to look
for the impala it had vanished. I was sure that we would
never see it again, but we walked in the direction toward
which its head had been pointed, and Judd ascended an
ant-hill to scan the surrounding country with his glasses.
He did so, and after a minute remarked that he could not
see the wounded impala when a sudden movement caused
us to look down, and there it was, lying at our very feet,
on the side of the ant-hill, unable to rise.

When, after arranging for this impala to be carried back

to the farm, we returned to where our horses had been left, the boys told us with much excitement that there was a large snake near by. Sure enough a few yards off, coiled up in the long grass under a small tree, was a python. I could not see it distinctly, and using a solid bullet I just missed the backbone, the bullet going through the body about its middle. Immediately the snake lashed at me with open jaws, and then, uncoiling, came gliding rapidly in our direction. I do not think it was charging; I think it was merely trying to escape. But Judd, who was utterly unmoved by lion, leopard, or rhino, evidently held this snake in respect, and yelled to me to get out of the way. Accordingly, I jumped back a few feet, and the snake came over the ground where I had stood; its evil genius then made it halt for a moment and raise its head to a height of perhaps three feet, and I killed it by a shot through the neck. The porters were much wrought up about the snake, and did not at all like my touching it and taking it up, first by the tail and then by the head. It was only twelve feet long. We tied it to a long stick and sent it in by two porters.

Kermit had a bit of deserved good luck. While the main body of us went down the river-bed, he and McMillan, with a few natives, beat up a side ravine, down the middle of which ran the usual dry watercourse fringed with patches of brush. In one of these they put up a leopard, and saw it slinking forward ahead of them through the bushes. Then they lost sight of it, and came to the conclusion that it was in a large thicket. So Kermit went on one side of it and McMillan on the other, and the beaters approached to try and get the leopard out. But the leopard did not wait to be driven. Without any warning, out he came and charged straight at Kermit, who stopped him when he was but six yards off with a bullet in the forepart of the body. The leopard turned, and as he galloped back Kermit hit him again, crippling him in the hips. The wounds were fatal, and they would have knocked the fight out of any animal less plucky and savage than the leopard, but, not even in Africa, is there a beast of more unflinching courage than this spotted cat. The beaters were much excited by the sight of the charge and one of them, who was on McMillan's side of the thicket, went too near it, and out came the wounded leopard at him. It was badly crippled or it would have got the beater at once. As it was, it was slowly over-taking him as he ran through the tall grass, when McMillan, standing on an ant-heap, shot it again. Yet, in spite of having this third bullet in it, it ran down the beater and seized him, worrying him with teeth and claws. It was weak because of its wounds, and the powerful savage wrenched himself free, while McMillan fired into the beast again, and back it went through the long grass into the thicket. There was a pause, and the wounded beater was removed to a place of safety, while a messenger was sent on to us to bring up the Boer dogs. But while they were waiting, the leopard, on its own initiative, came again straight at Kermit, and this time it dropped dead to Kermit's bullet. No animal could have shown a more fearless and resolute temper. It was an old female, but small, its weight being a little short of seventy pounds.

The rivers that bounded Juja Farm, not only the Athi, but the Nairobi and Rewero, contained hippopotami and crocodiles in the deep pools. Early one morning Judd and I rode off across the plains, through the herds of grazing game seen dimly in the dawn, to the Athi. We reached the river, and, leaving our horses, went down into the wooded bottom, soon after sunrise. Judd had with him a Masai, a keen-eyed hunter, and I my two gun-bearers. We advanced with the utmost caution toward the brink of a great pool. As we crept noiselessly up to the steep bank which edged the pool, the sight was typically African. On the still water floated a crocodile, nothing but his eyes and nostrils visible. The bank was covered with a dense growth of trees, festooned with vines. Among the branches sat herons. A little cormorant dived into the water and a very small and brilliantly colored king-fisher with a red beak and large turquoise crest, perched unheedingly within a few feet of us. Here and there a dense growth of the tall and singularly graceful papyrus rose out of the water, the feathery heads, which crowned the long smooth green stems, waving gently to and fro.

We scanned the waters carefully, and could see no sign of hippos, and, still proceeding with the utmost caution, we moved a hundred yards farther down to another lookout. Here the Masai detected a hippo head a long way off on the other side of the pool. We again drew back and started cautiously forward to reach the point opposite which he had seen the head.

But just as we had about reached the point at which we had intended to turn in toward the pool, there was a succession of snorts in our front and the sound of the trampling of heavy feet and of a big body being shoved through a dense mass of tropical bush. My companions called to me in loud whispers that it was a rhinoceros coming at us, and to "Shoot, shoot." In another moment the rhinoceros appeared, twitching its tail and tossing and twisting its head from side to side as it came toward us. It did not seem to have very good horns, and I would much rather not have killed it, but there hardly seemed any alternative, for it certainly showed every symptom of being bent on mischief. My first shot, at under forty yards, produced no effect whatever, except to hasten its approach. I was using the Winchester, with full-jacketed bullets. My second bullet went in between the neck and shoulder, bringing it to a halt. I fired into the shoulder again, and as it turned toward the bush I fired into its flank.

For a moment or two after it disappeared we heard the branches crash, and then there was silence. In such cover a wounded rhino requires cautious handling, and as quietly as possible we walked through the open forest along the edge of the dense thicket into which the animal had returned. The thicket was a tangle of thorn-bushes, reeds, and small, low-branching trees. It was impossible to see ten feet through it, and a man could only penetrate it with the utmost slowness and difficulty, whereas the movements of the rhino were very little impeded. At the far end of the thicket we examined the grass to see if the rhino had passed out, and sure enough there was the spoor, with so much blood along both sides that it was evident the animal was badly hit. It led across this space and into another thicket of the same character as the first. Again we stole cautiously along the edge some ten yards out. I had taken the heavy

Holland double-barrel, and with the safety-catch pressed forward under my thumb, I trod gingerly through the grass, peering into the thicket and expectant of developments. In a minute there was a furious snorting and crashing directly opposite us in the thicket, and I brought up my rifle. But the rhino did not quite place us, and broke out of the cover in front, some thirty yards away. I put both barrels into and behind the shoulder. The terrific striking force of the heavy gun told at once, and the rhino wheeled, and struggled back into the thicket, and we heard it fall. With the utmost caution, bending and creeping under the branches, we made our way in, and saw the beast lying with its head toward us. We thought it was dead, but would take no chances and I put in another, but as it proved needless, heavy bullet.

McMillan sent out an ox-wagon and brought it in to the house, where we weighed it. It was a little over two thousand two hundred pounds. It had evidently been in the neighborhood in which we found it for a considerable time, for a few hundred yards away we found its stamping-ground, a circular spot where the earth had been all trampled up and kicked about, according to the custom of rhinoceroses.

In the afternoon of the day on which we killed the rhino Judd took me out again to try for hippos, this time in the Rewero, which ran close by the house. We rode upstream a couple of miles. Then we sent back our horses and walked down the river-bank as quietly as possible, Judd scanning the pools, and the eddies in the running stream, from every point of vantage. Once we aroused a crocodile, which plunged into the water. The stream was full of fish, some of considerable size; and in the meadow-land on our side we saw a gang of big, black wild geese feeding. But we got within half a mile of McMillan's house without seeing a hippo, and the light was rapidly fading. Judd announced that we would go home, but took one last look around the next bend, and instantly sank to his knees, beckoning to me. I crept forward on all fours, and he pointed out to me an object in the stream, fifty yards off, under the overhanging branch of a tree, which jutted out from the steep bank opposite. In that light I should not myself have recognized it as a hippo head; but it was one, looking toward us, with the ears up and the nostrils, eyes, and forehead above water. I aimed for the center; the sound told that the bullet had struck somewhere on the head, and the animal disappeared without a splash. Judd was sure I had killed, but I was by no means so confident myself, and there was no way of telling until next morning, for the hippo always sinks when shot and does not rise to the surface for several hours. Accordingly, back we walked to the house.

At sunrise next morning Cuninghame, Judd, and I, with a crowd of porters, were down at the spot. There was a very leaky boat in which Cuninghame, Judd, and I embarked, intending to drift and paddle downstream while the porters walked along the bank. We did not have far to go, for as we rounded the first point we heard the porters break into guttural exclamations of delight, and there ahead of us, by a little island of papyrus, was the dead hippo. With the help of the boat it was towed to a convenient landing-place, and then the porters dragged it ashore. It was a cow, of good size for one dwelling in a small river, where they never approach the dimensions of those making their homes in a great lake like the Victoria Nyanza. This one weighed nearly two thousand eight hundred pounds, and I could well believe that a big lake bull would weigh between three and four tons.

Chapter 5

A Buffalo Hunt

THE NEXT hunt was for buffalo on the Kamiti, an affluent of the Nairobi, a queer little stream, running for most of its course through a broad swamp of tall papyrus, which often grew to a height of twenty feet, only inches apart. Thus it was impossible to see for more than a few feet or to penetrate the papyrus at all. The water and mud were hip deep. The semi-aquatic buffalo lived in the swamp and were able, because of their huge bulk and enormous strength, to plough through the mud and water and burst their way through the papyrus stems. They had made paths three feet deep in ooze and black water hither and thither through the swamp. Toward the lower end of the Kamiti, where it ran into the Nairobi, the stream emerged from the swamp as a rapid brown mass of water with only here and there a clump of papyrus on its bank.

One evening as I galloped through a world of dim shade and dying color, my horse suddenly halted on the brink of a deep ravine from out of which came the thunder of a cataract. I reined up on a jutting point. The snowy masses of the Nairobi Falls foamed over a ledge to my right, and below at my feet was a great pool of swirling water. Thick-foliaged trees, of strange shape and festooned with creepers, climbed the sheer sides of the ravine. A black-and-white eagle perched in a blasted treetop in front and the bleached skull of a long-dead rhinoceros glimmered white near the brink to one side. It was a sight I long remembered.

The most interesting birds we saw in this region were the black whydah-finches. The female is a dull-colored, ordinary-looking bird, somewhat like a female bobolink. The male in his courtship dress is clad in a uniform dark glossy suit, and his tail-feathers are almost like some of those of a barn-yard rooster, being over twice as long as the rest of the bird, with a downward curve at the tips. The long tail hampers the bird in its flight, and it is often held at rather an angle downward, giving the bird a peculiar and almost insect-like appearance. But the marked and extraordinary peculiarity was the custom the cocks had of dancing in artificially made dancing-rings. For a mile and a half beyond our camp, down the course of the Kamiti, the grass-land at the edge of the papyrus was thickly strewn with these dancing-rings. Each was about two feet in diameter, sometimes more, sometimes less. A tuft of growing grass perhaps a foot high was left in the center. Over the rest of the ring the grass was cut off close by the roots, and the blades strewn evenly over the surface of the ring. The cock bird would alight in the ring and hop to a height of a couple of feet, wings spread and motionless, tail drooping, and the head usually thrown back. As he came down he might or might not give an extra couple of little hops. After a few seconds he would repeat the motion, sometimes remaining almost in the same place, at other times going forward during and between the hops so as finally to go completely round the ring. As there were many scores of these dancing-places within a comparatively limited territory, the effect was rather striking when a large number of birds were dancing at the same time. As one walked along, the impression conveyed by the birds continually popping above the grass and then immediately sinking back, was somewhat as if a man was making peas jump in a tin tray by tapping on it. The favorite dancing times were in the early morning, and, to a less extent, in the evening. We saw dancing-places of every age, some with the cut grass which strewed the floor green and fresh, others with the grass dried into hay and the bare earth showing through.

But the game we were after was the buffalo-herd that haunted the papyrus swamp.

The first day we saw the buffalo, to the number of seventy or eighty, grazing in the open, some hundreds of yards from the papyrus swamp, and this shortly after noon. For a mile from the papyrus swamp the country was an absolutely flat plain, gradually rising into a gentle slope. We saw herds come out to graze at ten o'clock in the morning, and again at three in the afternoon. They usually remained out several hours, first grazing and then lying down. Flocks of the small white cow-heron usually accompanied them, the birds stalking about among them or perching on their backs; and occasionally the whereabouts of the herd in the papyrus swamp could be determined by seeing the flock of herons perched on the papyrus tops.

Not only the natives but the whites were inclined to avoid the immediate neighborhood of the papyrus swamp, for there had been one or two narrow escapes from unprovoked attacks by the buffalo.

The morning after making our camp, we started at dawn for the buffalo-ground, Kermit and I, Cuninghame and a Boer farmer with three big, powerful dogs. We walked near the edge of the swamp. The whydah-birds were continually bobbing up and down in front of us as they rose and fell on their dancing-places, while the Kavirondo cranes called mournfully all around. Before we had gone two miles, buffalo were spied, well ahead, feeding close to the papyrus. The line of the papyrus which marked the edge of the swamp was not straight, but broken by projections and indentations; and by following it closely and cutting cautiously across the points, the opportunity for stalking was good. As there was not a tree of any kind anywhere near, we had to rely purely on our shooting to prevent damage from the buffalo. Kermit and I had our double-barrels, with the Winchesters as spare guns, while Cuninghame carried a 577.

Cautiously threading our way along the edge of the swamp, we got within a hundred and fifty yards of the buffalo before we were perceived. There were four bulls, grazing close by the edge of the swamp, their black bodies glistening in the early sun-rays, their massive horns showing white, and the cow-herons perched on their backs. They stared sullenly at us with outstretched heads from under their great frontlets of horn. The biggest of the four stood a little out from the other three, and at him I fired, the bullet telling with a smack on the tough hide and going through the lungs. We had been afraid they would at once turn into the papyrus, but instead of this they started straight across our front directly for the open country. This was a piece of huge good luck. Kermit put his first barrel into the second bull, and I my second barrel into one of the others, after which it became impossible to say which bullet struck which animal, as the firing became general. They ran a quarter of a mile into the open, and then the big bull I had first shot, and which had no other bullet in him, dropped dead, while the other three, all of which were wounded, halted beside him. We walked toward them, rather expecting a charge; but when we were still over two hundred yards away they started back for the swamp, and we began firing. The distance being long, I used my Winchester. Aiming well before one bull, he dropped to the shot as if poleaxed, falling straight on his back with his legs kicking; but in a moment he was up again and after the others. Later I found that the bullet, a full-metal patch, had struck him in the head but did not penetrate to the brain, and merely stunned him for the moment. All the time we kept running diagonally to their line of flight. They were all three badly wounded, and when they reached the tall rank grass, high as a man's head, which fringed the papyrus swamp, the two foremost lay down, while the last one, the one I had floored with the Winchester, turned, and with nose outstretched began to come toward us. He was badly crippled, however, and with a soft-nosed bullet from my heavy Holland I knocked him down, this time for good. The other two then rose, and though each was again hit they reached the swamp, one of them to our right, the other to the left where the papyrus came out in a point.

We decided to go after the latter, and advancing very cautiously toward the edge of the swamp, put in the three big dogs. A moment after, they gave tongue within the papyrus; then we heard the savage grunt of the buffalo and saw its form just within the reeds; and as the rifles cracked, down it went.

Our three bulls were fine trophies. The largest, with the largest horns, was the first killed, being the one that fell to my first bullet; yet it was the youngest of the three. The other two were old bulls. The second one killed had smaller horns than the other, but the bosses met in the middle of the forehead for a space of several inches, making a solid shield.

Heller was soon on the ground with his skinning tent and skinners, and the Boer farmer went back to fetch the ox-wagon on which the skins and meat were brought into camp.

It was three days later before we were again successful with buffalo. On this occasion we started about eight in the morning, having come to the conclusion that the herd was more apt to leave the papyrus late than early. Our special object was to get a cow. We intended to take advantage of a small half-dried water-course, an affluent of the Kamiti, which began a mile beyond where we had killed our bulls, and for three or four miles ran in a course generally parallel to the swamp, and at a distance which varied, but averaged perhaps a quarter of a mile. When we reached the beginning of this watercourse, we left our horses and walked along it. Like all such watercourses, it wound in curves. The banks were four or five feet high, the bottom was sometimes dry and sometimes contained reedy pools, while at intervals there were clumps of papyrus. We caught a glimpse of several buffalo and crept up the watercourse until about opposite them. They were now lying down. There were patches where the grass was short, and other places where it was three feet high, and after a good deal of cautious crawling we had covered half the distance toward them, when one of them made us out, and several rose from their beds. They were still at least two hundred yards off—a long range for heavy rifles; but any closer approach was impossible, and we fired. Both the leading bulls were hit, and at the shots there rose from the grass not half a dozen buffalo, but seventy or eighty, and started at a gallop parallel to the swamp and across our front. In the rear were a number of cows and calves, and I at once singled out a cow and fired. She plunged forward at the shot and turned toward the swamp, going slowly and dead lame, for my bullet had struck the shoulder and had gone into the cavity of the chest. But at this moment our attention was distracted from the wounded cow by the conduct of the herd, which, headed by the wounded bulls, turned in a quarter-circle toward us, and drew up in a phalanx facing us with outstretched heads. It was not a nice country in which to be charged by the herd, and for a moment things trembled in the balance. There was a perceptible motion of uneasiness among some of our followers. "Stand steady! Don't run!" I called out. "And don't shoot!" called out Cuninghame; for to do either would invite a charge. A few seconds passed, and then the unwounded mass of the herd resumed their flight, and after a little hesitation the wounded bulls followed. We now turned our attention to the wounded cow, which was close to the papyrus. She went down to our shots, but the reeds and marsh-grass were above our heads when we drew close to the swamp. We loosed the two dogs. They took up the trail and went some little distance into the papyrus, where we heard them give tongue, and immediately afterward there came the angry grunt of the wounded buffalo. It had risen and gone off thirty yards into the papyrus, although mortally wounded—the frothy blood from the lungs was actually coming out of my first bullet-hole. Its anger now made it foolish, and it followed the dogs to the edge of the papyrus. Here we caught a glimpse of it. Down it went to our shots, and in a minute we heard the moaning bellow which a wounded buffalo often gives before dying.

Among the sights Theodore saw here was a forest of wild fig trees. This tree begins as a huge parasite vine and ends up as one of the largest and most stately, one of the greenest and most shady, trees in this part of Africa. Its chief victim is the mahogo-tree, a kind of sandalwood. "It grows up the mahogo as a vine and gradually, by branching, and by the spreading of the branches, completely envelops the trunk and also grows along each limb, and sends out great limbs of its own. Every stage can be seen, from that in which the big vine has begun to grow up along the still flourishing mahogo, through that in which the tree looks like a curious composite, the limbs and thick foliage of the fig branching out among the limbs and scanty foliage of the still living mahogo, to the stage in which the mahogo is simply a dead skeleton seen here and there through the trunk or the foliage of the fig. Finally nothing remains but the fig, which grows to be a huge tree."

Chapter 6

The Sotik

THE PARTY started south from Kijabe, a town northeast of Kapiti Plains, on June 5, 1909, to trek through "the thirst"—a waterless country—for a hunt in the Sotik, in the southernmost part of the Southern Hunting Preserve close to the border of German East Africa. The sixty miles across "the thirst" could have been ridden by horseback in a night, but it was a long tedious trip for the porters. Additional transportation was needed so four ox wagons were hired.

The march went on by both day and night, the longest halt being in the middle of the day. To spare the porters, and to save time, camp was not made. Theodore and Kermit took nothing but army overcoats, rifles and cartridges, and three canteens of water apiece. The oxen would be without water for three days.

The trail led first through open brush, or low, dry forest,

and then out on to the vast plains, where the withered
grass was dotted here and there with low, scantily leaved
thorn bushes from three to eight feet high. The dust rose
in clouds from the dry earth covering all of them. In the
distance herds of zebra and hartebeest gazed at them as they
passed.

Just before nightfall they halted on the farther side of a
dry watercourse. The safari "came up singing and whistling,
and the men put down their loads, lit fires, and with chatter
and laughter prepared their food. The horses were fed. We
had tea, with bread and cold meat—and a most delicious
meal it was—and then lay dozing beside the bush fires."

At half past eight, the moon having risen, they were off
again. Sometimes they rode, sometimes they walked to ease
their horses. Higher and higher rose the moon, and brighter
grew the flood of her light. They halted again at midnight.
The air was cool and the fires felt good. After two hours
sleep, with rifles ready in case of an attack by dangerous
animals, they were off again at three. For four more hours
they travelled steadily, first through the moonlight and then
through the reddening dawn. Jackals shrieked, and the
plains plover wailed and scolded as they circled round them.
When the sun was well up they halted again. "The horses
were fed, were given half a pail of water apiece, and were
turned loose to graze with the oxen. This was the last time
the oxen would feed freely, unless there was rain and this
was to be our longest halt." They started again after noon.
The country grew hilly and brushy. They travelled until
nearly sunset, when they halted at the foot of a steep divide,
beyond which their course lay across slopes that fell gradually to the stream for which they were heading.

The porters were given all of the food and water they wished. From here it was safe to start the safari and then leave it to come on by itself, while the ox-wagons came later. Black clouds had thickened in the west and gusts of rain blew in their faces. At one o'clock they halted, in the rain, for a couple of hours' rest. They lay down on the drenched grass, with saddle cloths over their feet, and their heads on their saddles, and slept comfortably. At three they mounted and pressed on until by six o'clock they crossed over the little Suavi River. It was half past ten before the safari arrived and the porters were told that they would have an extra day's rations as well as a day's rest. Camp was pitched and everyone soon asleep, though the lions moaned near by.

After a day's rest, they pushed on, in two days' easy travelling, to the river, Guaso Nyero, of the south. Here the camps were pleasant, by running streams of swift water. "One was really beautiful, in a grassy bend of a rapid little river, by huge African yew trees, with wooded cliffs in front."

They halted by the Guaso Nyero for several days. The day after reaching camp Theodore rode off by himself accompanied by two gun bearers and a dozen porters to carry in the game.

Half a mile from camp I saw a buck tommy with a good head and, as we needed his delicious venison for our own table, I dismounted and killed him as he faced me at two hundred and ten yards. I rode on toward two topi [a kind of antelope] I saw far in front. Bu there were zebra, hartebeest and wildebeest in between, all of which ran as did the topi. I was still walking after them when we made out two

eland bulls ahead and to our left. Leaving my horse and the
porters to follow slowly, the gunbearers and I walked quartering toward them. When I had come as close as I dared,
I motioned to the two gun bearers to continue walking, and
dropped on one knee. I had the little Springfield, and was
anxious to test the new sharp-pointed military bullet on
some large animal. The biggest bull was half facing me, just
two hundred and eighty yards off. The tiny ball broke his
back and the splendid beast, heavy as a prize steer, came
plunging and struggling to the ground. The other bull
started to run off, but after I had walked a hundred yards
forward, he actually trotted back toward his companion,
then halted, turned, and galloped across my front at a
distance of a hundred and eighty yards. Him too I brought
down with a single shot.

I was much pleased with my two prizes, for the National
Museum particularly desired a good group of eland. They
were splendid animals, like beautiful heavy cattle, with
sleek, handsome, striped coats, shapely heads, fine horns and
massive bodies.

At last we spied a herd of topi, distinguishable from the
hartebeest at a very long distance by their dark coloring, the
purples and browns giving the coat a heavy shading which
when far off, in certain lights, looks almost black. They did
not run clear away, but let me approach to distances varying
from 450 to 600 yards. I fired many times before getting my
topi at just 520 yards. It was a handsome cow, weighing 260
pounds. The beauty of its coat, in texture and coloring,
struck me afresh as I looked at the sleek creature stretched
out on the grass.

The next day, on a long hunt to a high, rocky hill, several miles away, they passed up three rhinos, a bull, a cow and a big calf, as they did not have unusual horns. Theodore missed a long shot at a hyena. Another rhino was passed four hundred yards to the leeward and left alive as it did not charge. Just opposite it they saw another hyena.

Tarlton, whose eye for distance was good, told me the hyena was over three hundred yards off. I put up the three-hundred-yard sight, and drew a rather coarse bead, and down went the hyena with its throat cut. As soon as I had pulled the trigger I wheeled to watch the rhino. It started round at the shot and gazed toward us with its ears cocked forward, but made no movement to advance.

While a couple of porters were dressing the hyena, I could not help laughing at finding that we were the center of a thoroughly African circle of deeply interested spectators. We were in the middle of a vast plain, covered with sun-scorched grass and here and there a stunted thorn. In the background were isolated barren hills, and the mirage wavered in the distance. Vultures wheeled overhead. The rhino, less than half a mile away, stared steadily at us. Wildebeest—their heavy fore quarters and the carriage of their heads making them look like bison—and hartebeest were somewhat nearer, in a ring all round us, intent upon our proceedings. Four topi became so much interested that they approached within two hundred and fifty yards and stood motionless. A buck tommy came even closer, and a zebra trotted by at about the same distance, uttering its queer bark or neigh. It continued its course past the rhino,

and started a new train of ideas in the latter's muddled rep-
tilian brain. Round it wheeled, gazed after the zebra, and
then evidently concluded that everything was normal, for
it lay down to sleep.

*A little while later Theodore killed a lioness, a large one
that weighed over three hundred pounds. The porters wished
to carry the body whole into camp. By now it was dark.
Again and again they heard lions. Before getting back to
camp they came to a Masai kraal, a big oval, with a thick
wall of thorn-bushes, eight feet high, with low huts just
inside it, and shelters for cattle and sheep in the center.*

The fires flamed here and there within, and as we approached we heard the talking and laughing of men and
women, and the lowing and bleating of the pent-up herds
and flocks. We hailed loudly, explaining our needs. At first
they were very suspicious. They told us we could not bring
the lion within, because it would frighten the cattle, but
after some parley consented to our building a fire outside,
and skinning the animal. They passed two brands over the
thorn fence, and our men speedily kindled a blaze, and
drew the lioness beside it. By this time the Masai were re-
assured, and a score of their warriors, followed soon by half
a dozen women, came out through a small opening in the
fence, and crowded close around the fire, with boisterous,
noisy good humor. They showed a tendency to chaff our
porters. But they were entirely friendly, and offered me cal-
abashes of milk. The men were tall, finely shaped savages,
their hair plastered with red mud, and drawn out into long-

ish ringlets. They were naked except for a blanket worn, not round the loins, but over the shoulders. The women had pleasant faces, and were laden with metal ornaments—chiefly wire anklets, bracelets, and necklaces—of many pounds weight.

Our gun-bearers worked at the skinning, and answered the jests of their war-like friends with the freedom of men who themselves followed a dangerous trade. The two horses stood quiet just outside the circle and, over all, the firelight played and leaped.

It was after ten when we reached camp, and I enjoyed a hot bath and a shave before sitting down to a supper of eland venison and broiled fowl. No supper ever tasted more delicious.

The next camp was in the middle of a vast plain, near some limestone springs, at one end of a line of dark acacias. Little rocky koppies, or hills bounded it on either side. From the tents game could be seen grazing on the open flats, or among the scattered wizened thorn trees.

During the next few days additional giraffes were killed to complete the specimens for the museums. They also needed rhinos with good horns.

One day, when Kermit and I were out alone with our gun-bearers we saw a rhino, a bull, with a stubby horn. "Look at him," said Kermit, "standing there in the middle of the African plain, deep in pre-historic thought."

At last a day came when I saw a rhino with a big body and a good horn. We had been riding for a couple of hours;

the game was all around us. At last Bakhari, the gun-bearer, pointed to a gray mass on the plain, and a glance through the glasses showed that it was a rhino lying asleep with his legs doubled under him. He proved to be a big bull, with a front horn nearly twenty-six inches long. When we were a hundred yards off he rose and faced us, huge and threatening, head up and tail erect. But he lacked heart after all. I fired into his throat, and instead of charging, he whipped round and was off at a gallop, immediately disappearing over a slight rise. We ran back to our horses, mounted, and galloped after him. He had a long start, and, though evidently feeling his wound, was going strong, and it was some time before we overtook him. I tried to gallop alongside, but he kept swerving, so jumping off (fortunately, I was riding Tranquillity) I emptied the magazine at his quarters and flank. Rapid galloping does not tend to promote accuracy of aim; the rhino went on; and, remounting, I followed, overtook him, and repeated the performance. This time he wheeled and faced round, evidently with the intention of charging, but a bullet straight in his chest took all the fight out of him, and he continued his flight. But his race was evidently run, and when I next overtook him I brought him down. In all we galloped four miles after this wounded rhino bull.

After getting the bull rhino, Heller needed a cow and calf to complete the group, and Kermit and I got him what he needed, one day when we were out alone with our gun-bearers. About the middle of the forenoon we made out the huge gray bulk of the rhino, standing in the bare plain, with not so much as a bush two feet high within miles, and we soon also made out her calf beside her. Getting the wind right we rode up within a quarter of a mile, and then dismounted and walked slowly toward her. It seemed impossible that on that bare plain we could escape even her dull vision, for she stood with her head in our direction. Yet she did not see us, and actually lay down as we walked toward her. Careful examination through the glasses showed that she was an unusually big cow, with thick horns of fair length—twenty-three inches and thirteen inches respectively. Accordingly we proceeded, making as little noise as possible. At fifty yards she made us out, and jumped to her feet with unwieldy agility. Kneeling I sent the bullet from the heavy Holland just in front of her right shoulder as she half faced me. It went through her vitals, lodging behind the opposite shoulder and, at once, she began the curious death waltz which is often, though by no means always, the sign of immediate dissolution in a mortally wounded rhino. We shot the calf, which when dying uttered a screaming whistle almost like that of a small steam-engine.

Next day we shifted camp to a rush-fringed pool by a grove of tall, flat-topped acacias at the foot of a range of low, steep mountains. Before us the plain stretched, and in front of our tents it was dotted by huge candelabra euphorbias.

Along toward mid-afternoon, of our first day's hunting here, we stopped at a little pool, to give the men and horses water. Kermit's horse suddenly went dead lame, and he went forward with us on foot, as we rode round the base of the first koppies. After we had gone a mile loud shouts called our attention to one of the men who had left with the lame horse. He was running back to tell us that they had just seen a big maned lion walking along in the open plain toward the body of a zebra he had killed the night before. Immediately Tarlton and I galloped in the direction indicated, while the heart-broken Kermit ran after us on foot, so as not to miss the fun. In a few minutes Tarlton pointed out the lion, a splendid old fellow, a heavy male with a yellow-and-black mane, and after him we went. There was no need to go fast. He was too burly and too savage to run hard, and we were anxious that our hands should be reasonably steady when we shot. The lion stopped and lay down behind a bush. Jumping off I took a shot at him at two hundred yards, but only wounded him slightly in one paw and, after a moment's sullen hesitation, off he went, lashing his tail. We mounted our horses and went after him. Tarlton lost sight of him, but I marked him lying down behind a low grassy ant-hill. Again we dismounted at a distance of two hundred yards, Tarlton telling me that now he was sure to charge.

Again I knelt and fired but the mass of hair on the lion made me think he was nearer than he was, and I undershot, inflicted a flesh wound that was neither crippling nor fatal. He was already grunting savagely and tossing his tail erect, with his head held low. At the shot the great sinewy beast came toward us with the speed of a greyhound. Tarlton then, very properly, fired, for lion-hunting is no child's play, and it is not good to run risks. Ordinarily it is a very mean thing to experience joy at a friend's miss but this was not an ordinary case, and I felt keen delight when the bullet from the badly sighted rifle missed, striking the ground many yards short. I was sighting carefully, from my knee, and I knew I had the lion all right, for though he galloped at a great pace, he came on steadily—ears laid back, and uttering terrific coughing grunts. There was now no question of making allowance for distance, nor, as he was out in the open, for the fact that he had not before been distinctly visible. The bead of my foresight was exactly on the center of his chest as I pressed the trigger, and the bullet went as true as if the place had been plotted with dividers. The blow brought him up all standing, and he fell forward on his head. The soft-nosed Winchester bullet had gone straight through the chest cavity, smashing the lungs and the big blood-vessels of the heart. Painfully he recovered his feet, and tried to come on, his ferocious courage holding out to the last. But he staggered, and turned from side to side, unable to stand firmly, still less to advance at a faster pace than a walk. He had not ten seconds to live but it is a sound principle to take no chances with lions. Tarlton hit him with his second bullet, probably in the shoulder, and with my next shot I broke his neck. I had stopped him when he was still a hundred yards away and certainly no finer sight could be imagined than that of this great maned lion as he charged. Kermit gleefully joined us as we walked up to the body. Only one of our followers had been able to keep up with him on his two miles' run. He had had a fine view of the charge, from one side, as he ran up, still three hundred yards distant. He could see all the muscles play as the lion galloped in, and then everything relax as he fell to the shock of my bullet.

The lion was a big old male, still in his prime. Between

uprights his length was nine feet four inches, and his weight 410 pounds, for he was not fat. We skinned him and started for camp, which we reached after dark. There was a thunder-storm in the southwest, and in the red sunset that burned behind us the rain-clouds turned to many gorgeous hues. Then daylight failed, the clouds cleared, and, as we made our way across the formless plain, the half-moon hung high overhead, strange stars shone in the brilliant heavens, and the Southern Cross lay radiant above the skyline.

Our next camp was pitched on a stony plain, by a wind-ing stream-bed still containing an occasional rush-fringed pool of muddy water.

At this camp we killed five poisonous snakes: a light-colored tree-snake, two puff-adders, and two seven-foot cobras. One of the latter three times "spat" or ejected its poison at us, the poison coming out from the fangs like white films or threads, to a distance of several feet. On the bigger puff-adder, some four feet long, were a dozen ticks, some swollen to the size of cherries.

One day Kermit had our first characteristic experience with a honey-bird; a smallish bird, with its beak like a gros-beak's and its toes like a woodpecker's, whose extraordinary habits as a honey-guide are known to all the natives of Africa throughout its range. Kermit had killed an eland bull, and while he was resting, his gun-bearers drew his attention to the calling of the honey-bird in a tree near by. He got up, and as he approached the bird, it flew into another tree in front and again began its twitter. This was repeated again and again as Kermit walked after it. Finally the bird darted round behind his followers, in the direction from which they had come, and, for a moment, they thought it had played them false. But immediately afterward they saw that it had merely overshot its mark, and had now flown back a few rods to the honey-tree, round which it was flitting, occasionally twittering. When they came toward the tree it perched silent and motionless in another, and thus continued while they took some honey—a risky business, as the bees were vicious. They did not observe what the bird then did; but Cuninghame told me that in one instance where a honey-bird led him to honey he carefully watched it and saw it picking up either bits of honey and comb, or else, more probably, the bee grubs out of the comb, he could not be certain which.

Chapter 7

Hippo Hunting on Lake Naivasha

THEODORE HAD killed almost all the specimens of the common game that were needed. From now on
he concentrated on game for meat, the skins and skeletons
of which were kept, and on fine specimens. "Now and then,
after a good stalk I would get a boar with unusually fine
tusks, a big gazelle with unusually long and graceful horns,
or a fine old wildebeest bull, its horns thick and battered,
its knees bare and calloused from its habit of going down on
them when fighting or threatening to fight."

At one point on the plains, near salt marshes where animals went to lick, a couple of rhinos charged the party.
Theodore calmly studied them, as they came on, to see if
their horns were worth saving. One of them—a cow—had
good horns. The wind shifted before the rhinos reached
them, and the huge beasts lost their scent. Then they had to
run the cow down. Her back horn was over two feet long.

302

From the camp on the Guaso Nyero they trekked in a little over four days to a point on Lake Naivasha where they intended to spend some time. The scenery was wild and beautiful. In the open places the ground was starred with flowers of many colors. Two or three times, in getting there, they "crossed singularly beautiful ravines, the trail winding through narrow clefts that were almost tunnels, and along the brinks of sheer cliffs, while the green mat of trees and vines was spangled with gay colored flowers."

Their camp was near the house of the Messrs. Attenborough, settlers on the shores of the lake. They had a steam launch and a big heavy rowboat which were used for hippohunting. At this camp Theodore presented the porters with twenty-five sheep, "as a recognition of their good conduct and hard work, whereupon they improvised long chants in my honor, and feasted royally."

The first day was spent in the rowboat in a series of lagoons. A broad belt of papyrus fringed the lagoons and jutted out between them. The straight green stalks with their feathery heads rose high and close, forming a mass so dense that it was practically impenetrable save where the huge bulk of the hippos had made tunnels. They saw no hippos that day.

On the second day we steamed down the lake, not far from the shore, for over ten miles, dragging the big, clumsy rowboat, in which Cuninghame had put three of our porters who knew how to row. Then we spied a big hippo walking entirely out of the water on the edge of the papyrus, at the farther end of a little bay which was filled with water-lilies. Thither we steamed, and when a few rods from the bay,

Cuninghame steered, Kermit carried his camera, and I steadied myself in the bow with the little Springfield rifle. The hippo was a self-confident, truculent beast. It went under water once or twice, but again came out to the papyrus and waded along the edge, its body out of water. We headed toward it, and thrust the boat in among the water-lilies, finding that the bay was shallow, from three to six feet deep. While still over a hundred yards from the hippo, I saw it turn as if to break into the papyrus, and at once fired into its shoulder, the tiny pointed bullet smashing the big bones. Round spun the great beast, plunged into the water, and with its huge jaws open came straight for the boat, floundering and splashing through the thick-growing water-lilies. I think that its chief object was to get to deep water; but we were between it and the deep water, and instead of trying to pass to one side it charged straight for the boat, with open jaws, bent on mischief. But I hit it again and again with the little sharp-pointed bullet. Once I struck it between the neck and shoulder; once, as it rushed forward with its huge jaws stretched to their threatening utmost, I fired right between them, whereat it closed them with the clash of a sprung bear trap, and then, when under the punishment it swerved for a moment, I hit it at the base of the ear, a brain shot which dropped it in its tracks. Meanwhile Kermit was busily taking photos of it as it charged, and, as he mentioned afterward, until it was dead he never saw it except in the "finder" of his camera.

Hitherto we had not obtained a bull hippo, and I made up my mind to devote myself to getting one, as otherwise the group for the museum would be incomplete. We steamed down the lake some fifteen miles to a wide bay, indented by smaller bays, lagoons, and inlets, all fringed by a broad belt of impenetrable papyrus, while the beautiful purple lilies, with their leathery-tough stems and broad surface-floating leaves, filled the shallows. At the mouth of the main bay we passed a floating island, a mass of papyrus perhaps a hundred and fifty acres in extent which had been broken off from the shore somewhere, and was floating over the lake as the winds happened to drive it.

In an opening in the dense papyrus masses we left the launch moored, and Cuninghame and I started in the row-boat to coast the green wall of tall, thick-growing, feather-topped reeds. Under the bright sunshine the shallow flats were alive with bird life. Gulls, both the gray-hooded and black-backed, screamed harshly overhead. The chestnut-colored lily-trotters tripped daintily over the lily-pads, and when they flew, had their long legs straight behind them, so that they looked as if they had tails like pheasants. Sacred ibis, white with naked black head and neck, stalked along the edge of the water, and on the bent papyrus small cormorants and herons perched. Everywhere there were coots and ducks, and crested grebes, big and little. Huge white pelicans floated on the water. Once we saw a string of flamingoes fly by, their plumage a wonderful red.

Immediately after leaving the launch we heard a hippo, hidden in the green fastness on our right, uttering a meditative soliloquy, consisting of a succession of squealing grunts. Then we turned a point, and in a little bay saw six or eight hippo, floating with their heads above water. There were two much bigger than the others, and Cuninghame, while of course unable to be certain, thought these were probably males. The smaller ones, including a cow and her calf, were not much alarmed, and floated quietly, looking at us, as we cautiously paddled and drifted nearer; but the bigger ones dove and began to work their way past us toward deep water. We could trace their course by the twisting of the lily-pads. Motionless the rowers lay on their oars; the line of moving lily-pads showed that one of the big hippo was about to pass the boat; suddenly the waters opened close at hand and a monstrous head appeared. "Shoot," said Cuninghame; and I fired into the back of the head just as it disappeared. It sank out of sight without a splash, almost without a ripple, the lily-pads ceased twisting; a few bubbles of air rose to the surface; evidently the hippo lay dead underneath. Poling to the spot, we at once felt the huge body with our oar-blades. But, alas, when the launch came round, and we raised the body, it proved to be that of a big cow.

So I left Cuninghame to cut off the head for the museum, and started off by myself in the boat with two rowers, neither of whom spoke a word of English. For an hour we saw only the teeming bird life. Then, in a broad, shallow lagoon, we made out a dozen hippo, two or three very big. Cautiously we approached them, and when seventy yards off I fired at the base of the ear of one of the largest. Down went every head, and utter calm succeeded. I had marked the spot where the one at which I shot had disappeared, and thither we rowed. When we reached the place, I told one of the rowers to thrust a pole down and see if he could touch the dead body. He thrust accordingly, and at once shouted that he had found the hippo. In another moment his face altered, and he shouted much more loudly that the hippo was alive. Sure enough, bump went the hippo against the bottom of the boat, the jar causing us all to sit suddenly down—for we were standing. Another bump showed that we had again been struck; and the shallow, muddy water boiled, as the huge beasts, above and below the surface, scattered every which way. Their eyes starting, the two rowers began to back water out of the dangerous neighborhood, while I shot at an animal whose head appeared to my left, as it made off with frantic haste, for I took it for granted that the hippo at which I had first fired (and which was really dead) had escaped. This one disappeared as usual, and I had not the slightest idea whether or not I had killed it. I had small opportunity to ponder the subject, for twenty feet away the water bubbled and a huge head shot out facing me, the jaws wide open. There was no time to guess at its intentions, and I fired on the instant. Down went the head, and I felt the boat quiver as the hippo passed underneath. Just here the lily-pads were thick, so I marked its course, fired as it rose, and down it went. But on the other quarter of the boat a beast, evidently of great size—it proved to be a big bull—now appeared, well above water, and I put a bullet into its brain.

I did not wish to shoot again unless I had to, and stood motionless, with the little Springfield at the ready. A head burst up twenty yards off, with a lily-pad plastered over one eye, giving the hippo an absurd resemblance to a discomfited prizefighter, and then disappeared with great agitation. Two half-grown beasts stupid from fright appeared, and stayed up for a minute or two at a time, not knowing what to do. Other heads popped up, getting farther and farther away. By degrees everything vanished, the water grew calm, and we rowed over to the papyrus, moored ourselves by catching hold of a couple of stems, and awaited events. Within an hour four dead hippos appeared: a very big bull and three big cows. Of course I would not have shot the latter if it could have been avoided but, under the circumstances, I do not see how it was possible to help it. The meat was not wasted. On the contrary, it was a godsend, not only to our own porters, but to the natives round about, many of whom were on short commons on account of the drought.

Bringing over the launch, we worked until after dark to get the bull out of the difficult position in which he lay. It was nearly seven o'clock before we had him fixed for towing on one quarter, the rowboat towing on the other, by which time two hippos were snorting and blowing within a very few yards of us, their curiosity much excited as to what was going on. The night was overcast; there were drenching rain-squalls, and a rather heavy sea was running, and I did not get back to camp until after three. Next day the launch fetched in the rest of the hippo meat.

Chapter 8

Elephant Hunting

ON JULY 24, Theodore and party went into the chief city on the railroad, Nairobi, where they remained until August 4, enjoying some of the luxuries of civilization. Then they returned to Lake Naivasha. From there, across high plateaus and mountain chains of the Aberdare range, they went north and east to Neri. Their last camp, over the range, was at 10,000 feet, and it got so cold (in this country almost on the equator) that water froze in the basins, and the porters slept in numbed discomfort. There was constant fog and rain, and, on the highest plateau, the bleak landscape, shrouded in driving mist, was dismal.

At Neri the district commissioner, Mr. Browne, arranged a Kikuyu dance in their honor. Two thousand warriors, and as many women, came in. The warriors were naked. Some carried gaudy blankets, others girdles of leopard skin. Their ox-hide shields were colored in bold patterns, their long-bladed spears quivered and gleamed. Their faces and legs were painted red and yellow, while the faces of the young men who were about to undergo the rite of circumcision were stained a ghastly white. The warriors wore bead necklaces and waist-belts and armlets of brass and steel, and spurred anklets of monkey skin. They chanted in unison a deep-toned chorus, and danced rhythmically in rings, while the drums throbbed and the horns blared. The women shrilled applause, and danced in groups by themselves.

At Neri they had secured some native, or 'Ndorobo guides to help find elephants.

Kermit and Tarlton went northward on a safari of their own, while Cuninghame, Heller, and Theodore headed northeast for Mt. Kenia itself. On the afternoon of the second they struck upward among the steep foothills of the mountain, riven by deep ravines. They pitched camp in an open glade, surrounded by the green wall of tangled forest, the forest of the tropical mountainsides.

For two days after reaching our camp in the open glade on the mountainside it rained. We were glad of this, because it meant that the elephants would not be in the bamboos, and Cuninghame and the 'Ndorobo went off to hunt for fresh signs. Cuninghame was as skilful an elephant-hunter as could be found in Africa, and was one of the very few white men able to help even the wild bushmen at their work. By the afternoon of the second day they were fairly well satisfied as to the whereabouts of the quarry.

The following morning a fine rain was still falling when

Cuninghame, Heller, and I started on our hunt; but by noon it had stopped. Of course we went in single file and on foot; not even a bear-hunter from the cane-brakes of the lower Mississippi could ride through that forest. We left our home camp standing, taking blankets and a coat and change of underclothing for each of us, and two small Whymper tents, with enough food for three days. I also took my wash kit and a book from the Pigskin Library. First marched the 'Ndorobo guides, each with his spear, his blanket round his shoulders, and a little bundle of corn and sweet potato. Then came Cuninghame, followed by his gun-bearer. Then I came, clad in khaki-colored flannel shirt and khaki trousers buttoning down the legs, with hobnailed shoes and a thick slouch-hat. I had intended to wear rubber-soled shoes, but the soaked ground was too slippery. My two gun-bearers followed, carrying the Holland and the Springfield. Then came Heller, at the head of a dozen porters and skinners.

For three hours our route lay along the edge of the woods. We climbed into and out of deep ravines in which groves of tree-ferns clustered. We waded through streams of swift water, whose course was broken by cataract and rapid. We passed through shambas, and by the doors of little hamlets of thatched beehive huts. We met flocks of goats and hairy, fat-tailed sheep guarded by boys; strings of burden-bearing women stood meekly to one side to let us pass; parties of young men sauntered by, spear in hand.

Then we struck into the great forest, and in an instant the sun was shut from sight by the thick screen of wet foliage. It was a riot of twisted vines, interlacing the trees and bushes. Only the elephant paths, which, of every age, crossed and recrossed it hither and thither, made it pass-able. One of the chief difficulties in hunting elephants in the forest is that it is impossible to travel, except very slowly and with much noise, off these trails, so that it is sometimes very difficult to take advantage of the wind and, although the sight of the elephant is dull, both its sense of hearing and its sense of smell are exceedingly acute.

Hour after hour we worked our way onward through tangled forest and matted jungle. There was little sign of bird or animal life. A troop of long-haired black-and-white monkeys bounded away among the tree-tops. Here and there brilliant flowers lightened the gloom. We ducked under vines and climbed over fallen timber. Poisonous nettles stung our hands. We were drenched by the wet boughs which we brushed aside.

Twice we got on elephant spoor, once of a single bull, once of a party of three. Then Cuninghame and the 'Ndorobo redoubled their caution. They would minutely examine the fresh dung and, above all they continually tested the wind, scanning the treetops, and lighting matches to see from the smoke what the eddies were near the ground. Each time after an hour's stealthy stepping and crawling along the twisted trail a slight shift of the wind in the almost still air gave our scent to the game, and away it went before we could catch a glimpse of it. The elephant paths led up hill and down—for the beasts are wonderful climbers—and wound in and out in every direction. They were marked by broken branches and the splintered and shattered trunks of the smaller trees, especially where the elephant had stood and fed, trampling down the bushes for many yards around. Where they had crossed the marshy valleys they had punched big round holes, three feet deep, in the sticky mud.

As evening fell we pitched camp by the side of a little brook at the bottom of a ravine, and dined ravenously on bread, mutton, and tea. The air was keen, and under our blankets we slept in comfort until dawn. Breakfast was soon over and camp struck and, once more, we began our cautious progress through the dim, cool archways of the mountain forest.

Two hours after leaving camp we came across the fresh trail of a small herd of perhaps ten or fifteen elephant cows and calves, but including two big herd bulls. At once we took up the trail. Cuninghame and his bush people consulted again and again, scanning every track and mark with minute attention. The signs showed that the elephants had fed in the shambas early in the night, had then returned to the mountain, and stood in one place resting for several hours, and had left this sleeping-ground some time before we reached it. After we had followed the trail a short while we made the experiment of trying to force our own way through the jungle, so as to get the wind more favorable; but our progress was too slow and noisy, and we returned to the path the elephants had beaten. Then the 'Ndorobo went ahead, travelling noiselessly and at speed. One of them was clad in a white blanket, and another in a red one, which were conspicuous; but they were too silent and cautious to let the beasts see them, and could tell exactly where they were and what they were doing by the sounds. When these trackers waited for us they would appear before us like ghosts. Once one of them dropped down from the branches above, having climbed a tree with monkey-like agility to get a glimpse of the great game.

At last we could hear the elephants, and under Cuninghame's lead we walked more cautiously than ever. The wind was right, and the trail of one elephant led close alongside that of the rest of the herd, and parallel thereto. It was about noon. The elephants moved slowly, and we listened to the boughs crack, and now and then to the curious internal rumblings of the great beasts. Carefully, every sense on the alert, we kept pace with them. My double-barrel was in my hands, and, whenever possible, as I followed the trail, I stepped in the huge footprints of the elephant, for where such a weight had pressed there were no sticks left to crack under my feet. It made our veins thrill thus for half an hour to creep stealthily along, but a few rods from the herd, never able to see it, because of the extreme denseness of the cover, but always hearing first one and then another of its members, and always trying to guess what each one might do, and keeping ceaselessly ready for whatever might befall. A flock of hornbills flew up with noisy clamor, but the elephants did not heed them.

At last we came in sight of the mighty game. The trail took a twist to one side, and there, thirty yards in front of us, we made out part of the gray and massive head of an elephant resting his tusks on the branches of a young tree. A couple of minutes passed before, by cautious scrutiny, we were able to tell whether the animal was a cow or a bull, and whether, if a bull, it carried heavy enough tusks. Then we saw that it was a big bull with good ivory. It turned its head in my direction and I saw its eye. I fired a little to one side of the eye, at a spot which I thought would lead to the brain. I struck exactly where I aimed, but the head of an elephant is enormous and the brain small, and the bullet missed it. However, the shock momentarily stunned the beast. He stumbled forward, half falling, and as he recovered I fired with the second barrel, again aiming for the brain. This time the bullet sped true, and as I lowered the rifle from my shoulder, I saw the great lord of the forest come crashing to the ground.

But at that very instant, before there was a moment's time in which to reload, the thick bushes parted immediately on my left front, and through them surged the vast bulk of a charging bull elephant, the matted mass of tough creepers snapping like packthread before his rush. He was so close that he could have touched me with his trunk. I leaped to one side and dodged behind a tree trunk, opening the rifle, throwing out the empty shells, and slipping in two cartridges. Meanwhile Cuninghame fired right and left, at the same time throwing himself into the bushes on the other side. Both his bullets went home, and the bull stopped short in his charge, wheeled, and immediately disappeared in the thick cover. We ran forward, but the forest had closed over his wake. We heard him trumpet shrilly, and then all sounds ceased.

Later, in commenting on this elephant charge, Cuninghame wrote, "Colonel Roosevelt never turned a hair. At any moment the cows might have blundered through the bushes over us, but Roosevelt never thought of that. He went right up to the old chap he had shot and gave it the coup de grace." Then, after getting another one, "he let himself loose, boyishly jubilant, waving his hat and dancing about. He had himself photographed with the elephant and was absolutely delighted. But half an hour later, when we were back in camp and the elephant turned over to taxidermists, he sat down and began to read Balzac. While he was on the job he was altogether wrapped up in it. As soon as it was over and someone else had taken charge he was busy about something else."

The 'Ndorobo, who had quite properly disappeared when this second bull charged, now went forward, and soon returned with the report that he had fled at speed, but was evidently hard hit, as there was much blood on the spoor. If we had been only after ivory we should have followed him at once, but there was no telling how long a chase he might lead us. As we desired to save the skin of the dead elephant entire, there was no time whatever to spare. It is a formidable task, occupying many days, to preserve an elephant for mounting in a museum, and if the skin is to be properly saved, it must be taken off without an hour's delay.

So back we turned to where the dead tusker lay, and I felt proud indeed as I stood by the immense bulk of the slain monster and put my hand on the ivory. The tusks weighed a hundred and thirty pounds the pair. There was the usual scene of joyful excitement among the gun-bearers—who had behaved excellently—and among the wild bush people who had done the tracking for us, and, as Cuninghame had predicted, the old Masai Dorobo, from pure delight, proceeded to have hysterics on the body of the dead elephant.

The scene was repeated when Heller and the porters appeared half an hour later. Then, chattering like monkeys, and as happy as possible, all, porters, gun-bearers, and 'Ndorobo alike, began the work of skinning and cutting up the quarry, under the leadership and supervision of Heller and Cuninghame, and soon they were all splashed with blood from head to foot. One of the trackers took off his blanket and squatted stark naked inside the carcass the better to use his knife. Each laborer rewarded himself by cutting off strips of meat for his private store, and hung them in red festoons from the branches round about. There was no let-up in the work until it was stopped by darkness.

Our tents were pitched in a small open glade a hundred yards from the dead elephant. The night was clear, the stars shone brightly, and in the west the young moon hung just above the line of tall tree-tops. Fires were speedily kindled and the men sat around them, feasting and singing in a strange minor tone until late in the night. The flickering light left them at one moment in black obscurity, and the next brought into bold relief their sinewy crouching figures, their dark faces, gleaming eyes and flashing teeth. When they did sleep, two of the 'Ndorobo slept so close to the fire as to burn themselves—an accident to which they were prone, judging from the many scars of old burns on their legs. I toasted slices of elephant's heart on a pronged stick before the fire, and found it delicious, for I was hungry, and the night was cold.

Since the task of preparing the elephant hide would take ten days, Theodore went on a hunt by himself in the neighborhood of Mt. Kenia. On September 3, after re-

joining the rest of the party, he received word that Admiral Peary had reached the North Pole. Theodore wrote, "A little more than a year had passed since I said goodby to Peary as he started on his Arctic quest. After leaving New York in the Roosevelt he had put into Oyster Bay to see us, and we had gone aboard the Roosevelt, had examined with keen interest how she was fitted for the boreal seas and the boreal winter, and had then waved farewell to the tall, gaunt explorer, as he stood looking toward us over the side of the stout little ship."

On a tributary of the Guaso Nyero a river north of Mt. Kenia which they reached on September 22, Theodore went ostrich hunting and killed both a cock and a hen for the National Museum. They also had a curious experience with a cow giraffe that, "indulging in a series of noon naps," let them get within ten feet of her. "Nearer I did not care to venture, as giraffe strike and kick very hard with their hoofs, and, moreover, occasionally strike with the head, the blow seemingly not being delivered with the knobby, skin-covered horns, but with the front teeth of the lower jaw." They pelted her with sticks and clods of earth which caused her to canter off for fifty yards or so and then she walked leisurely away with little concern.

Kermit and his safari joined the main group at Nairobi. On his trip he had killed a koodoo which, with its spiral horns and striped coat, is the stateliest and handsomest antelope in the world. He had also passed his twentieth birthday and, before doing so, had killed all the kinds of dangerous African game—lion, leopard, elephant, buffalo and rhino.

On October 26, the party headed for the Uasin Gishu plateau on the 'Nzoi river which flows southwest into Lake Victoria. The following day Theodore celebrated his own birthday on the march with not even an opportunity for a hunt. "The year before I celebrated my fiftieth birthday by riding my jumping horse, Roswell, over all the jumps in Rock Creek Park at Washington," he wrote.

A few days later they camped at the edge of a swamp about five miles from the 'Nzoi river. A few miles beyond this swamp they saw a small herd of elephants in the open. There were eight cows and two calves. Since they did not need another cow for the National Museum they watched them. "There was always a fascination about watching elephants. They are such giants, they are so intelligent—much more so than any other game, except perhaps the lion, whose intelligence has a very sinister bent—and they look so odd with their great ears flapping and their trunks lifting and curling." But these elephants were not destined to be lucky.

After leaving the elephants we were on our way back to camp when we saw a white man in the trail ahead and, on coming nearer, whom should it prove to be but Carl Akeley, who was out on a trip for the American Museum of Natural History in New York. We went with him to his camp, where we found Mrs. Akeley, Clark, who was assisting him, and Messrs. McCutcheon and Stevenson, who were along on a hunting trip. They were old friends and I was very glad to see them. McCutcheon, the cartoonist, had been at a farewell lunch given me by Robert Collier just before I left New York, and at the lunch we had been talking much of

George Ade, and the first question I put to him was, "Where is George Ade?" for if one unexpectedly meets an American cartoonist on a hunting trip in mid-Africa there seems no reason why one should not also see his crony, an American playwright.

"In 1909," Carl Akeley wrote, "I was about to return to Africa in behalf of the American Museum of Natural History to secure material for a group of elephants, and I had set my heart on including in that group an animal shot by Theodore Roosevelt. In response to my suggestion that he should secure an elephant for me, Roosevelt had arranged to meet me in Africa for an elephant hunt. However, I was later in reaching the game fields than I had anticipated. Roosevelt had already completed his elephant hunting for the Smithsonian Institution on and about Mount Kenia, and it looked for a time as though our plan would have to be abandoned. When later in the year I went to the Uasin Gishu Plateau, understanding that Roosevelt had gone on to Uganda, I had given up all hope of having an elephant hunt with the colonel."

Luck had brought the two together here in the elephant country at a time when a herd of elephants had just been seen. It was decided that Akeley would camp with Roosevelt and that they should start early the next morning on the hunt.

Next morning Akeley, Tarlton, Kermit, and I started on our elephant-hunt. We were travelling light. I took nothing but my bedding, wash-kit, spare socks, and slippers, all in a

roll of water-proof canvas. We went to where we had seen
the herd and then took up the trail, two or three other gun-
bearers walking ahead as trackers. The elephants had not
been in the least alarmed. The trail led up and down hills
and through open thorn-scrub, and it crossed and recrossed
the wooded watercourses in the bottoms of the valleys. At
last, after going some ten miles we came on signs where the
elephants had fed that morning, and four or five miles
farther on we overtook them. That we did not scare them
into flight was due to Tarlton. The trail went nearly across
wind. The trackers were leading us swiftly along it, when
suddenly Tarlton heard a low trumpet ahead and to the
right hand. We at once doubled back, left the horses, and
advanced toward where the noise indicated that the herd
was standing.

In a couple of minutes we sighted them. It was just noon.
There were six cows, and two well-grown calves—these last
being quite big enough to shift for themselves or to be awkward antagonists for any man of whom they could get hold.
They stood in a clump, each occasionally shifting its position or lazily flapping an ear. Now and then one would
break off a branch with its trunk, tuck it into its mouth, and
withdraw it stripped of its leaves. The wind blew fair, we
were careful to make no noise, and with ordinary caution
we had nothing to fear from their eyesight. The ground was
neither forest nor bare plain; it was covered with long grass
and a scattered open growth of small scantily leaved trees,
chiefly mimosas, but including some trees covered with
gorgeous orange-red flowers. After careful scrutiny we ad-

vanced behind an ant-hill to within sixty yards, and I stepped forward for the shot.

Akeley wished two cows and a calf. Of the two best cows one had rather thick, worn tusks; those of the other were smaller, but better shaped. The latter stood half facing me, and I put the bullet from the right barrel of the Holland through her lungs, and fired the left barrel for the heart of the other. Tarlton, and then Akeley and Kermit, followed suit. At once the herd started diagonally past us, but half halted and faced toward us when only twenty-five yards distant, an unwounded cow beginning to advance with her great ears cocked at right angles to her head. Tarlton called "Look out; they are coming for us." At such a distance a charge from half a dozen elephant is a serious thing; I put a bullet into the forehead of the advancing cow, causing her to lurch heavily forward to her knees and then we all fired. The heavy rifles were too much even for such big beasts, and round they spun and rushed off. As they turned I dropped the second cow I had wounded with a shot in the brain, and the cow that had started to charge also fell, though it needed two or three more shots to keep it down as it struggled to rise. The cow at which I had first fired kept on with the rest of the herd, but fell dead before going a hundred yards.

"Nothing that I know of Roosevelt [said Akeley] better illustrates his habit of coming out in the open and going straight to the point than the way in which he approached his elephants on that occasion. A herd, the trail of which he had crossed the day before, was easily overtaken. As we stood hidden by a great ant-hill, I picked out a cow for my group and pointed her out to Roosevelt. Of course I assumed that he would shoot from behind the ant-hill, well out of sight and protected, but at that time I did not know Roosevelt. The rule in elephant-hunting is to get as close as you can before shooting, and, to him, sixty yards did not seem close. He went around the hill and started straight toward the eight elephants. As Kermit and I followed, one on either side and a little behind him, I had an impulse to climb on his shoulder and whisper: 'Shoot her! Don't take her alive.' "

We pitched camp a hundred yards from the elephants and Akeley, working like a demon, and assisted by Tarlton, had the skins off the two biggest cows and the calf by the time night fell. I walked out and shot an oribi for supper. Soon after dark the hyenas began to gather at the carcasses and to quarrel among themselves as they gorged. Toward morning a lion came near and uttered a kind of booming, long-drawn moan, an ominous and menacing sound. The hyenas answered with an extraordinary chorus of yelling, howling, laughing, and chuckling, as weird a volume of noise as any to which I ever listened. At dawn we stole down to the carcasses in the faint hope of a shot at the lion. However, he was not there but, as we came toward one carcass, a hyena raised its head seemingly from beside the elephant's belly, and I brained it with the little Springfield. On walking up it appeared that I need not have shot at all. The hyena, which was swollen with elephant meat, had gotten inside the huge body, and had then bitten a hole through

the abdominal wall of tough muscle and thrust his head
through. The wedge-shaped head had slipped through the
hole all right, but the muscle had then contracted, and the
hyena was fairly caught, with its body inside the elephant's
belly, and its head thrust out through the hole. We took
several photos of the beast in its queer trap.

"While Tarlton and Kermit returned to camp for tools
with which to dress the skins," Akeley wrote, "Colonel
Roosevelt and I sat together in the shade resting. He had
not seen any one except the members of his own party for
a good many months, while I was fresh from the States,
fresh from Oyster Bay, and he talked to me of his wife and
children at home. It was then that I first caught a vision of
Roosevelt, the father and husband. I got a new view of the
man, a view that only his intimate friends were privileged to
see, a view that I wish every one might have. Had our trails
not crossed there on the Uasin Gishu, I might never have
known the inspiration of his friendship . . . for the wall between acquaintance and friendship crumbled away and re-
vealed to me the simplicity, the fineness, the bigness of
Roosevelt, the man."

Chapter 9

A Lion Hunt with Spears

From the 'Nzoi River the safari made a two-days' march southeast to a trading post run by a Scotchman, Mr. Kirke, who arranged for a party of Nandi warriors to show how they hunted lions.

The Nandi were a warlike pastoral tribe, close kin to the Masai in blood and tongue, in weapons and in manner of life. They had long been accustomed to kill with the spear lions which became man-eaters or which molested their cattle overmuch. When it was told them that if they wished they could come to hunt lions at Sergoi, eight hundred warriors volunteered, and much heartburning was caused in choosing the sixty or seventy who were allowed the privilege. They stipulated, however, that they should not be used merely as beaters, but should kill the lion themselves, and refused to come unless with this understanding.

We started immediately after breakfast. We carried our rifles, but our duty was merely to round up the lion and hold him, if he went off so far in advance that even the Nandi runners could not overtake him. We intended to beat the country toward some shallow, swampy valleys twelve miles distant.

In an hour we overtook the Nandi warriors, who were advancing across the rolling, grass plains in a long line, with intervals of six or eight yards between the men. They were splendid savages, stark naked, lithe as panthers, the muscles rippling under their smooth dark skins; all their lives they had lived on nothing but animal food, milk, blood, and flesh, and they were fit for any fatigue or danger. Their faces were proud, cruel, fearless and, as they ran they moved with long springy strides. Their head-dresses were fantastic; they carried ox-hide shields painted with strange devices; and each bore in his right hand the formidable war spear, used both for strapping and for throwing at close quarters. The narrow spear heads of soft iron were burnished till they shone like silver; they were four feet long, and the point and edges were razor-sharp. The wooden haft appeared for but a few inches. The long butt was also of iron, ending in a spike, so that the spear looked almost solid metal. Yet each sinewy warrior carried his heavy weapon as if it were a toy, twirling it till it glinted in the sun-rays. Herds of game, red hartebeests and striped zebra and wild swine, fled right and left before the advance of the line.

It was noon before we reached a wide, shallow valley, with beds of rushes here and there in the middle, and on either side high grass and dwarfed and scattered thorn-trees.

Down this we beat for a couple of miles. Then, suddenly, a maned lion rose a quarter of a mile ahead of the line and galloped off through the high grass to the right. All of us on horseback tore after him.

He was a magnificent beast, with a black and tawny mane, in his prime, teeth and claws perfect, with mighty thews, and savage heart. He was lying near a hartebeest on which he had been feasting. His life had been one unbroken career of rapine and violence and now the maned master of the wilderness, the terror that stalked by night, the grim lord of slaughter, was to meet his doom at the hands of the only foes who dared molest him.

It was a mile before we brought him to bay, to hold him until the spearmen could come. It was a sore temptation to shoot him but, of course, we could not break faith with our Nandi friends. We were only some sixty yards from him, and we watched him with our rifles ready, least he should charge either us, or the first two or three spearmen, before their companions arrived.

One by one the spearmen came up, at a run, and gradually began to form a ring around him. Each, when he came near enough, crouched behind his shield, his spear in his right hand, his fierce, eager face peering over the shield rim. As man followed man, the lion rose to his feet. His mane bristled, his tail lashed, he held his head low, the upper lip now drooping over the jaws, now drawn up so as to show the gleam of the long fangs. He faced first one way and then another, and never ceased to utter his murderous grunting roars. It was a wild sight—the ring of spearmen, intent, silent, bent on blood, and in the center the great man-killing beast, his thunderous wrath growing ever more dangerous.

At last the tense ring was complete, and the spearmen rose and closed in. The lion looked quickly from side to side, saw where the line was thinnest, and charged at his top-most speed. The crowded moment began. With shields held steady, and quivering spears poised, the men in front braced themselves for the rush and the shock and, from either hand, the warriors sprang forward to take their foe in flank. Bounding ahead of his fellows, the leader reached throwing distance, the long spear flickered and plunged. As the lion felt the wound he half turned, and then flung himself on the man in front. The warrior threw his spear. It drove deep into the life, for entering at one shoulder it came out of the opposite flank, near the thigh, a yard of steel through the great body. Rearing, the lion struck the man, bearing down the shield, his back arched, and for a moment, he slaked his fury with fang and talon. But on the instant I saw another spear driven clear through his body from side to side and, as the lion turned again, the bright spear blades darting toward him were flashes of white flame. The end had come. He seized another man, who stabbed him and wrenched loose. As he fell he gripped a spear head in his jaws with such tremendous force that he bent it double. Then the warriors were round and over him, stabbing and shouting, wild with furious exultation.

From the moment when he charged until his death I doubt whether ten seconds had elapsed, perhaps less; but what a ten seconds! The first half-dozen spears had done the work. Three of the spear blades had gone clear through the body, the points projecting several inches, and these, and one or two others, including the one he had seized in his jaws, had been twisted out of shape in the terrible death-struggle.

We at once attended to the two wounded men. Treating their wounds with antiseptic was painful, and so, while the operation was in progress, I told them, through Kirke, that I would give each a heifer. A Nandi prizes his cattle rather more than his wives. Each sufferer smiled broadly at the news, and forgot all about the pain of his wounds.

Then the warriors, raising their shields above their heads, and chanting the deep-toned victory song, marched with a slow, dancing step around the dead body of the lion. This savage dance of triumph ended a scene of as fierce interest and excitement as I ever hope to see.

The Nandi marched back by themselves, carrying the two wounded men on their shields. We rode to camp by a roundabout way, on the chance that we might see another lion. The afternoon waned and we cast long shadows before us as we rode across the vast lonely plain. The game stared at us as we passed; a cold wind blew in our faces, and the tall grass waved ceaselessly; the sun set behind a sullen cloud bank; and then, just at nightfall, the tents glimmered white through the dusk.

We tried to get the Nandi to stay with us for a few days and beat for lions. But this they refused to do, unless they were also to kill them. I did not care to assist as a mere spectator at any more lion-hunts, no matter how exciting— though to do so once was well worth while. So we moved on by ourselves, camping in likely places.

Chapter 10

The Great Rhinoceros of the Lado

AFTER THE lion hunt by the Nandi warriors the safari continued southward until it came to Londiani, the nearest point on the railroad. At this place Theodore said goodbye to most of the members of the safari as the party was to leave East Africa.

After a short hunt in the neighboring country the remaining members of the party went southeast, by the railroad, to Nairobi, where preparations were being made for a further hunt north of Lake Victoria in the Uganda region. Working like beavers they got everything ready—including additions to the Pigskin Library—and on December 18 took the train northwest toward Lake Victoria. On the following morning they reached Kismu, on the northeastern tip of the lake. This was in the Kavirondo country "where the natives, both men and women, as a rule, went absolutely naked." At noon they embarked on a steamer to cross the lake, going in a northwesterly direction. The next morning they crossed the equator. The entire region was practically deserted on account of sleeping sickness brought on by the bite of a fly. They landed twenty-four hours later at Entebbe, on the northwestern tip of the lake. From here the safari went northwest to Lake Albert Nyanza.

Christmas Day we passed on the march. There is not much use in trying to celebrate Christmas unless there are small folks to hang up their stockings on Christmas Eve, to rush gleefully in at dawn next morning to open the stockings, and after breakfast to wait in hopping expectancy until their elders throw open the door of the room in which the big presents are arranged, those for each child on a separate table.

At noon on January 5, 1910, the safari reached Butiaba, a sandpit and marsh on the shores of Lake Albert Nyanza. They had marched about one hundred and sixty miles from Lake Victoria. From here they took boats down the Nile to the Lado country. As they went northward, the waters of Lake Albert Nyanza "stretched behind us beyond the ken of vision, to where they were fed by streams from the Mountains of the Moon." On their left rose the frowning ranges over which the Congo forest lay like a shroud over the land. On the right was the mouth of the Victorian Nile, "alive with monstrous crocodiles, and its banks barren of human life because of the swarms of the fly whose bite brings the torment which ends in death." As night fell they entered the

White Nile, and steamed and drifted down the mighty stream.

The following morning, forty-eight hours after leaving Butiaba, on Lake Albert Nyanza, we disembarked from the little flotilla which had carried us—a crazy little steam-launch, two sailboats, and two big rowboats. We made our camp close to the river's edge, on the Lado side, in a thin grove of scattered thorn-trees. The grass grew rank and tall all about us. Our tents were pitched, and the grass huts of the porters built, on a kind of promontory, the main stream running past one side, while on the other was a bay. The nights were hot, and the days burning; the mosquitoes came with darkness, sometimes necessitating our putting on head nets and gloves in the evenings, and they would have made sleep impossible if we had not had mosquito bars. Nevertheless it was a very pleasant camp, and we thoroughly enjoyed it. It was a wild, lonely country, and we saw no human beings except an occasional party of naked savages armed with bows and poisoned arrows. Game was plentiful, and a hunter always enjoys a permanent camp in a good game country; for while the expedition is marching, his movements must largely be regulated by those of the safari, whereas at a permanent camp he is foot-loose.

The morning after making camp we started on a rhinoceros-hunt. At this time in this neighborhood, the rhinoceros seemed to spend the heat of the day in sleep, and to feed in the morning and evening, and perhaps throughout the night, and to drink in the evening and morning, usually at some bay or inlet of the river. In the morning they walked away from the water for an hour or two, until they came to a place which suited them for the day's sleep. Unlike the ordinary rhinoceros, the square-mouthed rhinoceros feeds exclusively on grass. Its dung is very different; we only occasionally saw it deposited in heaps, according to the custom of its more common cousin. The big, sluggish beast seemed fond of nosing the ant-hills of red earth, both with its horn and with its square muzzle. It may be that it licked them for some saline substance. It was apparently of less solitary nature than the prehensile-lipped rhino, frequently going in parties of four or five or half a dozen individuals.

We did not get an early start. Hour after hour we plodded on, under the burning sun, through the tall, tangled grass, which was often higher than our heads. Continually we crossed the trails of elephant and more rarely of rhinoceros, but the hard, sun-baked earth and stiff, tinder-dry long grass made it a matter of extreme difficulty to tell if a trail was fresh, or if to follow it. Finally, Kermit and his gun-bearer, Kassitura, discovered some unquestionably fresh footprints which those of us who were in front had passed over. Immediately we took the trail, my gun-bearer, Kongoni and Kassitura acting as trackers, while Kermit and I followed at their heels. Once or twice the two trackers were puzzled, but they were never entirely at fault. After half an hour Kassitura suddenly pointed toward a thorn-tree about sixty yards off. Mounting a low ant-hill I saw rather dimly through the long grass a big gray bulk, near the foot of the tree. It was a rhinoceros lying asleep on its side, looking like an enormous pig. It heard something and raised itself on its fore legs, in a sitting posture, the big ears thrown forward. I fired for the chest, and the heavy Holland bullet knocked it clean off its feet. Squealing loudly it rose again, but it was clearly done for, and it never got ten yards from where it had been lying.

At the shot four other rhino rose. One bolted to the right, two others ran to the left. Firing through the grass Kermit wounded a bull and followed it for a long distance, but could not overtake it. Days later, however, he found the carcass, and saved the skull and horns. Meanwhile I killed a calf, which was needed for the museum. The rhino I had already shot was a full-grown cow, doubtless the calf's mother.

There were some white egrets on the rhinos, and the bodies and heads of both the cow and calf looked as though they had been splashed with streaks of whitewash. One of the egrets returned after the shooting and perched on the dead body of the calf.

In the next few days Theodore and Kermit killed enough rhinos of this specie to have a complete collection for the Museum. At this camp hippos became more and more familiar. "They grunted and brayed to one another throughout the night, splashed and wallowed among the reeds, and came close to the tents during their dry-land rambles in the darkness. One night, in addition to the hippo chorus, we heard the roaring of lions and the trumpeting of elephants. We were indeed in the heart of the African wilderness."

They often saw elephants. One band, with five cows and four calves, marching across a patch of burnt ground ahead of them, offered some amusement. "One dropped behind and looked fixedly in our direction, probably having heard us talking. Then, with head aloft and tail stiffly erect, it hastened after the others, presenting an absurd likeness to a baboon. The four calves played friskily about, especially a very comical little pink fellow which accompanied the leading cow."

Chapter 11

Down the Nile: The Giant Eland

AFTER TWO more uneventful hunts, the party went northward by boat, on the Bahr el Jebel river which flows south into Lake Albert, to Nimule. From here, with a laden safari, Theodore and Kermit went northwest on a ten-days march and an eight-days' hunt in the Belgian Congo to hunt the "largest and handsomest and one of the least known of African antelopes, the giant eland." They went alone since all the other white men on the party were either down with dysentery or fever. They took sixty Uganda porters and a dozen mules. In addition they had seven black soldiers of the Belgian native troops, under a corporal. From Redjaf they marched two days west, stopping short of the River Koda, where the game drank.

The natives lived in pointed beehive huts in unfenced villages, with shambas [native huts] lying about them. They kept goats, chickens and a few cattle. The doors in the low
336

mud walls of the huts were but a couple of feet high and had to be entered on all fours. Black children scuttled into them in wild alarm as they passed. Skinny, haggard old men and women, almost naked, sat by fires and smoked long pipes.

One day, in the course of a long and fruitless hunt, they stopped to rest near one of the native villages. "Some chief and several of his people came out to see us. The chief proudly wore a dirty jersey and a pair of drawers. . . . Two women bore on their heads, as gifts for us, one a large earthenware jar of water, the other a basket of ground nuts. They were tall and well shaped. One as her sole clothing wore a beaded cord around her waist and a breech-clout consisting of half a dozen long, thickly leaved, fresh sprays of a kind of vine. The other, instead of this vine breech-clout, had hanging from her girdle in front a cluster of long-stemmed green leaves, and behind a bundle of long strings, carried like a horse's tail."

Each day they went out after the giant eland.

We would walk until we found tracks made that morning, and then the gun-bearers and the native guide would slowly follow them, hour after hour, under the burning sun. On the first day we saw nothing; on the next we got a moment's glimpse of an eland, trotting at the usual slashing gait. I had no chance to fire. By mid-afternoon on each day it was evident that further following of the trail we were on was useless, and we plodded campward, tired and thirsty. Gradually the merciless glare softened; then the sun sank crimson behind a chain of fantastically carved mountains in the distance; and the hues of the afterglow were drowned in the silver light of the moon, which was nearing the full.

On the third day we found the spoor of a single bull by eight o'clock. Hour after hour went by while the gun-bearers, even more eager than we, puzzled out the trail. At half past twelve we knew we were close on the beast, and immediately afterward caught a glimpse of it. Taking advantage of every patch of cover I crawled toward it on all fours, my rifle too hot for me to touch the barrel, while the blistering heat of the baked ground hurt my hands. At a little over a hundred yards I knelt and aimed at the noble beast. I could now plainly see his huge bulk and great, massive horns, as he stood under a tree. The pointed bullet from the little Springfield hit a trifle too far back and up, but made such a rip that he never got ten yards from where he was standing, and great was my pride as I stood over him, and examined his horns, twisted almost like a koodoo's, and admired his size, his finely modelled head and legs, and the beauty of his coat.

Meanwhile, Kermit had killed two eland, a cow on the first day, and on the second a bull even better than, although not quite so old, as mine.

It was no easy job in that climate, to care for and save the three big skins; but we did it.

On the last evening there was nothing to do, and we sat in the brilliant moonlight in front of our tents, while Kassitura played his odd little harp. Kermit and I strolled over to listen; and at once Kassitura began to improvise a chant in my honor, reciting how the Bwana Makuba had come, how he was far from his own country, how he had just

killed a giant eland, and so on and so on. Meanwhile, over
many little fires strips of meat were drying on scaffolds of
bent branches, and askaris and porters were gathered in
groups, chatting and singing, while the mighty tree near
which our tents were pitched cast a black shadow on the
silver plain. Then the shenzis, who had helped us, came to
receive their reward, and their hearts were gladdened with
red cloth and salt, and for those whose services had been
greatest there were special treasures in the shape of three
green-and-white umbrellas. It was a pleasant ending to a
successful hunt.

On the last day of February we started down the Nile,
slipping easily along on the rapid current, which wound and
twisted through stretches of reeds and marsh-grass and
papyrus.

Occasionally they saw crocodiles and water birds which
reminded Theodore of the time that he had gone up the
river thirty-seven years before. Now and then they passed
native villages, "the tall, lean men and women stark naked,
their bodies daubed with mud, grease and ashes to keep off
the mosquitoes." At night they sat on the deck and watched
the stars and dark, lonely river. "The swimming crocodiles
and plunging hippos made whirls and wakes of feeble light
that glimmered for a moment against the black water." The
health of the sick members gradually improved.

They reached Kartoum on the afternoon of March 14,
1910, and Theodore and Kermit parted with their comrades
of the trip. "During the year we spent together, there had
not been a jar, and my respect and liking for them had

grown steadily . . . Kermit's and my health throughout the trip had been excellent. He had been laid up for three days all told, and I for five."

Kermit and I kept about a dozen trophies for ourselves; otherwise we shot nothing that was not used either as a museum specimen or for meat—usually for both purposes. We were in hunting-grounds practically as good as any that have ever existed; but we did not kill a tenth, nor a hundredth, part of what we might have killed had we been willing. The mere size of the bag indicates little as to a man's prowess as a hunter, and almost nothing as to the interest or value of his achievement.

PART FIVE

Exploring The Brazilian Wilderness

Chapter 1

The Start: A Jaguar Hunt

ROOSEVELT RETURNED from his African adventures to find that the same group that had wished the lions to do their duty, had without any effective resistance from President Taft, thrown out all of his progressive measures and ideas, and had returned the party to its traditional "owners." In the election of 1912 he broke the Republican Party wide open by establishing his Bull Moose Party. This, together with a rising feeling over the country that the Republican Party was being used as an instrument to further vested interests, brought about the election of Woodrow Wilson.

In the spring of 1913 Roosevelt accepted invitations to address learned societies in Argentina and Brazil, and determined that in addition he would "come north through the middle of the continent into the valley of the Amazon" and see what he could see.

343

Roosevelt's expedition to Africa had been planned while he was President of the United States, and it had seemed to him proper that it should be made in the interests of the National Museum. As a private citizen he felt free to offer the scientific results of the Brazilian expedition to the American Museum of Natural History, an institution of which his father had been a founder.

The Museum recommended George K. Cherrie, a noted ornithologist and explorer, and Leo E. Miller, equally noted as a mammalogist, to accompany Roosevelt on the expedition. "No two better men for such a trip could have been found. Both were veterans of the tropical American forests." Anthony Fiala, a former Arctic explorer, was secured to assemble and take charge of the equipment. Kermit Roosevelt, who was bridge-building in Brazil, was also to go along.

In talking to Roosevelt, before going on the expedition, Cherrie told him that he occasionally took a drink. Theodore, who was writing, did not look up. Cherrie waited— what seemed like a very long time. Suddenly Theodore swung around in his chair.

"Cherrie, you say you drink?"

"I occasionally take a drink."

"What do you drink?"

"That depends a good deal on what is available."

"How much do you drink?"

"All that I want."

Theodore shook a warning finger at him. "Cherrie," he said, "just keep right on drinking."

This was the forthright honesty that Roosevelt wanted. He knew he had a man that he could depend upon.

For arms the naturalists took sixteen-bore shotguns, one of Cherrie's having a rifle barrel underneath. The firearms for the rest of the party were supplied by Kermit and myself, including my Springfield rifle, Kermit's two Winchesters, a 405 and 30-40, the Fox twelve-gauge shotgun, and another sixteen-gauge gun, and a couple of revolvers, a Colt and a Smith & Wesson. Each equipped himself with the clothing he fancied. Mine consisted of khaki, such as I wore in Africa, with a couple of United States army flannel shirts and a couple of silk shirts, one pair of hobnailed shoes with leggings, and one pair of laced leather boots coming nearly to the knee. Both the naturalists told me that it was well to have either the boots or leggings as a protection against snake bites, and I also had gauntlets because of the mosquitoes and sand flies. We intended where possible to live on what we could get from time to time in the country, but we took some United States army emergency rations, and also ninety cans, each containing a day's provisions for five men, made up by Fiala.

The trip I proposed to take can be understood only if there is a slight knowledge of South American topography. The great mountain chain of the Andes extends down the entire length of the western coast, so close to the Pacific Ocean that no rivers of importance enter it. The rivers of South America drain into the Atlantic. Southernmost South America, including over half of the territory of the Argentine Republic, consists chiefly of a cool, open plains country. Northward of this country, and eastward of the Andes, lies the great bulk of the South American continent, which is included in the tropical and the subtropical regions. Most of this territory is Brazilian. Aside from certain relatively small stretches drained by coast rivers, this immense region of tropical and subtropical America east of the Andes is drained by the three great river systems of the Plate, the Amazon, and the Orinoco. At their headwaters the Amazon and the Orinoco systems are actually connected by a sluggish natural canal. The headwaters of the northern affluents of the Paraguay and the southern affluents of the Amazon are sundered by a stretch of highland, which toward the east broadens out into the central plateau of Brazil. This plateau is a region partly of healthy, rather dry and sandy, open prairie, partly of forest. The great and low-lying basin of the Paraguay, which borders it on the south, is one of the largest, and the still greater basin of the Amazon, which borders it on the north, is the very largest of all the river-basins of the earth.

In these basins, but especially in the basin of the Amazon, and thence in most places northward to the Caribbean Sea, lie the most extensive stretches of tropical forest to be found anywhere. Much difficulty has been experienced in exploring these forests, because under the torrential rains and steaming heat the rank growth of vegetation becomes almost impenetrable, and the streams difficult of navigation.

Our purpose was to ascend the Paraguay as nearly as possible to the head of navigation, thence cross to the sources of one of the affluents of the Amazon, and if possible descend it in canoes built on the spot. The starting-point of our trip was to be Asuncion, in the state of Paraguay.

The Brazilian government, on learning of Roosevelt's intention, informed him, through its minister of foreign af-

fairs, Mr. Lauro Muller, *that it would like to cooperate in
the endeavor. Towards that end arrangements had been
made for Colonel Rondon, the foremost explorer in Brazil
to accompany him. Even more important it was suggested,
if Roosevelt wanted to make this a serious exploration, the
explorers attempt the descent of a river which started in the
unexplored portion of Western Matto Grasso—the south-
westernmost state in Brazil, bordering on both Paraguay
and Bolivia—and flowed "nobody knew whither, but which
the best-informed men believed would prove to be a very big
river, utterly unknown to geographers." Of course Theodore
jumped at such a challenge.*

On the afternoon of December 9 we left the attractive
and picturesque city of Asuncion to ascend the Paraguay.
With generous courtesy the Paraguayan Government had
put at my disposal the gunboat-yacht of the president himself, a most comfortable river steamer, and so the opening
days of our trip were pleasant in every way. The food was
good, our quarters were clean, we slept well, below or on
deck, usually without our mosquito-nettings, and in the daytime the deck was pleasant under the awnings.

Under the brilliant sky we steamed steadily up the mighty
river. The sunset was glorious as we leaned on the port rail-
ing and, after nightfall, the moon, nearly full and hanging
high in the heavens, turned the water to shimmering radi-
ance. On the mud-flats and sand bars, and among the green
rushes of bays and inlets, were stately water fowl—crimson
flamingoes and rosy spoonbills, dark-colored ibis and white
storks with black wings. Snowy egrets flapped across the
marshes. There were plenty of cayman that differed from

the crocodiles we had seen in Africa in that they were not alarmed by the report of a rifle when fired at, and that they lay with the head raised instead of stretched along the sand.

With me on the gunboat was an old Western friend, Tex Ricard of the Panhandle and Alaska and various places in between. He now had a large tract of land and some thirty-five thousand head of cattle in the Chaco (an ideal cattle country), opposite Concepcion, at which city he was to stop. He told me that horses did not do well in the Chaco but that cattle throve, and that while ticks swarmed on the east bank of the great river, they would not live on the west bank.

Late on the evening of the second day of our trip, just before midnight, we reached Concepcion. On this day, when we stopped to get wood or provisions, we caught many fish. They belonged to one of the most formidable genera of fish in the world, the piranha or cannibal fish, the fish that eats men when it gets chances. Farther north the piranha go in schools. At this point on the Paraguay they do not go in regular schools but swarm in all the waters and attain a length of eighteen inches or over. They are the most ferocious fish in the world. Even sharks or barracudas usually attack things smaller than themselves. But the piranhas habitually attack things much larger than themselves. They will snap a finger off a hand incautiously trailed in the water. They mutilate swimmers. They will rend and devour alive any wounded men. Those that we caught sometimes bit through the hooks, or double strands of copper wire that served as leaders, and got away. Those that we landed on deck lived for many minutes. As they flapped about they bit with vicious eagerness at whatever presented itself. One of them flapped into a cloth and seized with a bulldog grip. Another grasped one of its fellows. Another snapped at a piece of wood and left the teeth-marks deep therein. If cattle are driven into, or of their own accord enter, the water, they are commonly not molested. But if by chance some unusually big or ferocious specimen of these fearsome fishes does bite an animal the blood brings up every member of the ravenous throng and unless the attacked animal can immediately make its escape from the water it is devoured alive. The only redeeming feature about them is that they are themselves fairly good to eat, although with too many bones.

At the point where the Paraguay River begins to form the boundary, which they reached on the 12th of December, they met Colonel Rondon, with a shallow river steamer which was to take them farther up the river, and several other members of his party. These included Captain Megalhaes, Lieutenant Lyra, a medical doctor, and Lieutenant Filho of the army, and Doctor Oliveira, a geologist. Theodore and Colonel Rondon communicated with each other in French, which both spoke rather poorly. Kermit, who spoke Portuguese fluently, served as an interpreter.

They reached the city of Corumba on December 15th where they were joined by Cherrie and Miller who had already collected several hundred specimens of both birds and mammals.

While preparations were going forward for the trip, Theodore, Kermit and Colon Rondon went to the ranch of a

Brazilian, Senhor de Barros, for a jaguar hunt. Theodore described the flocks of jabiru storks which "whitened the marshes and lined the river banks. For such big birds they were not shy, and before flying they had to run a few paces and then launch themselves on the air. Once, at noon, a couple soared round overhead in wide rings, rising higher and higher. On another occasion, late in the day, a flock passed by, gleaming white with black points in the long afternoon lights, and with them were spoonbills, showing rosy amid their snowy companions."

Kermit had charge of two hounds which we owed to the courtesy of one of our Argentine friends. They were biggish, nondescript animals, obviously good fighters, and they speedily developed the utmost affection for all the members of the expedition, but especially for Kermit. One we named "Shenzi," the name given the wild bush natives by the Swahili, the semicivilized African porters. He was good-natured, rough, and stupid—hence his name. The other was called by a native name, "Trigueiro." The chance now came to try them. We were steaming between long stretches of coarse grass, about three feet high, when we spied from the deck a black object, very conspicuous against the vivid green. It was a giant ant-eater, one of the most extraordinary creatures of the latter-day world. It was about the size of a small black bear.

As soon as we saw it we pushed off in a rowboat, and landed only a couple of hundred yards distant from our clumsy quarry. The two dogs ran ahead, followed by Colonel Rondon and Kermit, with me behind carrying the rifle. In a minute or two the hounds overtook the cantering, shuffling creature, and promptly began a fight with it. The combatants were so mixed up that I had to wait another minute or so before I could fire without risk of hitting a dog. We carried our prize back to the bank and hoisted it aboard the steamer. The sun was just about to set, behind dim mountains, many miles distant across the marsh.

Soon afterward we reached one of the outstations of the huge ranch, and hauled up alongside the bank for the night. There was a landing-place, and sheds and corrals. Several of the peons or gauchos had come to meet us. After dark they kindled fires, and sat beside them singing songs in a strange minor key and strumming guitars. The red firelight flickered over their wild figures as they squatted away from the blaze, where the light and the shadows met.

At sunrise we were off for the "fazenda," the ranch of M. de Barros. The baggage went in an ox-cart. We rode small, tough ranch horses. The distance was some twenty miles. The whole country was marsh, varied by stretches of higher ground. For three or four miles we splashed through the marsh, now and then crossing boggy pools where the little horses labored hard not to mire down. Our dusky guide was clad in a shirt, trousers, and fringed leather apron, and wore spurs on his bare feet. He had a rope for a bridle, and two or three toes of each foot were thrust into little iron stirrups. Then for miles we rode through a beautiful open forest of tall, slender caranda palms, with other trees scattered among them. Green parakeets with black heads chattered as they flew. Noisy green and red parrots climbed among the palms and huge macaws, some entirely blue, others almost entirely red, screamed loudly as they perched in the trees or took wing at our approach.

After five or six hours' travelling we reached the ranch for which we were heading. In the neighborhood stood giant fig trees, singly or in groups, with dense, dark-green foliage. Ponds, overgrown with water plants, lay about. Wet meadow and drier pastureland, open or dotted with palms and varied with tree jungle, stretched for many miles on every hand. There were some thirty thousand head of cattle on the ranch, besides herds of horses and droves of swine, and a few flocks of sheep and goats.

The home buildings of the ranch stood in a quadrangle, surrounded by a fence or low stockade. One end of the quadrangle was formed by the ranchhouse itself, one story high, with whitewashed walls and red-tiled roof. Inside, the rooms were bare, with clean, whitewashed walls and palm-trunk rafters. There were solid wooden shutters on the unglazed windows.

We slept in hammocks or on cots, and we feasted royally on delicious Brazilian dishes.

On another side of the quadrangle stood another long, low white building with red-tiled roof. This held the kitchen and the living rooms of the upper-grade peons, the head men, the cook and jaguar hunters, with their families: dark-skinned men, their wives showing various strains of white, Indian and Negro blood. The children tumbled merrily in the dust, and were fondly tended by their mothers.

Opposite the kitchen stood a row of buildings, some whitewashed daub-and-wattle, with tin roofs, others of erect palm logs with palm-leaf thatch. These were the saddle-rooms, storehouse, chicken house, and stable.

The fourth end of the quadrangle was formed by a corral and a big wooden scaffolding on which hung hides and strips of drying meat. Extraordinary to relate, there were no mosquitoes at the ranch. Therefore, in spite of the heat, it was very pleasant.

The first hunt after jaguars while not successful was interesting. "The native hunters who accompanied us were swarthy men of mixed blood. They were barefooted and scantily clad, and each carried a long, clumsy spear and a keen machete, in the use of which he was an expert. Now and then, in the jungle, we had to cut out a path, and it was interesting to see one of them, although cumbered by his unwieldy spear, handling his half-broken little horse with complete ease while he hacked at limbs and branches."

A few days later one of the jaguar hunters rode in with the information that he had found fresh sign in the swamp nine miles away.

Next morning we rose at two, and had started on our jaguar-hunt at three. Colonel Rondon, Kermit, and I with the two trailers, made up the party, each on a weedy, under-sized marsh pony accustomed to traversing the vast stretches of morass. We were accompanied by a brown boy, with saddle-bags holding our lunch, who rode a long-horned trotting steer which he managed by a string through its nostril and lip. The two trailers each carried a clumsy spear.

We had a rather poor pack. Besides our own two dogs,

neither of which was used to jaguar hunting, there were the ranch dogs, which were well-nigh worthless, and then two jaguar hounds borrowed for the occasion from a ranch six or eight leagues distant. These were the only hounds on which we could place any trust, and they were led on leashes by the two trailers. One was a white bitch, the other, the best one we had, was a gelded black dog. They were lean, half-starved creatures with prick ears and a look of furtive wildness.

As our shabby little horses shuffled away from the ranch-house the stars were brilliant and the Southern Cross hung well up in the heavens, tilted to the right. The landscape was spectral in the light of the waning moon. At the first shallow ford, as horses and dogs splashed across, an alligator, some five feet long, floated unconcernedly among the splashing hoofs and paws. Evidently in the night he did not fear us. Hour after hour we shogged along. The night grew ghostly with the first dim gray of the dawn. The sky had become overcast. The sun rose red and angry through broken clouds as his disk flamed behind the tall, slender columns of the palms, and lit the waste fields of papyrus. The black monkeys howled mournfully. The birds awoke. Macaws, parrots, parakeets screamed at us and chattered at us as we rode by. Ibis called with wailing voices, and the plovers shrieked as they wheeled in the air. We waded across bayous and ponds, where white lilies floated on the water and thronging lilac-flowers splashed the green marsh with color.

At last, on the edge of a patch of jungle, in wet ground, we came on fresh jaguar tracks. Both the jaguar hounds challenged the sign. They were unleashed and galloped along the trail, while the other dogs noisily accompanied them. The hunt led right through the marsh. Evidently the jaguar had not the least distaste for water.

The pace quickened and the motley pack burst into yelling and howling, and then a sudden quickening of the note showed that the game had either climbed a tree or turned to bay in a thicket. The dogs had entered a patch of tall tree jungle, and as we cantered up through the marsh we saw the jaguar high among the forked limbs of a taruman tree. It was a beautiful picture—the spotted coat of the big, lithe, formidable cat fairly shone as it snarled defiance at the pack below. I did not trust the pack, the dogs were not stanch, and if the jaguar came down and started I feared we might lose it. So I fired at once, from a distance of seventy yards. At the shot the jaguar fell like a sack of sand through the branches and, although it staggered to its feet, it went but a score of yards before it sank down, and when I came up it was dead under the palms, with three or four of the bolder dogs riving at it.

The jaguar is the king of South American game, ranking on an equality with the noblest beasts of the chase of North America, and behind only the huge and fierce creatures which stand at the head of the big game of Africa and Asia.

This one was an adult female. It was heavier and more powerful than a full-grown male cougar, or African panther or leopard. It was a big, powerfully built creature, giving the same effect of strength that a tiger or lion does, and that the lithe leopards and pumas do not. Its flesh, by the way, proved good eating when we had it for supper, although it was not cooked in the way it ought to have been. I tried it because I had found cougars such good eating. I have always regretted that in Africa I did not try lion's flesh, which I am sure must be excellent.

Next day came Kermit's turn. About ten in the morning we came to a long, deep, winding bayou. On the opposite bank stood a capybara, looking like a blunt-nosed pig, its wet hide shining black. I killed it, and it slid into the water. Then I found that the bayou extended for a mile or two in each direction, and the two hunter guides said they did not wish to swim across for fear of the piranhas. Just at this moment we came across fresh jaguar tracks. It was hot, we had been travelling for five hours, and the dogs were much exhausted. The black hound in particular was nearly done up, for he had been led in a leash by one of the horsemen. He lay flat on the ground, panting, unable to catch the scent. Kermit threw water over him, thrust his nose into the jaguar's footprint. The game old hound at once and eagerly, responded. As he snuffed the scent he challenged loudly, while still lying down. Then he staggered to his feet and started on the trail, going stronger with every leap. Evidently the big cat was not far distant. Soon we found where it had swum across the bayou. Piranhas or no piranhas, we now intended to get across and we tried to force our horses in at what seemed a likely spot. The matted growth of water-plants, with their leathery, slippery stems, formed an un-pleasant barrier, as the water was swimming-deep for the horses. Kermit finally forced his horse through the tangled mass, swimming, plunging and struggling. He left a lane of clear water, through which we swam after him. The dogs splashed and swam behind us. On the other bank they struck the fresh trail and followed it at a run. It led into a long belt of timber, chiefly composed of low-growing nacury palms, with long, drooping, many-fronded branches. In silhouette they suggested coarse bamboos. The nuts hung in big clusters and looked like bunches of small, unripe bananas. Among the lower palms were scattered some big ordinary trees.

We cantered along outside the timber belt, listening to the dogs within, and in a moment a burst of yelling clamor from the pack told that the jaguar was afoot. These few minutes are the really exciting moments in the chase, with hounds, of any big cat that will tree. The furious baying of the pack, the shouts and cheers of encouragement from the galloping horsemen, the wilderness surroundings, the knowledge of what the quarry is—all combine to make the moment one of fierce and thrilling excitement. Besides, in this case, there was the possibility the jaguar might come to bay on the ground, in which event there would be a slight element of risk, as it might need straight shooting to stop a charge.

However, about as soon as the long-drawn howling and eager yelping showed that the jaguar had been overtaken, we saw him, a huge male, up in the branches of a great fig tree. A bullet behind the shoulder, from Kermit's 405 Winchester, brought him dead to the ground. He was heavier than the very big male horse-killing cougar I shot in Colorado, whose skull Hart Merriam reported as the biggest he had ever seen. He was very nearly double the weight of any of the male African leopards we shot. He was nearly or quite the weight of the smallest of the adult African lionesses we shot while in Africa. He had the big bones, the stout frame, and the heavy muscular build of a small lion, and was not lithe and slender and long like a cougar or leopard. The tail, as with all jaguars, was short, while the girth of the body was great. His coat was beautiful, with a satiny gloss, and the dark-brown spots on the gold of his back, head and sides were hardly as conspicuous as the black of the equally well-marked spots against his white belly.

This was a well-known jaguar who had indulged in cattle killing and, on one occasion during the floods, had taken up his abode near the ranchhouse and had killed a couple of cows and a young steer. The hunters had followed him, but he had made his escape, and for the time being had abandoned the neighborhood.

Others of our party found a deepish pond, a hundred yards or so long and thirty or forty across, tenanted by small caymans and by capybaras—the largest known rodent, a huge aquatic guinea-pig, the size of a small sheep. It also swarmed with piranhas. Undoubtedly the caymans were subsisting largely on these piranhas. But the tables were readily turned if any caymans were injured. When a capybara was shot and sank in the water, the piranhas at once attacked it, and ate the carcass in a few minutes. But much more extraordinary was the fact that when a cayman about five feet long was wounded the piranhas attacked and tore it, and actually drove it out on the bank to face its human foes.

Early one morning we came across two armadillos—the

big, nine-banded armadillo. They were feeding in an open space between two jungle clumps, which were about a hundred yards apart. One was on all fours, the other in a squatting position with its forelegs off the ground. The dogs raced at them. I had always supposed that armadillos merely shuffled along, and curled up for protection when menaced, and I was almost as surprised as if I had seen a turtle gallop when these two armadillos bounded off at a run, going as fast as rabbits. One headed back for the nearest patch of jungle which it reached. The other ran at full speed until it nearly reached the other patch, a hundred yards distant, the dogs in full cry immediately behind it. Then it suddenly changed its mind, wheeled in its tracks, and came back like a bullet right through the pack. Dog after dog tried to seize or stop it and turned to pursue it, but its wedge-shaped snout and armored body, joined to the speed at which it was galloping, enabled it to drive straight ahead through its pursuers, not one of which could halt it or grasp it, and it reached in safety its thorny haven.

I killed a wood-ibis on the wing with the handy little Springfield, and then lost all credit I had thus gained by a series of inexcusable misses, at long range, before I finally killed a jabiru. This great, splendid bird, standing about as tall as a man, shows fight when wounded, and advances against assailants, clattering its formidable bill. One day we found the nest of a jabiru in a mighty fig-tree, on the edge of a patch of jungle. It was a big platform of sticks, placed on a horizontal branch. There were four half-grown young standing on it. We passed it in the morning, when both parents were also perched alongside. In the afternoon, when

we passed it again, only one parent bird was present. It
showed no fear. I noticed that, as it stood on a branch near
the nest, its bill was slightly open. It was very hot, and I
suppose it had opened its bill just as a hen opens her bill
in hot weather.

We stayed at the ranch until a couple of days before
Christmas. Up to now the weather had been lovely. The
night before we left there was a torrential tropic downpour.
The following forenoon the baggage started, in a couple of
two-wheeled ox carts, for the landing where the steamboat
awaited us. Each cart was drawn by eight oxen. The huge
wheels were over seven feet high. Early in the afternoon we
followed on horseback. Next morning, with real regret, we
waved good-by to our dusky attendants, as they stood on the
bank, grouped around a little fire, beside the big, empty
ox-carts.

Chapter 2

The River of Tapirs

CHRISTMAS DAY saw the party steaming its way steadily north against the strong current of the Paraguay. The shallow little steamer, Nyoac, was jammed with men, dogs, rifles, partially cured skins, boxes of provisions, ammunition, tools, and photographic supplies, bags containing tents, cots, bedding, clothes, saddles, hammocks, and the other necessaries for a trip through the great wilderness, the "Matto Grasso" of western Brazil.

A side trip was taken to the São João fazendo, or ranch of Senhor João da Costa Marques. As they stepped ashore the American flag was run up to take its place beside that of Brazil.

A rodeo was planned for the next day. The party went hunting earlier and made no effort to get back for the rodeo, since it began raining so hard that they knew it had to be postponed. Riding through the woods Theodore had his

361

first introduction to fire ants which burnt his skin "like red-hot cinders, and left little sores."

We had been out about three hours when one of the dogs gave tongue in a large belt of woodland and jungle to the left of our line of march through the marsh. The other dogs ran to the sound, and after a while the long barking told that the thing, whatever it was, was at bay or else in some refuge. We made our way toward the place on foot. The dogs were baying excitedly at the mouth of a huge hollow log, and very short examination showed that there were two peccaries within, doubtless a boar and a sow. However, just at this moment the peccaries bolted from an unsuspected opening at the other end of the log, dove into the tangle, and instantly disappeared with the hounds in full cry after them. It was twenty minutes later before we again heard the pack baying. With much difficulty, and by the incessant swinging of the machetes, we opened a trail through the network of vines and branches. This time there was only one peccary, the boar. He was at bay in a half-hollow stump. The dogs were about his head, raving with excitement, and it was not possible to use the rifle. I borrowed the spear from Dom João, the younger, and killed the fierce little boar with it.

An hour or two afterward we unexpectedly struck the fresh tracks of two jaguars and at once loosed the dogs, who tore off yelling, on the line of the scent. Unfortunately, just at this moment the clouds burst and a deluge of rain drove in our faces. So heavy was the downpour that the dogs lost the trail and we lost the dogs. We found them again only owing to one of our *caboclos,* an Indian with a queer Mongolian face and no brain at all, apart from his special dealings with wild creatures, cattle and horses. Nothing escaped his eyes, and he rode anything anywhere.

Next morning the sky was leaden, and a drenching rain fell as we began our descent of the river. All that afternoon the rain continued. It was still pouring in torrents when we left the Cuyabá for the São Lourenco and steamed up the latter a few miles before anchoring. Dom João the younger had accompanied us in his launch. Next morning it was still raining, but we set off on a hunt, anyway, going afoot. A couple of brown *camaradas* led the way, and Colonel Rondon, Dom João, Kermit and I followed. We made our way slowly through the forest, the machetes playing right and left, up and down, at every step, for the trees were tangled in a network of vines and creepers. Some of the vines were as thick as a man's leg. Mosquitoes hummed about us, the venomous fire-ants stung us, the sharp spines of a small palm tore our hands—afterwards some of the wounds festered. Hour after hour we thus walked on through the Brazilian forest. We saw monkeys, the common yellowish kind. A couple were shot for the museum. Then we came on a party of coatis, which look like reddish, long-snouted, long-tailed, lanky raccoons. They were in the top of a big tree. One, when shot at and missed, bounced down to the ground, and ran off through the bushes—Kermit ran after it and secured it. He came back, to find us peering hopelessly up into a treetop, trying to place where the other coatis were. Kermit solved the difficulty by going up along some huge twisted lianas for forty or fifty feet and exploring the upper branches. Down came three other coatis, one being caught by the dogs and the other two escaping.

We heard the rush of a couple of tapirs, as they broke away in the jungle in front of the dogs, and headed for the river. But we never saw them. One of the party shot a bush-deer—a very pretty, graceful creature, smaller than our whitetail deer, but kin to it.

After we had been out four hours our camaradas got lost. Three times they traveled round in a complete circle and we had to set them right with the compass. About noon the rain, which had been falling almost without interruption for forty-eight hours, let up, and in an hour or two the sun came out. We went back to the river, and found our row-boat. In it the hounds—a motley and worthless lot—and the rest of the party were ferried across to the opposite bank, while Colonel Rondon and I stayed in the boat, on the chance that a tapir might be roused and take to the river. However none was found.

Next morning, January 1, 1914, we were up at five and had a good New Year's Day breakfast of hardtack, ham, sardines, and coffee before setting out on an all-day's hunt on foot. After an hour we found the fresh tracks of two jaguars. We soon found that the dogs would not by themselves follow the jaguar trail, nor would the camaradas, although they carried spears. Kermit was the one of our party who possessed the requisite speed, endurance and eyesight, and accordingly he led. Two of the dogs would follow the track half a dozen yards ahead of him but no farther, and two of the camaradas could just about keep up with him.

For an hour we went through thick jungles where the machetes were constantly at work. Then the trail struck off straight across the marshes. It was a hard walk. The sun was out. We were drenched with sweat. We were torn by the spines of the innumerable clusters of small palms with thorns like needles. We were bitten by the hosts of fire-ants, and by the mosquitoes, which we scarcely noticed where the fire-ants were found, exactly as all dread of the latter vanished when we were menaced by the big red wasps, of which a dozen stings will disable a man, and if he is weak or in bad health will seriously menace his life. In the marsh we were continually wading, now up to our knees, now up to our hips. Twice we came to long bayous so deep that we had to swim them, holding our rifles above water in our right hands. The floating masses of marsh grass, and the slimy stems of the water plants, doubled our work. One result of the swim was that my watch, a veteran of Cuba and Africa, came to an indignant halt. Then on we went, hampered by the weight of our drenched clothes while our soggy boots squelched as we walked. There was no breeze. In the undimmed sky the sun stood almost over-head. The heat beat on us in waves. By noon I could only go forward at a slow walk, and two of the party were worse off than I was. Kermit, with the dogs and two *camaradas* close behind him, disappeared across the marshes at a trot. At last, when he was out of sight, and it was obviously use-less to follow him, the rest of us turned back toward the boat. When we got there a relief party went back for the two men under the tree, and soon after it reached them Ker-mit also turned up with his hounds and his *camaradas* trailing wearily behind him. He had followed the jaguar trail until the dogs were so tired that even after he had bathed them, and then held their noses in the fresh footprints, they would pay no heed to the scent.

The next day the party once again began the ascent of the Paraguay. On January 5 they reached Caceres, where the easiest part of their journey ended. From there their journey was up the southward flowing Sepotuba, which in the Indian dialect means River of Tapirs.

On the morning of January 9 we started out for a tapir hunt. Tapirs were hunted with canoes, as they dwell in thick jungle and take to the water when hounds follow them. In this region there were extensive papyrus swamps and big lagoons, back from the river, and often the tapirs fled to these for refuge, throwing off the hounds. In these places it was exceedingly difficult to get them. Our best chance was to keep to the river in canoes, and paddle toward the spot in the direction of which the hounds, by the noise, seemed to be heading. We started in four canoes. Three of them were Indian dugouts, very low in the water. The fourth was our Canadian canoe—a beauty, light, safe, roomy, made of thin slats of wood and cement-covered canvas. Colonel Rondon, Fiala with his camera, and I went in this canoe, together with two paddlers. The bowsman was of nearly pure white blood; the steersman was of nearly pure Negro blood, and was evidently the stronger character and better man of the two. The other canoes carried a couple of ranchmen who had come up from Caceres with their dogs. These dugouts were manned by Indians and half-caste paddlers, and the ranchers, who were nearly white blood, also at times paddled vigorously.

The hounds were at first carried in two of the dugouts, and then let loose on the banks. We went upstream for a couple of hours against the swift current, the paddlers making good headway with their pointed paddles—the broad blade of each paddle was tipped with a long point, so that it could be thrust into the mud to keep the low dugout against the bank. The tropical forest came down almost like a wall, the tall trees laced together with vines, and the spaces between their trunks filled with a low, dense jungle. In most places it could only be penetrated by a man with a machete.

At last we landed at a point of ground where there was little jungle, and where the forest was composed of palms and was fairly open. The colonel strolled off in one direction, returning an hour later with a squirrel for the naturalists. Meanwhile Fiala and I went through the palm wood to a papyrus swamp.

While standing by the marsh we heard something coming along one of the game paths. In a moment a buck of the bigger species of bush-deer appeared, a very pretty and graceful creature. It stopped and darted back as soon as it saw us, giving us no chance for a shot. In another moment we caught glimpses of it running by at full speed, back among the palms. I covered an opening between two tree trunks. By good luck the buck appeared in the right place, giving me just time to hold well ahead of him and fire. At the report he went down in a heap, the umbrella-pointed

bullet going in at one shoulder, and ranging forward, breaking the neck.

This was an old buck. The antlers were single spikes, five
and six inches long. They were old and white and would
soon have been shed. We hung the buck in a tree.

The colonel returned, and not long afterward one of the
paddlers who had been watching the river called out to us
that there was a tapir in the water, a good distance upstream,
and that two of the other boats were after it. We jumped
into the canoe and the two paddlers dug their blades in the
water as they drove her against the strong current, edging
over for the opposite bank. The tapir was coming downstream at a great rate, only its queer head above water, while
the dugouts were closing rapidly on it, the paddlers uttering loud cries. As the tapir turned slightly to one side or the
other, the long, slightly upturned snout and strongly pronounced arch of the crest along the head and upper neck
gave it a marked and unusual aspect. I could not shoot, for
it was directly in line with one of the pursuing dugouts.
Suddenly it dived, the snout being slightly curved downward as it did so. Then we made it out clambering up the
bank. The branches partially hid it, and it was in deep
shadow, so that it did not offer a very good shot. My bullet
went into its body too far back, and the tapir disappeared
in the forest at a gallop as if unhurt, although the bullet
really secured it, by making it unwilling to trust to its speed
and leave the neighborhood of the water. Three or four of
the hounds by this time were swimming the river, and as
soon as the swimmers reached the shore they were put on
the tapir's trail and galloped after it, giving tongue. In a

couple of minutes we saw the tapir take to the water far upstream, and after it we went as fast as the paddles could urge us through the water. We were not in time to head it, but fortunately some of the dogs had come to the river's edge at the very point where the tapir was about to land, and turned it back. We were more than half the breadth of the river away from the tapir, and somewhat downstream, when it dived. It made an astonishingly long swim beneath the water this time, almost as if it had been a hippopotamus, for it passed completely under our canoe and rose between us and the hither bank. I shot it, the bullet going into its brain, while it was thirty or forty yards from the shore. It sank at once.

There was now nothing to do but wait until the body floated. I feared that the strong current would roll it downstream over the river-bed, but my companions assured me that this was not so, and that the body would remain where it was until it rose, which would be in an hour or two. They were right, except as to the time. For over a couple of hours we paddled, or anchored ourselves by clutching branches close to the spot, or else drifted down a mile and paddled up again near to shore, to see if the body had been caught anywhere. Then we crossed the river and had lunch at the lovely natural picnic ground where the buck was hung up. We had very nearly given up the tapir when it suddenly floated only a few rods from where it had sunk. With no little difficulty the big, round black body was hoisted into the canoe, and we all turned our prows downstream. The skies had been lowering for some time, and now—too late to interfere with the hunt or cause us any annoyance—a heavy downpour of rain came on and beat upon us. Little we cared, as the canoe raced forward, with the tapir and the buck lying in the bottom, and a dry, comfortable camp ahead of us.

The tapir was a big one. I did not wish to kill another, unless, of course, it became advisable to do so for food. On the other hand I did wish to get some specimens of the big, white-lipped peccary, the *quiexa* (pronounced "cashada") of the Brazilians, which would make our collection of the big mammals of the Brazilian forests almost complete.

Colonel Rondon had sent out one of our attendants, an old follower of his, a full-blood Parecis Indian, to look for tracks. He found the tracks of a herd of thirty or forty cashadas, and the following morning we started after them.

The horses were swum across the river, each being led beside a dugout. Then we crossed with the dogs. We went in single file, for no other mode of travel was possible, and this only with the help of the men swinging their machetes. Most of the time we were in forest or swampy jungle. Part of the time we crossed or skirted marshy plains. In one of them a herd of half-wild cattle were feeding. Herons, storks, ducks, and ibises were in these marshes and we saw one flock of lovely roseate spoonbills. In one grove the fig-trees were killing the palms, just as in Africa they kill the sandalwood trees.

Now and then we were bitten and stung by the venomous fire-ants. Once we were assailed by maribundi wasps, not the biggest kind, but about the size of our hornets. We were at the time passing through dense jungle, under tall trees, in a spot where the down timber, holes, tangled creepers, and thorns made the going difficult. Colonel Rondon and I were in the middle of the column, and the swarm attacked us. Both of us were badly stung on the face, neck, and hands, the colonel more severely than I was. He wheeled and rode to the rear and I to the front. Our horses were stung too.

At the close of the day, when we were almost back at the river, the dogs killed a jaguar kitten. There was no trace of the mother. Some accident must have befallen her, and the kitten was trying to shift for herself. She was very emaciated. In her stomach were the remains of a pigeon and some tendons from the skeleton or dried carcass of some big animal. The loathsome berni flies, which deposit eggs in living beings—cattle, dogs, monkeys, rodents, men—had been at it. There were seven huge, white grubs making big abscess-like swellings over its eyes. In 1909, on Colonel Rondon's hardest trip, every man of the party had from one to five grubs deposited in him, the fly acting with great speed, and driving its ovipositor through clothing. The grubs cause torture, although a couple of cross cuts with a lancet permit the loathsome creatures to be squeezed out.

In these forests the multitude of insects that bite, sting, devour, and prey upon other creatures, often with accompaniments of atrocious suffering, passes belief. The very pathetic myth of "beneficent nature" could not deceive even the least wise being if he once saw for himself the iron cruelty of life in the tropics. Of course "nature"—in common parlance a wholly inaccurate term, especially when used as if to express a single entity—is entirely ruthless, no less so as regards types than as regards individuals, and entirely indifferent to good or evil. She works out her ends or no ends with utter disregard of pain and woe.

The following morning at sunrise we started again. This time only Colonel Rondon and I went with a couple of trackers. We brought along four dogs which it was hoped might chase the cashadas. Two of them disappeared on the track of a tapir and we saw them no more. One of the others promptly fled when we came across the tracks of our game, and would not even venture after them in our company. The remaining one did not actually run away and occasionally gave tongue, but could not be persuaded to advance unless there was a man ahead of him.

After four hours of riding, one of the trackers suddenly stopped and pointed downward. He had found the fresh track of a herd of big peccaries crossing from left to right. There were apparently thirty or forty in the herd.

The tracker slipped off his horse, changed his leggings for sandals, threw his rifle over his arm, and took the trail of the herd, followed by the one dog. The peccaries had gone into a broad belt of forest, with a marsh on the farther side. The other tracker led the colonel and me, all of us on horseback, at a canter round this belt to the marsh side, thinking the peccaries had gone almost through it. But we could hear nothing. The dog only occasionally barked, and then not loudly. Finally we heard a shot. The other tracker had found the herd, which showed no fear of him. He had backed out and fired a single shot. We all three went into the forest on foot toward where the shot had been fired. It was a dense jungle and stiflingly hot. We could not see clearly for more than a few feet, or move easily without free use of the machetes. Soon we heard the ominous groaning of the herd, in front of us, and almost on each side. Then the first tracker appeared with the dog at his rear. We moved slowly forward, toward the sound of the fierce moaning grunts which were varied at times by a castanet chattering of the tusks. Then we dimly made out the dark forms of the peccaries moving very slowly to the left. My companions each chose a tree to climb at need and pointed out one for me. I fired at the half-seen form of a hog, through the vines, leaves, and branches. The colonel fired. I fired three more shots at other hogs. The tracker also fired. The peccaries did not charge. Instead, walking and trotting with bristles erect, groaning and clacking their tusks, they disappeared into the jungle. We could not see one of them clearly and not one was left dead. But a few paces on we came across one of the wounded ones, standing at bay by a palm trunk, and I killed it. The dog would not even trail the wounded one but one of the trackers did. With eyes almost as quick and sure as those of a wild beast he had watched after every shot, and was able to tell the results in each case. He said that in addition to the one I had just killed I had wounded two others so seriously that he did not think they would go far, that Colonel Rondon and he himself had each badly wounded one. He showed the trails each wounded animal had taken. The event justified him. In a few minutes we found my second one dead. Then we found the tracker's. Then we found my third one alive and at bay, and I killed it with another shot. Finally we found the colonel's. I told him I should ask the authorities of the American Museum to mount his and one or two of mine in a group to com-memorate our hunting together.

The queer custom of the people in the interior of Brazil of gelding their hunting dogs was doubtless the chief reason why there were so few hounds worth their salt in the more serious kind of hunting, where the quarry was the jaguar or big peccary. Thus far we had seen but one dog as good as the ordinary cougar hound or bear-hound in such packs as those with which I had hunted in the Rockies and in the cane-brakes of the lower Mississippi. It could hardly be otherwise when every dog that showed himself worth any-thing was promptly put out of the category of breeders— the theory apparently being that the dog would then last longer. All the breeding was from worthless dogs, and no dog of proved worth left descendants.

On the 13th of January the party broke camp and headed upstream for Tapirapoan. The cooking—"and it was good cooking"—was done at a funny little open-air fireplace, with two or three cooking-pots, on the stern of a houseboat. The trip was pleasant and interesting, although there was not much to do on the boat. Colonel Rondon studied a work on applied geographical astronomy. Theodore varied his reading from Quentin Durwood to Gibbon and the Chanson de Roland.

Shortly before noon on January 16, they reached Tapir-apoan.

It was an attractive place, gaily bedecked with flags, not only those of Brazil and the United States, but of all the other American republics, in our honor. Here we were to begin our trip overland, on pack-mules and pack-oxen, scores of which had been gathered to meet us. Several days were needed to apportion the loads and arrange for the several divisions in which it was necessary that so large a party should attempt the long wilderness march, through a country where there was not much food for man or beast, and where it was always possible to run into a district in which fatal cattle or horse diseases were prevalent.

At the camp the heat was great—from ninety-one degrees to one hundred and four degrees Fahrenheit—and the air very heavy, being saturated with moisture. But there were no mosquitoes, and we were very comfortable. Thanks to the neighborhood of a ranch, we fared sumptuously, with plenty of beef, chickens, and fresh milk. Two of the Brazilian dishes were delicious: canja, a thick soup of chicken and rice, the best soup a hungry man ever tasted, and beef chopped in rather small pieces and served with a well-flavored but simple gravy.

The Brazilian Government had waiting for me a very handsome silver-mounted saddle and bridle. I was much pleased with both. However, my exceedingly rough and shabby clothing made an incongruous contrast.

All the skins, skulls, and alcoholic specimens, and all the baggage not absolutely necessary, were sent back down the Paraguay and to New York. The separate baggage-trains, under the charge of Captain Amilcar, were organized to go in one detachment. The main body of the expedition, consisting of the American members, and of Colonel Rondon,

Lieutenant Lyra, and Doctor Cajazeira, with their baggage and provisions formed another detachment.

We were now in the land of the vampire bats that suck the blood of living creatures, clinging to or hovering against the shoulder of a horse or cow, or the hand or foot of a sleeping man, and making a wound from which the blood continues to flow long after the bat's thirst has been satiated. South America makes up for its lack, relatively to Africa and India, of large man eating carnivora by the extraordinary ferocity or bloodthirstiness of certain small creatures of which the kinsfolk elsewhere are harmless. It is only here that fish no bigger than trout kill swimmers, and bats the size of the ordinary "flittermice" of the northern hemisphere drain the life-blood of big beasts and man himself.

Chapter 3

Across the Wilderness

THE MAIN body of the expedition began its overland journey across the Plan Alto on January 21, 1914. The first day they made twelve miles, crossed the Sepotuba River, and camped beside it in country covered with an open forest of low, twisted trees resembling the crosstimbers of Texas and Oklahoma. From there they went westward through dense tropical forests in which trails had to be cut with machetes.

The Plan Alto is the high central plain of Brazil, "the healthy land of dry air, of cool nights, of clear running brooks." Here they saw rheas—the South American ostrich —and small pampas-deer which furnished excellent venison. During the afternoon of the third day they crossed the divide between the basins of the Paraguay and the Amazon. From then on the course was northward to east of north.

Quite naturally at night the discussions of the party turned on where the river they were going to descend—the Rio da Duvida or River of Doubt—would come out. If it flowed northwest into the Gy-Parana river, their journey would be short and their exploration of minor importance; if it flowed into a river lower down, for instance the Madeira —which in turn flowed into the Amazon—their journey would be extremely long and the importance of their exploration of major importance to geographers.

Their trip now was to the east of the northward-flowing Rio Sacre. Each night they camped on one of the tributary brooks that fed it. Their chief bother was the various insects from the "pium" fly to the inch-and-a-half long black ant which plagued them constantly.

We came across many queer insects. One red grasshopper when it flew seemed as big as a small sparrow. In other places multitudes of active little green grasshoppers frightened the mules. At our camping place we saw an extraordinary colony of spiders. It was among some dwarf trees, standing a few yards apart from one another. When we reached the camping place, early in the afternoon, no spiders were out. They were under the leaves of the trees. Their webs were for the most part broken down. But at dusk they came out, two or three hundred of them, and at once began to repair the old and spin new webs. Each spun its own circular web, and sat in the middle, and each web was connected on several sides with other webs, while those nearest the trees were hung to them by spun ropes, so to speak. The result was a kind of sheet of web consisting of scores of wheels, in each of which the owner and proprietor sat.

Praying mantis were common, and one evening at supper one had a comical encounter with a young dog, a jovial
near-puppy of Colonel Rondon's, named Cartucho. Cartucho was lying with his head on the ox-hide that served as
a table, waiting with poorly dissembled impatience for his
share of the banquet. The mantis flew down on the ox-hide
and proceeded to crawl over it, taking little flights from one
corner to another. Whenever it thought itself menaced, it
assumed an attitude of seeming devotion and real defiance.
Soon it lit in front of Cartucho's nose. Cartucho cocked his
big ear forward, stretched his neck, and cautiously sniffed
at the new arrival, not with any hostile design, but merely
to find out whether it would prove to be a playmate. The
mantis promptly assumed an attitude of prayer. This struck
Cartucho as both novel and interesting, and he thrust his
sniffing black nose still nearer. The mantis dexterously
thrust forward first one and then the other armed fore leg,
touching the intrusive nose, which was instantly jerked
back and again slowly and inquiringly brought forward.
Then the mantis suddenly flew in Cartucho's face, whereupon Cartucho, with a smothered yelp of dismay, almost
turned a back somersault. The triumphant mantis flew back
to the middle of the ox-hide, among the plates, where it
reared erect and defied the laughing and applauding company.

On the morning of the 29th, after six hours' march, we
came to the crossing of the Rio Sacre at the beautiful water-
fall appropriately called the Salto Bello. The falls themselves were very lovely. Just above them was a wooded
island, but the river joined again before it raced forward for

the final plunge. There was a sheer drop of forty or fifty yards with a breadth two or three times as great, and the volume of water was large. On the left side a cliff extended for several hundred yards below the falls. Green vines had flung themselves down over its face, and they were met by other vines thrusting upward from the mass of vegetation at the foot, glistening in the perpetual mist from the cataract, and clothing even the rock surfaces in vivid green. The river, after throwing itself over the rock wall, rushed off in long curves at the bottom of a thickly wooded ravine, the white water churning among the black boulders. There was a perpetual rainbow at the foot of the falls. The masses of green water that were hurling themselves over the brink dissolved into shifting, foaming columns of snowy lace.

There was a small Parecis Indian village at the falls. They were to all appearance an unusually cheerful, good-humored, pleasant-natured people. The colonel was received as a valued friend and as a leader who was to be followed and obeyed.

The men had adopted, and were wearing, shirts and trousers, but the women had made little change in their clothing. A few wore print dresses, but obviously only for ornament. Most of them, especially the girls and young married women, wore nothing but a loin cloth in addition to bead necklaces and bracelets. The nursing mothers—and almost all the mothers were nursing—sometimes carried the child slung against their side or hip, seated in a cloth belt, or sling, which went over the opposite shoulder of the mother.

In each house there were several families, and life went

on with no privacy but with good humor, consideration,
and fundamentally good manners. The man or woman who
had nothing to do lay in a hammock or squatted on the
ground leaning against a post or wall. The children played
together, or lay in little hammocks, or tagged round after
their mothers. They came trustfully up to us to be petted or
given some small trinket.

In our family we had always relished Oliver Hereford's
nonsense rhymes, including the account of Willie's displeas-
ure with his goat:

> *I do not like my billy goat,*
> *I wish that he was dead;*
> *Because he kicked me, so he did,*
> *He kicked me with his head.*

Well, these Parecis Indians enthusiastically played football with their heads. The game was not only native to
them, but I had never heard or read of its being played by
any other tribe or people. They used a light hollow rubber
ball, of their own manufacture. It was circular and about
eight inches in diameter. The players divided into two sides,
and stationed much as in association football, and the ball
was placed on the ground to be put in play as in football.
Then a player ran forward, threw himself flat on the ground,
and butted the ball toward the opposite side. This first butt,
when the ball was on the ground, never lifted it much and
it rolled and bounded toward the opponents. One or two
of the latter ran toward it, one throwing himself flat on his
face, and butted the ball back. Usually this butt lifted it,
and it flew back in a curve well up in the air. An opposite

player, rushing toward it, caught it on his head with such a swing of his brawny neck, and such precision and address that the ball bounded back through the air as a football soars after a drop-kick. If the ball flew off to one side or the other it was brought back, and again put in play. Often it would be sent to and fro a dozen times, from head to head, until finally it rose with such a sweep that it passed far over the heads of the opposite players and descended behind them. Then shrill, rolling cries of good-humored triumph arose from the victors, and the game instantly began again with fresh zeal.

There were, of course, no such rules as in a specialized ball game of civilization, and I saw no disputes. There might be eight or ten, or many more, players on each side. The ball was never touched with the hands or feet, or with anything except the top of the head. It was hard to decide whether to wonder most at the dexterity and strength with which it was hit or butted with the head, as it came down through the air, or at the reckless speed and skill with which the players threw themselves headlong on the ground to return the ball if it came low down. Why they did not grind off their noses I cannot imagine. Some of the players hardly ever failed to catch and return the ball if it came in their neighborhood, and with such a vigorous toss of the head that it often flew in a great curve for a really astonishing distance.

That night a pack-ox got into the tent in which Kermit and I were sleeping, entering first at one end and then at the other. It is extraordinary that he did not waken us, but we slept undisturbed while the ox deliberately ate our shirts, socks, and underclothes! It chewed them into rags. One of my socks escaped, and my undershirt, although chewed full of holes, was still good for some weeks' wear, but the other things were in fragments.

In the morning Colonel Rondon arranged for us to have breakfast over on benches under the trees by the waterfall, whose roar, lulled to a thunderous murmur, had been in our ears before we slept and when we waked. There could have been no more picturesque place for the breakfast of such a party as ours.

The party also visited the nearby Falls of Utiarity—so named by their discoverer, Colonel Rondon, after the sacred falcon of the Parecis. These falls were far superior in beauty and majesty to the Salto Bello falls. They were twice as high and twice as broad. There was also a large settlement of Parecis Indians here.

The men held a dance in the late afternoon. For this occasion most, but not all, of them cast aside their civilized clothing, and appeared as doubtless they would all have appeared had none but themselves been present. They were absolutely naked except for a beaded string round the waist. Most of them were spotted and dashed with red paint, and on one leg wore anklets which rattled. A number carried pipes through which they blew a kind of deep stifled whistle in time to the dancing. One of them had his pipe leading into a huge gourd, which gave out a hollow, moaning boom. Many wore two red or green or yellow macaw feathers in their hair, and one had a macaw feather stuck transversely through the septum of his nose. They circled slowly round and round, chanting and stamping their feet, while the anklet rattles clattered and the pipes droned. They advanced to the wall of one of the houses, again and again chanting and bowing before it. I was told this was a demand for drink. They entered one house and danced in a ring around the cooking-fire in the middle of the earth floor. I was told that they were then reciting the deeds of mighty hunters and describing how they brought in the game. They drank freely from gourds and pannikins of fermented drink made from mandioc which were brought out to them. During the first part of the dance the women remained in the houses, and all the doors and windows were shut and blankets hung to prevent the possibility of seeing out. But during the second part all the women and girls came out and looked on. They were themselves to have danced when the men finished, but were overcome with shyness at the thought of dancing with so many strangers looking on. The children played about with unconcern throughout the ceremony, one of them throwing high in the air, and again catching in his hands, a loaded feather, a kind of shuttlecock.

From this point we were to enter a still wilder region, the land of the naked Nhambiquaras. On February 3 we started with the mule-train and two ox-carts. We had now begun the difficult part of the expedition. The pium flies were becoming a pest. There was much fever and beriberi in the country we were entering. The feed for the animals was poor. The rains had made the trails slippery and diffi-cult and many, both of the mules and oxen, were already weak, and some had to be abandoned. We left the canoe, the motor, and the gasoline. We had hoped to try them on the Amazonian rivers, but we were obliged to cut down everything that was not absolutely indispensable. We drove with us a herd of oxen for food.

After going about fifteen miles we camped beside the swampy headwaters of a little brook. In the late afternoon the piums were bad but we had gloves and heat nets, and were not bothered. The frogs in the swamp uttered a peculiar loud noise. Miller told of a little tree-frog in Columbia which swelled itself out with air, until it looked like the frog in Aesop's fables, and then brayed like a mule. Cherrie told of a huge frog in Guiana that uttered a short, loud roar.

Their march the next day was through country in which skeletons of mules and oxen were seen everywhere, and once or twice, graves of men encircled by barbed wire. The following morning their mules were ferried over the Burity River, on whose bank they had camped, and the oxen were forced to swim. The distance covered, from now on, was short because the stock had to be driven a considerable distance from camp to find enough subsistence for them to live on. The baggage was cut down to make the loads lighter. The camp on the fourth night was on an open grassy space, beside a clear, cool, rushing little river, in which they all enjoyed a refreshing swim. That night, beside a campfire, they enjoyed "a delicious dinner of soup, beef, beans, rice and coffee."

The next night they camped by another little river—all these being affluents of the Juruena, the name by which the upper Tapajos was known.

The following day they had to march twenty miles under the tropical sun in the middle of the day. The dogs got so hot that they periodically ran off, cooled themselves under a shady place, and then caught up with the march. They reached the Juruena in the middle of the afternoon.

At the Juruena we met a party of Nhambiquaras, very friendly and sociable, and very glad to see Colonel Rondon. They were originally exceedingly hostile and suspicious, but the colonel's unwearied thoughtfulness and good temper, joined with his indomitable resolution, enabled him to avoid war and to secure their friendship and even their aid.

Nowhere in Africa did we come across wilder or more absolutely primitive savages, although these Indians were pleasanter and better featured than any of the African tribes at the same stage of culture. Both sexes were well made and rather good looking, with fairly good teeth, although some of them seemed to have skin diseases. They were a laughing, easy-tempered crew, and the women were as well fed as the men, and were obviously well treated, from the savage standpoint. They were absolutely naked. In many savage tribes the men go absolutely naked, but the women wear a breech clout or loin cloth, but among the Nhambiquaras the women were more naked than the men. The women did not wear a stitch of any kind anywhere on their bodies. They did not have on as much as a string, or a bead, or even an ornament in their hair. They were all, men and women, boys and well-grown young girls, as entirely at ease and unconscious as so many friendly animals. All of them— men, women, and children, laughing and talking—crowded around us, whether we were on horseback or on foot. They flocked into the house, and when I sat down to write surrounded me so closely that I had to push them gently away. The women and girls often stood holding one another's hands, or with their arms over one another's shoulders or around one another's waists, offering an attractive picture. The men had holes pierced through the septum of the nose and through the upper lip, and wore a straw through each hole. The women were not marked or mutilated.

It seems like a contradiction in terms, but it is nevertheless a fact that the behavior of these completely naked women and men was entirely modest. There was never an indecent look or a consciously indecent gesture. They had no blankets or hammocks, and when night came simply lay down in the sand. Colonel Rondon stated that they never wore a covering by night or by day, and if it was cool slept one on each side of a small fire. Their huts were merely slight shelters against the rain.

The moon was nearly full, and after nightfall a few of the Indians suddenly held an improvised dance for us in front of our house. There were four men, a small boy, and two young women or grown girls. Two of the men and the boy were practically naked, and the two young women were absolutely so. All of them danced in a circle, without a touch of embarrassment or impropriety. The two girls kept hold of each other's hands throughout, dancing among the men as modestly as possible, and with the occasional interchange of a laugh or jest, in as good taste and temper as in any dance in civilization. The dance consisted in slowly going around in a circle, first one way, then the other, rhythmically beating time with the feet to the music of the song they were chanting. The chants—there were three of them— were measured and rather slowly uttered melodies, varied with an occasional half-subdued cry. The women continually uttered a kind of long-drawn wailing or droning.

I was not enough of a musician to say whether it was an overtone or the sustaining of the burden of the ballad. The young boy sang better than any of the others. It was a strange and interesting sight to see these utterly wild, friendly savages circling in their slow dance, and chanting their immemorial melodies, in the brilliant tropical moonlight, with the river rushing by in the background, through the lonely heart of the wilderness.

The Indians stayed with us, feasting, dancing, and singing until the early hours of the morning. They then suddenly and silently disappeared in the darkness, and did not return. In the morning we discovered that they had gone off with one of Colonel Rondon's dogs. Probably the temptation had proved irresistible to one of their number, and the others had been afraid to interfere and also afraid to stay in or return to our neighborhood.

In the morning two days later we resumed our march. It soon began to rain and we were drenched when, some fifteen miles on, we reached the river where we were to camp. After the great heat we felt quite cold in our wet clothes, and gladly crowded round a fire which was kindled under a thatched shed, beside the cabin of the ferryman. The ferryboat was so small that it took some time the next day to cross.

After leaving the Juruena the ground became somewhat

more hilly, and the scrubby forest was less open, but otherwise there was no change in the monotonous, and yet to me rather attractive landscape.

That evening round the campfire Colonel Rondon mentioned how the brother of one of the soldiers with us—a Parecis Indian—had been killed by a jararaca snake. Snakes frequently came into camp after nightfall. Cherrie killed one rattlesnake which had swallowed the skinned bodies of four mice he had prepared for specimens.

There were many swollen rivers to cross at this point of our journey. Some we waded at fords. Some we crossed by rude bridges. The larger ones, such as the Juina, we crossed by ferry, and when the approaches were swampy, and the river broad and swift, many hours might be consumed in getting the mule-train, the loose bullocks, and the ox-cart over. We had few accidents, although we once lost a ferry-load of provisions, which was quite a misfortune in a country where they could not be replaced.

At one camp three Nhambiquaras paid us a visit at breakfast time. They left their weapons behind them before they appeared, and shouted loudly while they were still hid by the forest, and it was only after repeated answering calls of welcome that they approached. Always in the wilderness friends proclaim their presence—a silent advance marks a foe. Our visitors were men, and stark naked, as usual. They ate greedily of the food offered thcm. They had with them a big mandioc cake, some honey, and a little fish. One of them wore a high helmet of puma-skin, with the tail hanging down his back—handsome head gear which he gladly bartered for several strings of bright coral-red beads.

The party journeyed northwest and on February 15 stopped at the little village of Campos Novos to collect specimens for several days. Then they pushed on in the same direction to Vilhena which they reached in a couple of more days. Here the trail went in and out of steep valleys covered with magnificent woods in which giant rubber trees towered above all of them. "Great azure butterflies flitted through the open, sunny glades, and the bell-birds, sitting motionless, uttered their ringing calls from the dark stillness of the columned groves."

From Vilhena they traveled in a northward direction, across a nearly level plateau, after which they plunged into thick forests where there was little feed for the animals. "The loose bullocks furnished us abundance of fresh beef, although of a decidedly tough quality. One of the biggest of the bullocks was attacked one night by a vampire bat, and next morning his withers were literally bathed in blood."

The third night out from Vilhena they emerged from the close-growing forest to a beautiful open country, where grassy slopes, dotted with trees, came down on either side of a little brook which was one of the headwaters of the Dúvida.

Next day we journeyed to the telegraph station at Bonofacio, through alternate spells of glaring sunshine and heavy rain. On the way we stopped at an aldea—village—of Nhambiquaras. We first met a couple of men going to hunt, with bows and arrows longer than themselves. A rather comely young woman, carrying on her back a wickerwork basket, or creel, supported by a forehead band, and accom-

panied by a small child, was with them. At the village there
were a number of men, women and children. Although as
completely naked as the others we had met, the members of
this band were more ornamented with beads, and wore ear-
rings made from the inside of mussel-shells or very big snail-
shells. They were more hairy than the ones we had so far
met. The women, but not the men, completely removed
the hair from their bodies—and looked more, instead of
less, indecent in consequence.

The chief, whose body was painted red with the juice of
a fruit, had what could fairly be styled a mustache and im-
perial, and one old man looked somewhat like a hairy Ainu,
or perhaps even more like an Australian black fellow. My
companion told me that this probably represented an in-
fusion of Negro blood, and possibly of mulatto blood, from
runaway slaves of the old days, when some of the Matto
Grosso mines were worked by slave labor. They also thought
it possible that this infiltration of African Negroes might be
responsible for the curious shape of the bigger huts, which
were utterly unlike their flimsy, ordinary shelter, and bore
no resemblance in shape to those of the other Indian tribes
of this region, whereas they were not unlike the ordinary
beehive huts of the agricultural African Negroes.

There were in this village several huts or shelters open at
the sides, and two of the big huts. These were of closely
woven thatch, circular in outline, with a rounded dome, and
two doors a couple of feet high opposite each other, and no
other opening. There were fifteen or twenty people to each
hut. Inside were their implements and utensils, such as
wicker baskets (some of them filled with pineapples),

gourds, fire-sticks, wooden knives, wooden mortars, and a board for grating mandioc, made of a thick slab of wood, inset with sharp points of a harder wood.

From the Brazilians one or two of them had obtained blankets, and one a hammock. They had also obtained knives, which they sorely needed, for they were not even in the Stone Age. One woman shielded herself from the rain by holding a green palm-branch down her back. Another had on her head what we at first thought to be a monkey-skin headdress. But it was a little, live, black monkey. It stayed habitually with its head above her forehead, and its arms and legs spread so that it lay moulded to the shape of her head. Both the woman and the monkey showed some reluctance about having their photographs taken.

Chapter 4

The River of Doubt

BONOFACIO WAS at the end of the government-owned telegraph line and thus was the jumping off place into an unknown and unexplored wilderness. On February 24, the entire party assembled on a brook that flowed into the River of Doubt. They were only six miles from their place of embarkation. Captain Amilcar, Miller and a number of others were to march three days to the Gy-Paraná and descend it, and continue down the Madeira to Manaos. Colonel Rondon, Lieutenant Lyra, the medical doctor who had joined them, Cherrie, Kermit and Theodore, with sixteen paddlers, in seven canoes, were to descend the River of Doubt, and find out whether it led into the Gy-Paraná, into the Madeira, or into the Tapajos. If within a few days it led into the Gy-Paraná, they were to return and descend the Ananas river, whose outlet was also unknown.

Theodore and his party took provisions for about fifty days—not full rations, for they hoped in part to live on the country. Their baggage was cut as low as they thought possible. Cherrie, Kermit and Theodore took the naturalist's fly to sleep under, and also a light tent for anyone who might become sick. Rondon, Lyra, and the doctor took a small tent of their own. In addition there were medicines, bedding, instruments for determining the altitude and longitude, and a few books. "Lyra's were in German, consisting of two tiny volumes of Goethe and Schiller; Kermit's were in Portuguese; mine, all in English, included the last two volumes of Gibbon, the plays of Sophocles, More's Utopia, Marcus Aurelius, and Epictetus."

If our canoe voyage was prosperous we would gradually lighten the loads by eating the provisions. If we met with accidents, such as losing canoes and men in the rapids, or losing men in encounters with Indians, or if we encountered overmuch fever and dysentery, the loads would lighten themselves. We were all armed. We took no cartridges for sport. Cherrie had some to be used sparingly for collecting specimens. The others were to be used—unless in the unlikely event of having to repel an attack—only to procure food. The food and the arms we carried represented all reasonable precautions against suffering and starvation. If the course of the river proved very long and difficult, if we lost our boats over falls or rapids, or had to make too many and too long portages, or were brought to a halt by impassable swamps, then we would have to reckon with starvation as a possibility. Anything might happen. We were about to go into the unknown, and no one could say what it held.

On February 27, 1914, shortly after midday, we started down the River of Doubt into the unknown. We were quite uncertain whether after a week we should find ourselves in the Gy-Paraná, or after six in the Madeira, or after three months we knew not where. That was why the river was rightly christened the Dúvida.

As our laden dugouts swung into the stream, Amilcar and Miller and all the others of the Gy-Paraná party were on the banks and the bridge to wave farewell and wish us good-by and good luck. It was the height of the rainy reason, and the swollen torrent was swift and brown. Our camp was at about twelve degrees one minute latitude south and sixty degrees fifteen minutes longitude west of Greenwich. Our general course was to be northward toward the equator, by waterway, through the vast forest.

We had seven canoes, all of them dugouts. One was small, one was cranky, and two were old, water-logged, and leaky. The other three were good. The two old canoes were lashed together, and the cranky one was lashed to one of the others. Kermit with two paddlers went in the smallest of the good canoes, Colonel Rondon and Lyra with three other paddlers in the next largest. The doctor, Cherrie and I were in the largest with three paddlers. The remaining eight *camaradas* were equally divided between our two pairs of lashed canoes. Although our baggage was cut as low as possible the seven dugouts were overloaded.

The paddlers were a strapping set. They were expert rivermen of the forest, skilled veterans in wilderness work. They were lithe as panthers and brawny as bears. They swam like

water dogs. They were equally at home with pole and paddle, with axe and machete, and one was a good cook, while
most of them were good men around the camp. They looked
like pirates in the pictures of Howard Pyle or Maxfield Par-
rish. One or two of them had been pirates, and one worse
than a pirate, but most of them were hard-working, willing,
and cheerful. They were white—or, rather, the olive of
southern Europe—black, copper-colored, and of all inter-
mediate shades.

The actual surveying of the river was done by Colonel
Rondon and Lyra, with Kermit as their assistant.

The first half-day's work was slow. The general course
of the stream was a trifle east of north, but at short intervals it bent and curved literally toward every point of the
compass. Kermit landed nearly a hundred times, and we
made but nine and a third kilometres.

My canoe, running ahead of the surveying canoes, ran
only a couple of hours. Then we halted to wait for the
others. After a couple of hours more, as the surveyors had
not turned up, we landed and made camp at a spot where
the bank rose sharply for a hundred yards to a level stretch
of ground. The axmen cleared a space for the tents which
were pitched, then the baggage was brought up from the
moored canoes, and a fire built. The woods were soundless.
Through them ran old tapir trails, but there was no fresh
sign. Before nightfall the surveyors arrived. There were a
few piums and gnats, and a few mosquitoes, but not enough
to make us uncomfortable. Small stingless bees, of slightly
aromatic odor, crawled over our faces and hands. They were
such tame, harmless little things that when they tickled too

much I always tried to brush them away without hurting them. It was a pleasant night, the air almost cool, and we slept soundly.

Next morning the two surveying canoes left immediately after breakfast. An hour later the two pairs of lashed canoes pushed off. I kept our canoe to let Cherrie collect. The most interesting birds he shot were a cotinga, brilliant turquoise blue with a magenta-purple throat, and a big woodpecker, black above and cinnamon below with an entirely red head and neck.

It was almost noon before we started. As we drifted and paddled down the swirling brown current, through the vivid rain-drenched green of the tropic forest, the trees leaned over the river from both banks. Butterflies of every hue fluttered overhead. The day was overcast, with showers of rain. When the sun broke through rifts in the clouds, its shafts turned the forest to gold.

In mid-afternoon we came to the mouth of a big and swift affluent entering from the right. It was undoubtedly the Bandeira, which we had crossed well toward its head, some ten days before, on our road to Bonofacio. This evening we made camp on a flat of dry ground, densely wooded, directly on the edge of the river and five feet above it. It was fine to see the speed and sinewy ease with which the choppers cleared an open space for the tents. Next morning, when we bathed, we dived into deep water right from the shore, and from the moored canoes.

The following day, March 1, there was much rain. Our course was somewhat west of north and we made twenty and a half kilometres. We passed signs of Indian habitation. There were abandoned palm-leaf shelter on both banks. On the left bank we came to two or three old Indian fields, grown up with coarse fern and studded with the burned skeletons of trees. At the mouth of a brook which entered from the right some sticks stood in the water, marking the site of an old fish-trap. At one point we found the tough vine hand-rail of an Indian bridge running right across the river, a couple of feet above it. Evidently the bridge had been built at low water. Three stout poles had been driven into the stream bed in a line at right angles to the current. The bridge had consisted of poles fastened to these supports, leading between them and from the support at each end, to the banks. The rope of tough vines had been stretched as a handrail, necessary with such precarious footing. The rise of the river had swept away the bridge, but the props and the rope handrail remained.

In the afternoon, from the boat, Cherrie shot a large dark-gray monkey with a prehensile tail. It was very good eating. We camped on a dry level space, but a few feet above, and close beside the river—so that our swimming-bath was handy. The trees were cleared and camp was made with orderly hurry. One of the men almost stepped on a poisonous coral snake, which would have been a serious thing, as his feet were bare. But I had on stout shoes, and the fangs of these serpents—unlike those of the pit-vipers—are too short to penetrate good leather. I promptly put my foot on him, and he bit my shoe with harmless venom.

At this camp the carregadores ants completely devoured the doctor's undershirt, ate holes in his mosquito net, and ate the strap of Lyra's gun case.

The following day was almost without rain. It was delightful to drift and paddle slowly down the beautiful tropical river. Until mid-afternoon the current was not very fast, and the broad, deep, placid stream bent and curved in every direction, although the general course was northwest. At last the slow current quickened. Faster it went, and faster, until it began to run like a mill-race, and we heard the roar of rapids ahead. We pulled to the right bank, moored the canoes, and while most of the men pitched camp two or three of them accompanied us to examine the rapids.

We soon found them to be a serious obstacle. There were many curls, and one or two regular falls, perhaps six feet high. It would have been impossible to run them, and they stretched for nearly a mile. The carry, however, which led through woods and over rocks in a nearly straight line, was somewhat shorter. It was not an easy portage over which to carry heavy loads and drag heavy dugout canoes. At the point where the descent was steepest there were great naked flats of friable sandstone and conglomerate. Other parts were bare and had been worn by the weather into fantastic shapes—one projection looked like an old-fashioned beaver hat upside down. In this place, where the naked flats of rock showed the projection of the ledge through which the river had cut its course, the torrent rushed down a deep, sheer-sided, and extremely narrow channel. At one point it was less than two yards across, and for quite a distance not more than five or six yards. Yet only a mile or two above the rapids the deep, placid river was at least a hundred yards wide. It seemed impossible that so broad a river could in so short a space of time contract its dimensions to the width of a strangled channel through which it now poured its entire volume.

We spent March 3rd and 4th and the morning of the 5th in portaging around the rapids. We were bitten by huge horseflies the size of bumblebees. More serious annoyance was caused by the pium and boroshuda flies during daylight, and by the polvora sand-flies after dark. The boroshudas were the worst pests. They brought blood at once, and left marks that lasted for weeks. I did my writing in head net and gauntlets.

We started downstream again early in the afternoon of March 5. Our hands and faces were swollen from the bites and stings of the insect pests at the sand-flat camp, and it was a pleasure once more to be in the middle of the river, where they did not come, in any numbers, while we were in motion. Just before reaching camp Cherrie shot a jacu, a handsome bird somewhat akin to, but much smaller than a turkey. After he had taken its skin, its body made an excellent canja [stew]. The giant ants were rather too plentiful around this camp. One stung Kermit. It was almost like the sting of a small scorpion, and pained severely for a couple of hours.

On the following day we made nineteen kilometres, the river twisting in every direction, but in its general course running a little west of north. Once we stopped at a bee tree to get honey. The tree was a towering giant, of the kind called milk-tree, because a thick milky juice runs freely from any cut. Our camaradas eagerly drank the white fluid that flowed from the wounds made from the axes. I tried it. The taste was not unpleasant, but it left a sticky feeling in the mouth. The helmsman of my boat, Luiz, a powerful Negro, chopped into the tree, balancing himself with springy ease on a slight scaffolding. The honey was in a hollow, and had been made by medium-sized stingless bees. At the mouth of the hollow they had built a curious entrance of their own, in the shape of a spout of wax about a foot long. At the opening the walls of the spout showed the wax formation, but elsewhere it had become in color and texture indistinguishable from the bark of the tree. The honey was delicious, sweet and yet with a tart flavor. The comb differed much from that of our honey-bees. The honey-cells were very large, and the brood-cells, which were small, were in a single instead of a double row.

About three o'clock I was in the lead, when the current began to run more quickly. We passed over one or two decided ripples, and then heard the roar of rapids ahead, while the stream began to race. We drove the canoe into the bank. Later, Rondon, Lyra and Kermit started downstream to explore. They returned in an hour, with the information that the rapids continued for a long distance, with falls and steep pitches of broken water, and that the portage would take several days. We made camp just above the rapids. Ants swarmed, and some of them bit savagely.

The 7th, 8th and 9th we spent in carrying the loads and dragging and floating the dugouts past the series of rapids at whose head we had stopped. I would have found the time most tedious if Kermit had not lent me the Oxford Book of French Verse. Eustache Deschamp, Joachim du Bellay, Ronsard, the delightful La Fontaine, the delightful but appalling Villon, and many others comforted me much.

"The plans for the Brazilian expedition came into being so unexpectedly that father could not choose his library with the usual care," Kermit wrote in The Happy Hunting Grounds. "He brought Gibbon's Decline and Fall of the Roman Empire in the Everyman's Edition, and farmed out a volume to each of us, and most satisfactory it proved to all. He also brought Marcus Aurelius and Epictetus, but when he tried to read them during the descent of the Rio da Duvida, they only served to fill him with indignation at their futility. Some translations of Greek plays, not those of Gilbert Murray, for which he had unstinted praise, met with but little better success, and we were nearly as badly off for reading matter as we were for provisions . . . At last the time came when there was nothing left but the Oxford books of English and French verse . . . For French verse father had never cared. He said it didn't sing sufficiently. 'The Song of Roland' was the one exception he granted. It was, therefore, a still greater proof of distress when he borrowed the Oxford book of French verse. He always loved to tell afterward that when he first borrowed it he started criticizing and I had threatened to take it away if he continued to assail my favorites. In spite of all this he found it infinitely preferable to Epictetus and Marcus Aurelius, and, indeed, became very fond of some of the selections. Villon and Ronsard particularly interested him."

On the 10th we again embarked and made a kilometre and a half, spending most of the time in getting past two more rapids. Next morning we found that during the night we had met with a serious misfortune. We had halted at the foot of the rapids. The canoes were moored to trees on the bank, at the tail of the broken water. The two old canoes were water-logged and heavy, and one of them was leaking. In the night the river rose. The leaky canoe, which at best was too low in the water, must have gradually filled from the wash of the waves. It sank, dragging down the other. They began to roll, bursting their moorings, and in the morning they had disappeared. A canoe was launched to look for them, but, rolling over the boulders on the rocky bottom, they had at once been riven asunder. The big fragments that we soon found floating in eddies or along the shore showed that it was useless to look farther. We called these rapids Broken Canoe Rapids.

There was no alternative. We had to build either one large or two small canoes. It was raining heavily as the men started to explore in different directions for good canoe trees. Three were found close to the camp, one of them five feet in diameter. The axmen immediately attacked this one under the superintendence of Colonel Rondon. Lyra and Kermit started in the opposite direction to hunt. Lyra killed a jacu for us, and Kermit killed two monkeys for the men.

On the 12th I spent the day in the woods, for the most part near the river, but saw no game. In the season of the rains game was away from the river and fish were scarce and turtles absent. While bursting through a tangle I disturbed a nest of wasps whose resentment was active. In escaping I heedlessly stepped among the outliers of a small party of the carnivorous foraging ants. In my haste, grasping a branch, I shook down a shower of fire-ants. Then I was bitten by a giant ant the pain of which stayed with me for three hours. All of us were bitten or stung by different sorts of insects, and our clothes in the steaming jungles were wet when we went to bed and usually wet when we got up.

On the morning of the 14th the canoe was finished, dragged down to the water, and launched soon after midday. An hour later we were under way. The descent was marked, and the swollen river raced along. Several times we passed great whirlpools, sometimes shifting, sometimes steady. Half a dozen times we ran over rapids, and, although they were not high enough to have been obstacles to loaded Canadian canoes, two of them were serious to us. Our heavily laden, clumsy dugouts were sunk to within three or four inches of the surface of the river, and, although they were buoyed on each side with bundles of burity-palm branch stems, they shipped a great deal of water in the rapids. The two biggest rapids we just barely made, and after each we had hastily to push ashore in order to bail.

The following morning, the 15th of March, we started in good season. For six kilometres we drifted and paddled down the swift river without incident. At times we saw lofty Brazilian nut trees rising above the rest of the forest. Back from the river these trees grew to enormous proportions, towering like giants. There were great rubber trees also, their leaves always in sets of threes. The roar of broken water announced that once more our course was checked by dangerous rapids. Round a bend we came to them, a wide descent of white water, with an island in the middle, at the upper edge.

Kermit, as usual, was leading in his canoe. It was the

smallest and least seaworthy of all. He had in it little except a week's supply of our boxed provisions and a few tools. His dog, Trigueiro was with him. Beside himself the crew consisted of João, the helmsman, and Simplicio, the bowsman. Both were Negroes and exceptionally good men in every way. Kermit halted his canoe on the left bank, above the rapids, and waited for the colonel's canoe. Then the colonel and Lyra walked down the bank to see what was ahead. Kermit took his canoe across to the island to see whether the descent could be better accomplished on the other side. Having made his investigation, he ordered the men to return to the bank he had left, and the dugout was headed upstream accordingly. Before they had gone a dozen yards, the paddlers digging their paddles with all their strength into the swift current, one of the shifting whirlpools came downstream, whirled them around, and swept them so close to the rapids that no human power could avoid going over them. As they were drifting into them broadside on, Kermit yelled to the steersman to turn her head, so as to take them in the only way that offered any chance whatever of safety. The water came aboard, wave after wave, as they raced down. They reached the bottom with the canoe upright, but so full as barely to float, and the paddlers urged her toward the shore. They had nearly reached the bank when another whirlpool or whirling eddy tore them away and hurled them back to midstream, where the dugout filled and turned over. João, seizing the rope, started to swim ashore. The rope was pulled from his hand, but he reached the bank. Poor Simplicio must have been pulled under at once and his life beaten out on the boulders beneath the raging torrent. He never rose again, nor did we ever recover his body. Kermit clutched his rifle, his favorite 405 Winchester with which he had done most of his hunting in Africa and America, and climbed on the bottom of the upset boat. In a minute he was swept into the second series of rapids, and whirled away from the rolling boat, losing his rifle. The water beat his helmet down over his head and face and drove him beneath the surface, and when he rose at last, he was almost drowned, his breath and strength almost spent. He was in swift but quiet water, and swam toward an overhanging branch. His jacket hindered him, but he knew he was too nearly gone to be able to get it off, and, thinking with the curious calm one feels when death is but a moment away, he realized that the utmost his failing strength could do was to reach the branch. He reached and clutched it, and then almost lacked strength to haul himself out on the land. Good Trigueiro had faithfully swum alongside him through the rapids, and now himself scrambled ashore.

It was a very narrow escape. Kermit was a great comfort and help to me on the trip but the fear of some fatal accident befalling him was always a nightmare to me. He was to be married as soon as the trip was over, and it did not seem to me that I could bear to bring bad tidings to his betrothed and to his mother.

Simplicio was unmarried. Later we sent to his mother all the money that would have been his had he lived. The following morning we put on one side of the post erected to mark our camping-spot the following inscription in Portuguese:

"IN THESE RAPIDS DIED POOR SIMPLICIO."

On an expedition such as ours death is one of the accidents that may at any time occur, and narrow escapes from death are too common to be felt as they would be felt elsewhere. One mourns sincerely, but mourning cannot interfere with labor. We immediately proceeded with the work of the portage.

Kermit, accompanied by João, went three or four miles down the river, looking for the body of Simplicio and for the sunk canoe. He found neither. He found that a couple of kilometres below there was another stretch of rapids, and following them, found that they were worse than the ones we had just passed. We camped at the foot of the rapids we had just passed.

The morning of the 16th was dark and gloomy. Through sheets of blinding rain we left our camp of misfortune for another camp where misfortune also awaited us. Less than half an hour took our dugouts to the head of the rapids below. As Kermit had explored the left hand side, Colonel Rondon and Lyra went down the right-hand side and found a channel which led round the worst part, so that they deemed it possible to let down the canoes by ropes on the bank. While the loads were being brought down, two of our best water-men started to take down the canoe. Colonel Rondon walked ahead to see anything he could about the river. He was accompanied by one of the dogs, Lobo. After walking about a kilometre he heard ahead a kind of howling noise, which he thought was made by spider monkeys. He walked in the direction of the sound and Lobo ran ahead. In a minute he heard Lobo yell with pain, and then, still yelping, come toward him, while the creature that was howling also approached evidently in pursuit. In a moment a second yell from Lobo, followed by silence, announced that he was dead, and the sound of the howling when near convinced Rondon that the dog had been killed by an Indian, doubtless with two arrows. Probably the Indian was howling to lure the spider-monkeys toward him. Rondon fired his rifle in the air, to warn off the Indian or Indians, who in all probability had never seen a civilized man, and certainly could not imagine that one was in the neighborhood. He then returned to the foot of the rapids, where the portage was still going on, and in company with Lyra, Kermit and Antonio Parecis, the Indian, walked back to where Lobo's body lay. Sure enough he found him, slain by two arrows. One arrow-head was in him, and near by was a strange stick used in the very primitive method of fishing of all these Indians. Antonio recognized its purpose. The Indians, who were apparently two or three in number, had fled. Some beads and trinkets were left on the spot to show that we were not angry and were friendly.

Meanwhile, Cherrie stayed at the head and I at the foot of the portage, as guards. Two canoes were brought down safely. The next one was the new canoe, which was very large and heavy, and made of wood that would not float. In the rapids the rope broke, and the canoe was lost, one of the men nearly drowning. It was a bad thing to lose the canoe, but it was even worse to lose the rope and pulleys. This meant that it would be physically impossible to hoist big canoes up even small hills or rocky hillocks, such as had been frequent beside the many rapids we had encountered. It was not wise to spend the four days necessary to build new canoes where we were in danger of attack from the Indians. Moreover, new rapids might be near, in which case the new canoes would hamper us. Yet the four remaining canoes would not carry all the loads and all the men, no matter how we cut the loads down.

We had been gone eighteen days. We had used over a third of our food. We had gone only one hundred and twenty-five kilometres, and it was probable that we had at least five times, perhaps six or seven times, this distance still to go. We had taken a fortnight to descend rapids amounting in the aggregate to less than seventy yards of fall—a very few yards of fall makes a dangerous rapid when the river is swollen and swift and there are obstructions. We had only one aneroid to determine our altitude, and therefore could make merely a loose approximation to it, but we probably had between two and three times this descent in the aggregate of rapids ahead of us. So far the country had offered little in the way of food except palm tops. We had lost four canoes and one man. We were in the country of wild Indians, who shot well with their bows. It behooved us to go warily, but also to make all speed possible, if we were to avoid serious trouble.

The best plan seemed to be to march thirteen men down along the bank, while the remaining canoes, lashed two and two, floated down beside them. If after two or three days we found no bad rapids, and there seemed a reasonable chance of going some distance at decent speed, we could then build the new canoes. We left all the baggage we could. We were already down as far as comfort would permit but we now struck off much of the comfort. Cherrie, Kermit and I had been sleeping under a very light fly. There was another small light tent for one person, kept for possible emergencies. This was given to me for my cot, and all five of the others swung their hammocks under the big fly. This meant that we left two big and heavy tents behind. A box of surveying instruments was also abandoned. Each of us got his personal belongings down to one box or duffel-bag.

The following morning Colonel Rondon, Lyra, Kermit, Cherrie and nine of the camaradas started in a single file down the bank, while the doctor and I went in the two double canoes, with six camaradas, three of them invalids with swollen feet. We halted continually, as we went about three times as fast as the walkers. After forty minutes' actual going in the boats we came to some rapids. The unloaded canoes ran them without difficulty, while the loads were portaged. In an hour and a half we were again under way, but in ten minutes came to other rapids, where the river ran among islands, and there were several big curls. The clumsy, heavily laden dugouts, lashed in couples, were unwieldy and hard to handle. The rapids came just round a sharp bend, and we got caught in the upper part of the swift water and had to run the first set of rapids in consequence. We, in the leading pair of dugouts, were within an ace of coming to grief on some big boulders against which we were swept by a cross current at the turn. All of us paddling hard—scraping and bumping—we got through by the skin of our teeth, and managed to make the bank and moor our dugouts. It was a narrow escape from grave disaster. The second pair of lashed dugouts profited by our experience, and made the run—with risk, but with less risk—and moored beside us. Then all the loads were taken out, and

the empty canoes were run down through the least dangerous channels among the islands.

   This was a long portage, and we camped at the foot of
the rapids. Here a little river, a rapid stream of volume equal
to the Dúvida at the point where we first embarked, joined
from the west. Colonel Rondon and Kermit came to it first,
and the colonel named it Rio Kermit. There was a waterfall
about six or eight feet high just above the junction. Here
we found plenty of fish. Lyra caught two pacu, good-sized,
deep-bodied fish. They were delicious eating. Antonio the
Parecis said that these fish never came up heavy rapids in
which there were falls they had to jump. We could only
hope that he was correct, as in that case the rapids we
would encounter in the future would rarely be so serious
as to necessitate our dragging the heavy canoes overland.
But events showed that he was mistaken. The worst rapids
were ahead of us.

   There was no longer any question that the Dúvida was
a big river, a river of real importance. It was not a minor
affluent of some other affluent. But we were still wholly in
the dark as to where it came out.

   On the morning following our camping by the mouth of
the Rio Kermit, Colonel Rondon took a good deal of pains
in getting a big post set up at the entry of the smaller river
into the Dúvida. Then he summoned me, and all the others,
to attend the ceremony of its erection. We found the
camaradas drawn up in line, and the colonel preparing to
read aloud "the orders of the day." To the post was nailed
a board with "Rio Kermit" on it, and the colonel read the
orders reciting that by the direction of the Brazilian Gov-

ernment, and inasmuch as the unknown river was evidently a great river, he formally christened it the Rio Roosevelt. This was a complete surprise to me. Both Lauro Müller and Colonel Rondon had spoken to me on the subject, and I had urged, and Kermit had urged, as strongly as possible, that the name be kept as Rio da Dúvida. We felt that the River of Doubt was an unusually good name, and it is always well to keep a name of this character.

True, the worst was still ahead. They kept going down the river. On the 19th they found trees with wood that would float and built two small canoes. Then, after these were finished, they resumed their hazardous journey.

Chapter 5

Rio Teodoro

THE MIGHTIEST river in the world is the Amazon. It runs from west to east, from the sunset to the sunrise, from the Andes to the Atlantic. The main stream flows almost along the equator, while the basin which contains its affluents extends many degrees north and south of the equator. We were within the southern boundary of this great equatorial forest, on a river which was not merely unknown but unguessed at, no geographers having ever suspected its existence.

On the morning of March 22 we started in our six canoes. Twenty minutes after starting we came to the first rapids. Here every one walked except the three best paddlers, who took the canoes down in succession—an hour's job. We came to a small steep fall which we did not dare run in our overladen, clumsy, and cranky dugouts. After portaging around it, after having the boats in motion only an hour and a half, we came to a long stretch of rapids which it took us six hours to descend. We camped at the foot of it.

Opposite us was an Indian village, evidently inhabited only during the dry season. The marks on the stumps of trees showed that these Indians had axes and knives, and there were old fields in which maize, beans and cotton had been grown. Rubber trees were plentiful. At one point in the stream, to our great surprise, we saw flying fish.

The next few days were repetitions of those that went before except that food supplies were becoming dangerously low. Rations were cut down except for the tops of palms which helped fill the camaradas. The hard work, the bites of insects and lack of sufficient food was taking its toll on all of the party. As they hoped for surcease, the rapids became worse. Two of the men came down with fever. Another one of them, Julio, the strongest of the lot, became more and more surly and began to shirk his work. The food was pieced out with honey, a few small cocoanuts, and Brazil nuts. Occasionally a few fish were caught. Then an exploring party that went ahead for some miles came back with the disquieting news that they were now in a range of mountains, and that the river ran through the first range in a gorge, some three kilometres long, with ground so rough and steep that it would be impossible to drag the canoes over it and difficult enough to carry the loads over it.

Kermit, who was the only man with much experience of rope work, was the only man who believed we could get the canoes down at all. It was, of course, possible that we should have to build new ones at the foot to supply the place of any that were lost or left behind. In view of the length and character of the portage and of all the unpleasant possibilities that were ahead and of the need of keeping every pound of food, it was necessary to reduce weight in every possible way and to throw away everything except the barest necessities.

We cut to the bone. We kept the fly for all six of us to sleep under. Kermit's shoes had gone, and he took the pair I had been wearing, while I put on my spare pair. In addition to the clothes I wore, I kept one set of pajamas, a spare pair of drawers, a spare pair of socks, half a dozen handkerchiefs, my washkit, my pocket medicine case, and a little bag containing my spare spectacles, gun grease, some adhesive plaster, some needles and thread, and my purse and letter of credit, to be used at Manaos. All of these went into the bag containing my cot, blanket, and mosquito net. I also carried a cartridge bag containing my cartridges, head net and gauntlets. Kermit cut down even closer.

The last three days of March we spent in getting to the foot of this gorge. Lyra and Kermit, with four of the best watermen, handled the empty canoes. The walls of the gorge were so sheer that at the worst places they had to cling to narrow shelves on the face of the rock, while letting the canoes down with ropes.

Meanwhile Rondon surveyed and cut a trail for the burden bearers, and superintended the portage of the loads. The rocky sides of the gorge were too steep for laden men to attempt to traverse them. Accordingly the trail had to go over the top of the mountain, both the ascent and the descent of the rock-strewn, forest-clad slopes being very steep. The work was not only difficult and laborious in the extreme but also hazardous.

There were tracks of tapir, deer, and agouti around, and if we had taken two or three days to devote to nothing else than hunting them we might perchance have killed something. But the chance was much too uncertain, the work we were doing was too hard and wearing, and the need of pressing forward altogether too great to permit us to spend any time in such manner. A couple of curassows [large birds] and a big monkey were killed by the colonel and Kermit. The head, feet, tail, skin, and entrails were boiled for the gaunt and ravenous dogs. The flesh gave each of us a few mouthfuls, and how good those mouthfuls tasted!

On the third day Lyra and Kermit, with their daring and hard-working watermen, after wearing labor, succeeded in getting five canoes through the worst of the rapids to the chief fall. The sixth had its bottom beaten out on the jagged rocks of the broken water. On this night, although I thought I had put my clothes out of reach, both the termites and the carregadores ants got at them, ate holes in one boot, ate one leg of my drawers, and riddled my handkerchief. I now had nothing to replace anything that was destroyed.

On April 2 we once more started, wondering how soon we should strike other rapids in the mountains ahead, and whether in any reasonable time we should, as the aneroid indicated, be so low down that we should necessarily be in a plain where we could make a journey of at least a few days without rapids. We had been exactly a month going through an uninterrupted succession of rapids. During that month we had come only about one hundred and ten kilometres, and had descended nearly one hundred and fifty metres. In a straight line northward toward our supposed destination, we had not made more than a mile and a quarter a day.

Conditions, however, did not change. That day they made only three kilometres. Most of the party walked all the time. Then they struck another series of rapids that took them four days to descend. Another canoe was lost. Kermit and Lyra had been in the water for many days. Their clothes were never dry. Their shoes were rotten. The bruises on their feet and legs had become sores. On their bodies some of the insect bites had become festering wounds, as was true for all of the party. Poisonous ants, biting flies, ticks, wasps, bees were a perpetual torment.

Under such conditions whatever is evil in men's natures comes to the front. The camarada, Julio, in addition to shirking his work, constantly begging for favors, and shamming sickness, had now begun to steal food from the others. Alone of the whole party, and thanks to the stolen food, he had kept in full flesh and bodily vigor.

One of our best men was a huge Negro named Paixão—Paishon—a corporal and acting sergeant in the engineer corps. He was a stern disciplinarian. One evening he detected Julio stealing food and smashed him in the mouth. Julio came crying to us, his face working with fear and malignant hatred. After investigation he was told that he had gotten off uncommonly light.

The men had three or four carbines, which were sometimes carried by those who were not their owners. On this morning, at the outset of the portage. Pedrinho discovered Julio stealing some of the men's dried meat. Shortly afterward Paishon rebuked him for, as usual, lagging behind. By the time we had reached the place where the canoes were tied to the bank, we sat down and waited for the last loads to be brought along the trail. Paishon had just brought in a load, left it on the ground with his carbine beside it, and returned on the trail for another load. Julio came in, put down his load, picked up the carbine, and walked back on the trail, muttering to himself but showing no excitement. We thought nothing of it, for he was always muttering, and, occasionally, one of the men saw a monkey or big bird and tried to shoot it, so it was never surprising to see a man with a carbine.

In a minute we heard a shot. A short time later three or four of the men came up the trail to tell us that Paishon was dead, having been shot by Julio, who had fled into the woods. Colonel Rondon and Lyra were ahead. I sent a messenger for them, directed Cherrie and Kermit to stay where they were and guard the canoes and provisions, and started down the trail with the doctor—an absolutely cool and plucky man, with a revolver but no rifle—and a couple of the camaradas. We soon passed the dead body of poor Paishon. He lay in a huddle, in a pool of his own blood, where he had fallen, shot through the heart. I feared that Julio had run amuck, and intended merely to take more lives before he died, and that he would begin with Pedrinho, who was alone and unarmed in the camp we had left. When we came to the camp the doctor quietly walked by me, remarking, "My eyes are better than yours, colonel. If he is in sight I'll point him out to you, as you have the rifle." However, he was not there, and the others soon joined us with the welcome news that they had found the carbine.

The murderer had stood to one side of the path and killed his victim, when a dozen paces off, with deliberate and malignant purpose. Then evidently his murderous hatred had at once given way to his innate cowardice, and, perhaps hearing some one coming along the path, he fled in panic terror into the wilderness. A tree had knocked the carbine from his hand. His footsteps showed that after going some rods he had started to return, doubtless for the carbine, but had fled again, probably because the body had been discovered.

França, the cook, quoted out of the melancholy proverbial philosophy of the people the proverb, "No man knows the heart of any one," and then expressed with deep conviction a weird ghostly belief I had never encountered before: "Paishon is following Julio now, and will follow him until he dies. Paishon fell forward on his hands and knees, and when a murdered man falls like that his ghost will follow the slayer as long as the slayer lives."

We did not attempt to pursue the murderer. We could not legally put him to death, although he was a soldier who in cold blood had just deliberately killed a fellow soldier. If we had been near civilization we would have done our best to bring him in and turn him over to justice. But we were in the wilderness, and how many weeks' journey was ahead of us we could not tell. Our food was running low, sickness was beginning to appear among the

men, and both their courage and their strength were gradually ebbing. Our first duty was to save the lives and the
health of the men of the expedition, who had honestly been
performing, and had still to perform, so much perilous
labor. If we brought the murderer in he would have to be
guarded night and day on an expedition where there were
always loaded firearms about, and where there would continually be opportunity and temptation for him to make an
effort to seize food and a weapon and escape, perhaps mur-
dering some other good man. He could not be shackled
while climbing along the cliff slopes; he could not be
shackled in the canoes, where there was always a chance
of upset and drowning; and standing guard would be an
additional and severe penalty on the weary, honest men
already exhausted by overwork. The expedition was in peril,
and it was wise to take every chance possible that would
help secure success. Whether the murderer lived or died
in the wilderness was of no moment compared with the duty
of doing everything to secure the safety of the rest of the
party.

For the two days following we were always on the watch
against his return, for he could have readily killed some one
else by rolling rocks down on any of the men working on
the cliff sides or in the bottom of the gorge. But we did not
see him until the morning of the third day. We had passed
the last of the rapids of the chasm, and the four boats were
going downstream when he appeared behind some trees
on the bank and called out that he wished to surrender and
be taken aboard.

Colonel Rondon's boat was far in advance. He did not

stop nor answer. I kept on in similar fashion with the rear boats, for I had no intention of taking the murderer aboard, to the jeopardy of the other members of the party, unless Colonel Rondon told me that it would have to be done in pursuance of his duty, as an officer of the army and a servant of the government of Brazil. At the first halt Colonel Rondon came up to me and told me this was his view of his duty, but he had not stopped because he wished first to consult me as the chief of the expedition. I answered that I did not believe that in justice to the good men of the expedition we should jeopardize their safety by taking the murderer along, and that if the responsibility was mine I should refuse to take him, but that he, Colonel Rondon, was the superior officer of both the murderer and of all the other enlisted men and army officers on the expedition, and in return was responsible for his actions to his own governmental superiors and to the laws of Brazil, and that in view of this responsibility he must act as his sense of duty bade him. Accordingly, at the next camp he sent back two men, expert woodsmen, to find the murderer and bring him in. They failed to find him.

That day we got only halfway down the rapids. There was no good place to camp. But at the foot of one steep cliff there was a narrow, boulder-covered slope where it was possible to sling hammocks and cook. A slanting spot was found for my cot, which had sagged until by this time it looked like a broken-backed centipede.

The men were growing constantly weaker under the endless strain of exhausting labor. Kermit was having an attack of fever, and Lyra and Cherrie had touches of dysentery.

All three continued to work. While in the water trying to help with an upset canoe I had by my own clumsiness bruised my leg against a boulder and the resulting inflammation was somewhat bothersome. I now had a sharp attack of fever, but thanks to the excellent care of the doctor, was over it in about forty-eight hours. Kermit's fever grew worse and he too was unable to work for a day or two. We could walk over the portages however.

Roosevelt was entirely too modest both about his sickness and his helping. Cherrie, in describing this situation later, said, "I don't think any of us would have come out had the Colonel not been with us. And yet the Colonel almost stayed there. There were a good many days, a good many mornings when I looked at Colonel Roosevelt and said to myself, he won't be with us tonight. I would say the same thing in the evening, he can't possibly live until morning. I can't speak for the others, but I know as far as Kermit and myself were concerned, the fact that the Colonel was with us gave us energy to do things we couldn't possibly have done otherwise." Cherrie then went on to describe how, when Theodore received his bruise on the leg, it had been because he rushed into the water at a cry that the canoes were about to be crushed among some boulders and, in turn, had his own leg injured but the canoes were saved. "At that time," Cherrie went on, "the Colonel received a severe bruise on one of his legs, a wound that troubled him from that time forward. Indeed, it was the first night after that accident that he was seriously ill, his temperature going up to something like one hundred and five degrees. From that time on he was a very sick man."

Cherrie stated that he and Kermit had to watch the Colonel to keep him from giving his food to the men. "Whenever either Kermit or I would protest about his giving his portion of food to the canoemen he would say, 'I can't do anything to help and they need the food.' We had to watch him constantly, and reached the point where if he didn't eat all of his share either Kermit or I would take what was left and guard it until a later meal. We had so very little that every mouthful counted."

At the point when it seemed that they would have to abandon their canoes—and each man go on his own, Colonel Roosevelt turned to Cherrie and said, "Cherrie, I want you and Kermit to go ahead. We have reached a point where some of us must stop. I feel I am only a burden to the party."

Had they abandoned their canoes at this point it is doubtful if any of them would have reached safety. The next expedition sent out by the government was annihilated by the Indians.

After many other portages and hard going, on April 6, they portaged past another set of rapids, which proved to be the last of the rapids of the chasm. For some kilometres they kept passing hills, and feared lest at any moment they might again find themselves fronting another mountain gorge. It might have been impossible to have made it with the men as sick and dispirited as they were.

The hills gradually sank into a level plain, and the river carried us through it at a rate that enabled us during the remainder of the day to reel off thirty-six kilometres. At last, at four in the afternoon, we came to the mouth of a big river running in from the right. We thought it was probably the Ananas, but, could not be certain. We camped on the point of land between the two rivers. It was extraordinary to realize that here about the eleventh degree we were on such a big river, utterly unknown to the cartographers and not indicated by even a hint on any map.

We spent a day at this spot, determining our exact position by the sun, and afterward by the stars, and sending on two men to explore the rapids in advance. They returned with the news that there were big cataracts in them, and that they would form an obstacle to our progress. They had also caught a huge catfish, which furnished an excellent meal for everybody in camp. This evening the view across the broad river, from our camp where the two rivers joined, was very lovely. For the first time, we had an open space in front of and above us, so that after nightfall the stars, and the great waxing moon, were glorious overhead, and against the rocks in midstream the broken water gleamed like tossing silver.

For four or five days there were more rapids, more portages, more work, but there were more fish caught and more game killed and food built up the strength of the men. "How I longed for a big Maine birchbark," Theodore wrote, "such as that in which I once went down the Mattawamkeg at high water! It would have slipped down these rapids as a girl trips through a country dance. But our loaded dugouts would have shoved their noses under every curl."

Once they had to wait a day because Kermit's dog, Trigueiro, failed to show up. But that day they caught twenty-eight big fish, mostly piranhas, and everybody had enough to eat for supper and for breakfast the next morning. A day or so later the men found some new nuts of which they liked the taste, but which made all who ate them sick.

It was a rather sorry crew that embarked the following morning, April 15. But it turned out a red-letter day. On this day after running two hours and a half we found on the left bank a board on a post with the initials J.A. to show the farthest point up which a rubber man had reached and claimed as his own. An hour further down we came on a newly built house in a little planted clearing. No one was home, but the house of palm thatch was clean and cool. A couple of dogs were on the watch, and the belongings showed that a man, and a woman, and a child lived there and had just left. Another hour brought us to a similar house where dwelt an old black man who showed the innate courtesy of the Brazilian peasant. In mid-afternoon we stopped at another clean, cool, picturesque house of palm thatch. The inhabitants fled at our approach, fearing an Indian raid, for they were absolutely unprepared to have any one come from the unknown regions upstream. They returned and were most hospitable and communicative. We spent the night there. Said Antonio to Kermit, "It seems like a dream to be in a house again and hear the voices of men and women, instead of being among those mountains and rapids."

The river was known to them as the Castanho and was the left or western branch of the Aripuanan. This name was used by the rubber gatherers only and was unknown to the geographers. We were, according to our informants, about fifteen days' journey from the confluence of the two rivers. We had come over three hundred kilometres in forty-eight days, over absolutely unknown ground. We had seen no human being, although we had twice heard Indians. Six weeks had been spent in steadily slogging our way down through the interminable series of rapids. It was astonishing before, when we were on a river of about the size of the upper Rhine or Elbe, to realize that no geographer had any idea of its existence. But, after all, no civilized man of any grade had ever been on it. Here, however, was a river with people dwelling along the banks, some of whom had lived in the neighborhood for eight or ten years, and yet on no standard map was there a hint of the river's existence. We were putting on the map a river, running through between five and six degrees of latitude, of which no geographer, in any map published in Europe or the United States or Brazil, had even admitted the possibility of the existence.

We had passed the period when there was a chance of peril, of disaster, to the whole expedition. We no longer had to face continual anxiety, the need of constant economy with food, the duty of labor with no end in sight, and bitter uncertainty of the future.

Roosevelt spent a good part of the trip to the Amazon lying flat on his back in a canoe. The after effects of the fever still hung on and his leg, which had been bruised, gave him much pain. It had abscessed and the doctor had cut it open and put in a drainage tube. "I could hardly hobble and was pretty well laid up," he wrote. "But there is no 'stop, conductor,' while a battery's changing ground." It was not ideal lying in a canoe with the sun beating down, with occasional downpours of drenching rain, but it was so much better than what had gone before that it seemed a privilege. Besides home beckoned:

The north was calling strongly to the three men of the north—Rocky Dell Farm to Cherrie, Sagamore Hill to me, and to Kermit the call was stronger still. In our home country spring had now come, the wonderful northern spring of long glorious days, of brooding twilights, of cool delightful nights. Robin and bluebird, meadow lark and song sparrow, were singing in the mornings, the maple buds were red, flowers and bloodroot were blooming while the last patches of snow still lingered. The rapture of the hermit thrush in Vermont, the serene golden melody of the wood thrush on Long Island, would be heard before we were there to listen. Each man to his home, and to his true love! Each was longing for the homely things that were so dear to him, for the home people who were dearer still, and for the one who was dearest of all.

Epilogue

ONLY HIS indomitable will had kept Theodore from giving up in those days on the River of Doubt—now officially named Rio Téodoro by the Brazilian government. Perhaps it was the knowledge that Kermit would never leave him that kept him going.

When he returned to the United States in the middle of May, 1914, he was a sick man, fifty-five pounds lighter than when his trip began. His greatest adventure was over and, with the beginning of World War One, his hunting days were at an end, though his love for the outdoors was as strong as it had ever been. Theodore was at his most eloquent in this creed for the strenuous life, published in 1916, some three years before his death.

The man should have youth and strength who seeks adventure in the wide, waste spaces of the earth, in the marshes, and among the vast mountain masses, in the northern forests, amid the steaming jungles of the tropics, or on the deserts of sand or of snow. He must long greatly for the lonely winds that blow across the wilderness, and for sunrise and sunset over the rim of the empty world. His heart must thrill for the saddle and not for the hearthstone. He must be helmsman and chief, the cragsman, the rifleman, the boat steerer. He must be the wielder of axe and of paddle, the rider of fiery horses, the master of the craft that leaps through white water. His eye must be true and quick, his hand steady and strong. His heart must never fail nor his head grow bewildered, whether he face brute and human foes, or the frowning strength of hostile nature, or the awful fear that grips those who are lost in trackless lands. Wearing toil and hardship shall be his; thirst and famine he shall face, and burning fever. Death shall come to greet him with poison-fang or poison-arrow, in shape of charging beast or of scaly things that lurk in lake and river; it shall lie in wait for him among untrodden forests, in the swirl of wild waters, and in the blast of snow blizzard or thunder-shattered hurricane.

Not many men can with wisdom make such a life their permanent and serious occupation. Those whose tasks lie along other lines can lead it for but a few years. For them it must normally come in the hardy vigor of their youth, before the beat of the blood has grown sluggish in their veins.

Nevertheless, older men also can find joy in such a life, although in their case it must be led only on the outskirts of adventure, and although the part they play therein must be that of the onlooker rather than that of the doer. The feats of prowess are for others. It is for other men to face the peril of unknown lands, to master unbroken horses, and to hold their own among their fellows with bodies of supple strength. But much, very much, remains for the man who has "warmed both hands before the fire of life," and who, although he loves the great cities, loves even more the fenceless grass-land, and the forest-clad hills.

The grandest scenery of the world is his to look at if he chooses; and he can witness the strange ways of tribes who have survived into an alien age from an immemorial past, tribes whose priests dance in honor of the serpent and worship the spirits of the wolf and the bear. Far and wide, all the continents are open to him as they never were to any of his forefathers; the Nile and the Paraguay are easy of access, and the border-land between savagery and civilization; and the veil of the past has been lifted so that he can dimly see how, in time immeasurably remote, his ancestors—no less remote—led furtive lives among uncouth and terrible beasts, whose kind has perished utterly from the face of the earth. He will take books with him as he journeys; for the keenest enjoyment of the wilderness is reserved for him who enjoys also the garnered wisdom of the present and the past. He will take pleasure in the companionship of the men of the open; in South America, the daring and reckless horsemen who guard the herds of the grazing country, and the dark-skinned paddlers who guide their clumsy dugouts down the dangerous equatorial rivers; the white and red and half-breed hunters of the Rockies, and of the Canadian woodland; and in Africa the faithful black gun-bearers who have stood steadily at his elbow when the lion came on with coughing grunts, or when the huge mass of the charging elephant burst asunder the vine-tangled branches.

The beauty and charm of the wilderness are his for the asking, for the edges of the wilderness lie close beside the beaten roads of present travel. He can see the red splendor of desert sunsets, and the unearthly glory of the afterglow on the battlements of desolate mountains. In sapphire gulfs of ocean he can visit islets, above which the wings of myriads of sea-fowl make a kind of shifting cuneiform script in the air. He can ride along the brink of the stupendous cliff-walled canyon, where eagles soar below him, and cougars make their lairs on the ledges and harry the big-horned sheep. He can journey through the northern forests, the home of the giant moose, the forests of fragrant and murmuring life in summer, the iron-bound and melancholy forests of winter.

The joy of living is his who has the heart to demand it.